FEASTING ON THE WORD

THE LITERARY TESTIMONY OF
THE BOOK OF MORMON

RICHARD DILWORTH RUST

Deseret Book Company
Salt Lake City, Utah
and
Foundation for Ancient Research and Mormon Studies
Provo, Utah

Library of Congress Cataloging-in-Publication Data
Rust, Richard Dilworth.
    Feasting on the Word : the literary testimony of the Book of
Mormon / by Richard Dilworth Rust.
        p.   cm.
    Includes bibliographical references and index.
    ISBN 1-57345-204-1 (hardback)
    1. Book of Mormon—Criticism, interpretation, etc.   I. Title.
BX8627.R87   1997
289.3'22—dc21   96-45159
                                                                CIP

Printed in the United States of America
10 9   8   7   6   5   4   3   2   1   72082

To David Rust and Bradley Kramer
for their unflagging encouragement

If ye shall follow the Son, with full purpose of heart, . . . then cometh the baptism of fire and of the Holy Ghost; and then can ye speak with the tongue of angels. . . .

Angels speak by the power of the Holy Ghost; wherefore, they speak the words of Christ. Wherefore, I said unto you, feast upon the words of Christ; for behold, the words of Christ will tell you all things what ye should do.

2 Nephi 31:13; 32:3

Contents

Contents

Acknowledgments

The initial idea for this book came from John Seelye, to whom I am grateful, as I am to other colleagues from the Department of English at the University of North Carolina: Hugh Holman and Lewis Leary, both deceased now, who gave early encouragement, and George Lensing, who provided a useful perspective on one chapter.

For reading the book manuscript in part or in whole and providing helpful suggestions, I am indebted to Richard Cracroft, Page Davis, Richard Haglund, Christopher Harlos, Bradley Kramer, Neal Lambert, Robert E. Lee, Donald Parry, Bruce and Nancy Preece, Robert Rees, David Rust, Robert F. Smith, Kary Smout, John Welch, and readers for FARMS (Foundation for Ancient Research and Mormon Studies). John Welch also has my deep gratitude for helping shepherd the development and publication of this book.

Editors Melvin Thorne, Jessica Taylor, and especially Stephanie Terry at FARMS were of great help in revising the manuscript. Suzanne Brady, my editor at Deseret Book, has been wonderfully supportive of this project.

My indebtedness extends to, but is not limited to, Paul Dixon, Eugene England, Mitchell Harris, T. Walter Herbert Jr., Ed Ingebretsen, Randall Jones, Bruce Jorgensen, Benson Parkinson, Noel Reynolds, Joseph Rust, Beverly and Karl Snow, Phillip Snyder, Stephen Tanner, Mark Thomas, Robert K. Thomas,

Gordon Thomasson, and Pamela and David Winters. My mother, Alta Cutler Rust, has steadily supported me.

Finally, I am continually grateful to my wife and companion, Patricia Brighton Rust.

CHAPTER 1

"To Come Forth in Due Time"

INTRODUCTION

My love of great literature and my testimony of the saving principles of the gospel of Jesus Christ converge in seeing the Book of Mormon as sacred literature. To take a literary approach enhanced by spiritual sensitivity is to engage our full capacities in understanding and feeling. It is to delight in how something is said in a way that reveals its essence. This approach is appropriate and helpful in respect to the Book of Mormon. In this work of literature, God-directed prophets speak to us in the most powerful and effective ways possible by interconnecting truth, goodness, and beauty.

By literature I mean belles lettres in its literal sense, "beautiful letters." In the words of Ralph Waldo Emerson, literature is "the record of the best thoughts."[1] Wordsworth called poetic literature "the breath and finer spirit of all knowledge."[2] Poetry, Robert Frost wrote, is saying "matter in terms of spirit and spirit in terms of matter," or "saying one thing in terms of another."[3] Orson F. Whitney considered the essence of poetry to be "in thought, sentiment, and the power of suggestion. It is the music of ideas, as well as the music of language." It is, he said, "the power by which we appreciate and sympathize with all that is good, pure, true, beautiful and sublime."[4] Literature engages all our senses; it involves not only thinking but also feeling. Through literature we imaginatively touch, taste, hear, and see.

Many parts of the Book of Mormon have a literary appeal. They bid us to taste and hear, to experience spirit in terms of matter. In the book we are often put in the situation of the Nephites visited by the resurrected Savior: they "did see with their eyes and did feel with their hands" (3 Nephi 11:15). We are encouraged to "receive the pleasing word of God, and feast upon his love" (Jacob 3:2).

As an example of "feasting upon the pleasing word of God" (Jacob 2:9), Jacob poetically adapts Isaiah to encourage us to

> Hearken diligently unto me,
> and remember the words which I have spoken;
> and come unto the Holy One of Israel,
> and feast upon that which perisheth not, neither can be
>   corrupted,
> and let your soul delight in fatness.
>
> (2 Nephi 9:51; cf. Isaiah 55:2)[5]

This poignant appeal and other poetic segments like it are woven into the fabric of the Book of Mormon. These materials were selected and designed by inspired writers "to come forth in due time," as Moroni puts it in the title page, for people living in a later age. When I say "designed," I mean not only planned with a purpose but shaped artistically so that form and content are totally integrated, as they are in Milton's *Paradise Lost,* Handel's *Messiah,* or Michelangelo's paintings in the Sistine Chapel. With respect to *Paradise Lost,* for example, the majesty of Milton's theme to "justify the ways of God to men" requires the magnitude of the epic form and the stateliness of unrhymed English heroic verse. With Handel's *Messiah,* the exalted oratorio form carries the profound scriptural messages.

The purpose of the chapters that follow is to set forth a literary testimony of the Book of Mormon, to show how the impact of *what* the Book of Mormon says often is created through *how* it is said. The interconnection of beauty with truth and goodness invites us to Christ. That is, literary elements such as form, imagery, poetry, and narrative help teach and motivate us in ways that touch our hearts and souls as well as our minds.[6] We "see feelingly," as Gloucester puts it in another context in Shakespeare's *King Lear;* we gain what Nathaniel Hawthorne calls "heart-knowledge."[7]

Nephi understood the heart-knowledge that comes through pondering with our heart scriptural truths and delighting with our soul in the beautiful ways in which those truths are presented. In what has been called a psalm, Nephi says,

> For my soul delighteth in the scriptures,
> and my heart pondereth them,
> and writeth them for the learning and the profit of my children.
> Behold, my soul delighteth in the things of the Lord;
> and my heart pondereth continually upon the things which I
> have seen and heard.
>
> (2 Nephi 4:15–16)

This engagement of heart and soul is part of the Creator's plan to appeal to all our senses. For example, he has given us fruit, such as strawberries and apples, for the "benefit and the use of man, both to please the eye and to gladden the heart; . . . for taste and for smell, to strengthen the body and to enliven the soul" (D&C 59:18–19). His works are both useful and beautiful; they have both "strength and beauty" (Psalm 96:6). Indeed, as with the strawberries, their beauty often attracts us to their use. Author of the beautiful, the Lord "hath made every thing beautiful in his time" (Ecclesiastes 3:11). Zion is "the perfection of beauty" (Psalm 50:2).

This beauty extends to God's words. "How sweet are thy words unto my taste!" says the Psalmist, "yea, sweeter than honey to my mouth!" (Psalm 119:103). That is the experience of Lehi and Nephi in the dream vision of the tree of life: the beauty of the tree was "far beyond, yea, exceeding of all beauty; and the whiteness thereof did exceed the whiteness of the driven snow" (1 Nephi 11:8). To partake of this beautiful fruit is a soul-filling experience: "I beheld that it was most sweet, above all that I ever before tasted. Yea, and I beheld that the fruit thereof was white, to exceed all the whiteness that I had ever seen. And as I partook of the fruit thereof it filled my soul with exceedingly great joy" (1 Nephi 8:11–12). Symbolically the love of God, the tree with its fruit is also the word of God, as Alma understands: "But if ye will nourish the word, yea, nourish the tree as it beginneth to grow, by your faith with great diligence, and with patience, looking forward to the fruit thereof, it shall take root; and behold it shall be a tree springing up unto everlasting life" (Alma 32:41).

The Book of Mormon is itself a tree of life—a work of beauty and purity, with its words to be feasted upon. A literary approach helps reveal that beauty. In reading of another's experience, we often understand it better through comparison or a figure of speech. Thus when Alma says, "ye have tasted this light" (Alma 32:35), we come closer to sensing what it means to experience the "light of truth" (D&C 93:29). The book allows us to share the experience of Mormon, who for his part "tasted and knew of the goodness of Jesus" (Mormon 1:15). For those who seek after anything virtuous, lovely, or of good report, the book combines the qualities of the good, the beautiful, and the true. Just as Zion is challenged by Isaiah to "put on [her] beautiful garments" (2 Nephi 8:24), so we might consider that the Book of Mormon has beautiful garments in the way it is presented.

Beauty in the Book of Mormon takes many forms. In Nephi's psalm, the repeated words and phrases appeal to our auditory delight in rhythm and repetition. Through imagination, the reader responds to Nephi's metaphors, his saying one thing in terms of another. "My soul will rejoice in thee," he says, "my God, and the rock of my salvation" (2 Nephi 4:30). He continues with a series of metaphors that present concrete images relating to such experiences as being delivered, shaking, having one set of gates closed and another set open, and walking in a narrow path. These make it more possible for us to identify with him:

O Lord, wilt thou redeem my soul?
Wilt thou deliver me out of the hands of mine enemies?
Wilt thou make me that I may shake at the appearance of sin?
May the gates of hell be shut continually before me,
because that my heart is broken and my spirit is contrite!
O Lord, wilt thou not shut the gates of thy righteousness before
    me,
that I may walk in the path of the low valley,
that I may be strict in the plain road!
O Lord, wilt thou encircle me around in the robe of thy
    righteousness!
O Lord, wilt thou make a way for mine escape before mine
    enemies!
Wilt thou make my path straight before me!
Wilt thou not place a stumbling block in my way—
but that thou wouldst clear my way before me,
and hedge not up my way, but the ways of mine enemy.
                  (2 Nephi 4:31–33)

The power of Nephi's words is most apparent when the passage is read aloud and also when it is recognized as poetry with its primary appeal to feeling.[8] I discovered this quality through my own experience: when my family and I read the Book of Mormon together each morning, I recognized the intense nature of passages such as Nephi's psalm. Later, when I searched the Book of Mormon for its poetry, I better understood why I was responding with my feelings to these passages. I also experienced this intensity vicariously through the response of a certain friend, who was a graduate student in public health and a Blackfoot Indian. I had wanted to see how a Native American would respond to hearing the Book of Mormon, and as I read Nephi's psalm to my friend, I could see how he was visibly moved. Afterwards he told me he felt a stirring of emotions related to how he felt as a boy hearing chants and drum beats. Especially, he said, he could feel and identify with Nephi's joy and sorrow.

Read aloud, Nephi's words convey emotionally his depth of feeling. They become music that stirs the spirit more directly than would words simply read with the eyes.

> Yea, I know that God will give liberally to him that asketh.
> Yea, my God will give me, if I ask not amiss;
> therefore I will lift up my voice unto thee;
> yea, I will cry unto thee,
>   my God, the rock of my righteousness.
> Behold, my voice shall forever ascend up unto thee,
>   my rock and mine everlasting God.
> (2 Nephi 4:35)

Though we have the Book of Mormon in printed form, a number of evidences suggest that much of its content was originally transmitted orally. A "voice" from the dust, the book records what various prophets heard and taught. Alma remembered word for word what Abinadi taught and then related it to his followers; likewise, the chosen disciples of the Savior remembered the sermon he gave the people at the temple and then repeated it from memory the next day. The parting testimony of Nephi is "the voice of one crying from the dust" (2 Nephi 33:13). Alma the Younger asks the people if they can imagine to themselves that they "hear the voice of the Lord" speaking to them at judgment day (Alma 5:16). "The good shepherd doth call you," he goes on to say (Alma 5:38). Many of the direct words of Christ are contained in the Book of Mormon—words we are intended to hear with our ears as well as see with our eyes. There is much merit in listening to the Book of Mormon as well as reading it.

When we read or listen to the Book of Mormon as a whole, we discover more readily those elements we might well call literary—poetry, chiasms, repetitions, word choice, imagery, and the like—and feel the character of the book. Thus, while my Book of Mormon references will be to the current edition,[9] occasionally I will group sentences together in the spirit of the first printed edition (1830). In that edition, the Book of Mormon is made up of many fewer chapters than are in the current edition. For example, the First Book of Nephi contains seven chapters in the 1830 edition; it has twenty-two in the 1981 edition. Paragraphs in the 1830 edition are longer, sometimes a couple of pages in length. It was not until the 1879 edition that Orson Pratt divided the Book of Mormon into our present-day chapters and verses. Although this division makes it easier to cite specific passages, the earlier arrangement better allows us to experience the narrative flow of the book.

Indeed, through a variety of means, the Lord has made the Book of Mormon as memorable as possible for us. In this richly varied work we learn the value of freedom through the compelling story of Captain Moroni and his title of liberty. We learn of the dangers of secret combinations through the chilling accounts of Kishkumen and Gadianton and then through the frightening details of the story of Akish in the book of Ether. The nature of deception is exposed in the dramatic encounters between Jacob and Sherem, Alma and Nehor, and Alma and Korihor. Further, we are shown—not simply told—how covenanted people can avoid being deceived. Rhetorical and poetic power are behind Mormon's great sermon on faith, hope, and charity. And the destruction of the world (meaning the wicked) and the glory of Christ's second coming are set forth figuratively in the events of Third Nephi, just as the Millennium is prefigured in the first part of Fourth Nephi.[10]

Made up of diverse books, the Book of Mormon as a complete whole is a single "voice"—that of Jesus Christ who inspired Mormon and others regarding what should be included in the book and how they should present it. This primary author of the Book of Mormon knew that it would come forth just before his second coming. Fulfilling specific purposes, the Book of Mormon was designed for our day.

DESIGNED FOR *OUR* DAY

"The Book of Mormon . . . was written for our day," President Ezra Taft Benson asserted. "Under the inspiration of God, who sees all things from the beginning," he said, Mormon "abridged centuries of records, choosing the stories, speeches, and events that would be most helpful to us."[11] Hugh Nibley has similarly said that "the matter in the Book of Mormon was selected, as we are often reminded, with scrupulous care and with particular readers in mind. For some reason there has been chosen for our attention a story of how and why two previous civilizations on this continent were utterly destroyed."[12] Our own world at the end of the twentieth century, Nibley believes, "is the world with which the Book of Mormon is primarily concerned."[13]

In its teachings and concerns the book is clearly relevant to our own times, but it is more than that: coming out of one age, the Book of Mormon materials have been shaped and selected by inspired prophet-artists for people living in another age. The Book of Mormon is like a lovely modern home made of bricks from older structures. The bricks may have interest in themselves, but they are now a part of new buildings with new form and function. In other words, the Book of Mormon contains carefully selected and integrated "bricks" of history, sermons, letters, and prophecies, shaped specifically and intentionally into a beautiful "house" designed for the latter days. Though its doctrines are timeless and appropriate for various periods, the Book of Mormon is just coming into its own. "In its descriptions of the problems of today's society, it is as current as the morning newspaper, and much more definitive, inspired, and inspiring concerning the solutions of those problems," said President Gordon B. Hinckley.[14]

Of course Mormon and Moroni were writing for a future time. They had to be. Mormon did most of his writing during the long lull before what he knew would be an exterminating battle, and Moroni's writings are those of the lone wanderer destined to bury his precious work in the earth. From title page to parting words, father and son make clear that what they are inspired to include is first to the latter-day Lamanites and then to latter-day Gentiles and Jews. They speak as though "from the dead" to an audience living many generations hence (Mormon 9:30). In prophetic collapsed time, Moroni speaks to this audience "as if ye were present, and yet ye are not. But behold, Jesus Christ hath shown you unto me, and I know your doing" (Mormon 8:35).

Writers such as Moroni and his father are, however, actually secondary authors of the Book of Mormon; the primary author is Jesus Christ. As Mormon affirms, "I . . . do write the things which have been commanded me of the Lord" (3 Nephi 26:12). Again, the premortal Savior told Joseph of Egypt, the great patriarch, that Joseph Smith would write "the words which are expedient in my wisdom should go forth unto the fruit of thy loins" (2 Nephi 3:19).

The Book of Mormon is a time capsule, written in ancient America but designed for a latter-day audience. Considered in its entirety, the book is neither an abridgment in the common meaning of "condensation" nor is it a history as such. Rather, it emphasizes doctrinal teachings and examples, with most of the book devoted to the 150 years before Christ's coming. More than half the thousand-year span of Nephite history is covered in less than four pages—which would be a poor balance if the book claimed to be simply history. But it does not. It has come forth "that these things [elements listed as preparatory to the second coming of Christ] might be known among you, O inhabitants of the earth" (D&C 133:36); it heralds the fulfillment of the covenant of restoration so that "ye need not say that the Lord delays his coming unto the children of Israel" (3 Nephi 29:2); and it prepares us for the Millennium, being written so "that evil may be done away, and that the time may come that Satan may have no power upon the hearts of the children of men" (Ether 8:26).

9

DESIGNED FOR OUR DAY

Not only is the Book of Mormon intended for our day but it is also shaped artistically through ancient literary forms that appeal to us today. In the Book of Mormon, as in other great works of literature, effective presentation is essential to convey purpose. This point is well made by President Boyd K. Packer. He tells how as a mission president he wanted to teach his missionaries the importance of presentation. He showed the assembled missionaries a beautifully decorated cake representing the gospel, but then he served the cake by grabbing a fistful of it and throwing it at an elder. There were no takers for a second piece until he produced a crystal dish, silver fork, linen napkin, and silver serving knife and then cut a piece carefully and put it neatly on the crystal plate before serving it. His lesson was that for the message to be received, the messenger must take care to serve it well.[15]

Through inspiration, those who wrote and compiled the Book of Mormon paid attention to how it is served. The Lord's "keystone of our religion" is beautifully prepared for us, with its narratives, rhythms, and imagery helping engage all our senses (especially our spiritual sense) in gaining its truths. Language directed to the intellect alone is not enough. Particularly in its poetry, the Book of Mormon, in the words of Samuel Taylor Coleridge, "brings the whole soul of man into activity."[16] With content often determining form and form revealing content, profound concerns are presented in ways that reach us deeply.

As literature, or belles lettres, the Book of Mormon has that medium's advantages, which include memorability, ability to capture a reader's attention, power to influence feelings or emotions, and capacity to do justice to the complexity of life.[17] The Book of Mormon is a work of immediacy that, as significant literature does, *shows* as well as *tells*.

Narrations, sermons, letters, prophecies, and dialogues are presented as living voices. Nephi involves me in his world and allows me to identify with him when he begins his narration with "I, Nephi." Mormon calls on me to recognize the point of his narrations with expressions such as "and thus *we* see." And as though time has collapsed, Moroni forthrightly declares, "I speak unto you as if ye were present, . . . and I know *your* doing" (Mormon 8:35).[18]

Because so many discourses and dialogues are presented directly in the Book of Mormon, distances break down and time dissolves. I become an implied participant with Ammon in the court of Lamoni; I join the crowd listening to Alma respond to Korihor with pure testimony and the power of God; and, especially, I am there when the Savior descends to the gathered Nephites and Lamanites at Bountiful. With much direct quotation, Jesus Christ speaks to me in his own voice. "Another Testament of Jesus Christ" is not only *about* Christ but *by* him.

Some might think that because Nephi affirms the plainness of his writing (see, for example, 2 Nephi 25:7; 33:6), it is unliterary. Quite the contrary. Nephi uses poetic and rhetorical rhythms and structures with powerful effectiveness. By the word "plain" he means "easy to understand" (1 Nephi 14:23; 16:29)—and, indeed, impossible to be misunderstood (2 Nephi 25:7, 28). Perhaps it is Nephi's claim to such a style, however, that has kept many from thinking about the book in literary terms. As Nibley has commented, it contains none of the "fantastic imagery, the romantic descriptions, and the unfailing exaggerations that everyone expected in the literature of [Joseph Smith's] time."[19]

The Book of Mormon has a power of effectiveness that paradoxically is hidden because it is so obvious—much as Edgar Allan Poe's purloined letter was hidden in plain sight and thus overlooked. The expressions and rhythms of the Book of Mormon are all intended—if not always consciously by writers such as Nephi and Moroni, at least by the primary author of the book. Indeed, I become more and more convinced that every sentence counts in the Book of Mormon.

STYLE AND TONE

The writers of the Book of Mormon show an intense concern for style and tone—for the way they communicate and for their relationship to the matter communicated and to their audience. Like the prophet Alma, each writer desires to be able to "speak with the trump of God, with a voice to shake the earth," yet realizes that "I am a man, and do sin in my wish. . . . I do not glory of myself, but I glory in that which the Lord hath commanded me" (Alma 29:1, 3, 9). Alma's tone is one of humility. Other writers also are humble and feel inadequate in writing. That is especially true of the last writer, Moroni: "If there are faults they are the mistakes of men," Moroni writes in the title page; "wherefore, condemn not the things of God."[20] He thus appeals directly to his reader to be accepting of his imperfections. In a prayer he laments: "Lord, the Gentiles will mock at these things, because of our weakness in writing. . . . Thou hast also made our words powerful and great, even that we cannot write them; wherefore, when we write we behold our weakness, and stumble because of the placing of our words" (Ether 12:23, 25). The Lord responds, "My grace is sufficient for the meek, that they shall take no advantage of your weakness" (Ether 12:26).

Moroni's words to a future audience, however, are the opposite of what we might consider weak: In cadences of ascending power he boldly declares that

> the eternal purposes of the Lord shall roll on, until all his promises shall be fulfilled. . . . O ye pollutions, ye hypocrites, ye teachers, who sell yourselves for that which will canker, why have ye polluted the holy church of God? Why are ye ashamed to take upon you the name of Christ? . . . And now, behold, who can stand against the works of the Lord? Who can deny his sayings? Who will rise up against the almighty power of the Lord? Who will despise the works of the Lord? Who will despise the children of Christ? Behold, all ye who are despisers of the works of the Lord, for ye shall wonder and perish. (Mormon 8:22, 38; 9:26)

12

Although Moroni earlier has lamented his limitations in writing, in his last words he beautifully integrates expressions of Isaiah:

> And awake, and arise from the dust, O Jerusalem; yea, and put on thy beautiful garments, O daughter of Zion; and strengthen thy stakes and enlarge thy borders forever, that thou mayest no more be confounded, that the covenants of the Eternal Father which he hath made unto thee, O house of Israel, may be fulfilled. Yea, come unto Christ, and be perfected in him, and deny yourselves of all ungodliness; and if ye shall deny yourselves of all ungodliness, and love God with all your might, mind and strength, then is his grace sufficient for you, that by his grace ye may be perfect in Christ; and if by the grace of God ye are perfect in Christ, ye can in nowise deny the power of God. And again, if ye by the grace of God are perfect in Christ, and deny not his power, then are ye sanctified in Christ by the grace of God, through the shedding of the blood of Christ, which is in the covenant of the Father unto the remission of your sins, that ye become holy, without spot. (Moroni 10:31–33; compare Isaiah 52:1; 54:2)

A model for communication is Jesus, who, Moroni reports, "told me in plain humility, even as a man telleth another in mine own language, concerning these things; and only a few have I written, because of my weakness in writing" (Ether 12:39–40). Two concepts in this report are repeated throughout the Book of Mormon: plain speech and inability to write about some things. "I have spoken plainly unto you," Nephi says, "that ye cannot misunderstand"; "my soul delighteth in plainness," he continues, "for after this manner doth the Lord God work among the children of men" (2 Nephi 25:28; 31:3). Yet Nephi also delights in the words of Isaiah, which "are not plain unto you," although "they are plain unto all those that are filled with the spirit of prophecy" (2 Nephi 25:4). In the Book of Mormon we have both the plain and the veiled language, and we learn about each from the other.

Mormon's inability to write about certain things often has to do with confinement of space; in other instances, though,

Mormon is either forbidden to write or the words are so exalted that man cannot speak or write them. As an example of the latter, in a scene in which a mob is intent on killing two prophets named Nephi and Lehi, the piercing voice of God twice calls on the people to repent. The third time, the voice "did speak unto them marvelous words which cannot be uttered by man" (Helaman 5:33).

This event prefigures the scene not long afterward in which a multitude visited by the resurrected Jesus twice hear a voice from heaven but do not understand it; nevertheless, "notwithstanding it being a small voice it did pierce them that did hear to the center, insomuch that there was no part of their frame that it did not cause to quake; yea, it did pierce them to the very soul, and did cause their hearts to burn" (3 Nephi 11:3). The third time they hear the voice, it says simply yet profoundly, "Behold my Beloved Son, in whom I am well pleased, in whom I have glorified my name—hear ye him" (3 Nephi 11:7). Here at the meeting point between the mortal and divine we feel the intense power both of the word and of divine communication beyond speech. The people do hear Jesus, and later in responding to his prayers, they have an experience that transcends mortal language: "And their hearts were open and they did understand in their hearts the words which he prayed. Nevertheless, so great and marvelous were the words which he prayed that they cannot be written, neither can they be uttered by man" (3 Nephi 19:33–34).

The experiences of the Nephites with the resurrected Savior show the extreme possibilities and limitations of communication. Christ expounded unto the multitude all things, "both great and small," and "even babes did open their mouths and utter marvelous things" (3 Nephi 26:1, 16). Yet the things the babes said "were forbidden that there should not any man write them" (3 Nephi 26:16); those people who were filled with the Holy Ghost "saw and heard unspeakable things, which are not lawful to be written" (3 Nephi 26:18); and, as he has been commanded,

Mormon records only "a lesser part of the things which [the Savior] taught the people" (3 Nephi 26:8).

The styles Mormon and other narrators employ range widely, from the simple and unadorned to the lofty and poetic.[21] The tones range from humblest pleading to denunciation: "Behold, mine arm of mercy is extended towards you, and whosoever will come, him will I receive," Jesus says; "O ye wicked and perverse and stiffnecked people," Moroni declares, "why have ye built up churches unto yourselves to get gain?" (3 Nephi 9:14; Mormon 8:33). These styles and tones will be of interest in the chapters that follow as we read and analyze the integrated form and content of such pieces as the epigrammatic poetry of Lehi, the intricate psalm of Nephi, the rhetorically persuasive sermons of Jacob, the chiastic speech of King Benjamin, the dramatic encounter between Alma and Korihor, the lament of Mormon, and the parting testimony of Moroni.

PURPOSES OF THE BOOK OF MORMON

Literary elements in the Book of Mormon such as form, word choice, imagery, poetry, and narrative are part of the God-designed nature of the book to develop the primary purposes set out in the title page. The first of these purposes is to show the Lamanites, identified as a remnant of the house of Israel, the "great things the Lord hath done for their fathers" (especially Nephi and Lehi) and to help them "know the covenants of the Lord," which assure them "that they are not cast off forever." Second, the book is designed to convince "the Jew and Gentile that Jesus is the Christ, the Eternal God, manifesting himself unto all nations." Of course, what is true for one of the three audiences of the Book of Mormon can be applied to another.

The title page can be considered a table of contents for the Book of Mormon. Its major ideas are repeated elsewhere in Nephi's writings as well as in those of Mormon and Moroni, and those ideas give force to the major concerns of the book. For example, in extended comments about himself and his role, Mormon says that his work helps fulfill the prayers of the holy ones that the gospel would come in the latter days to the Lamanites. Mormon acknowledges the great thing the Lord has done in delivering Lehi and his family ("he brought our fathers out of the land of Jerusalem") and connects it with the deliverance of souls ("he hath given me and my people so much knowledge unto the salvation of our souls" [3 Nephi 5:20]). God shall "bring a remnant of the seed of Joseph [present-day Lamanites] to the knowledge of the Lord their God"; he shall restore to them "the knowledge of the covenant that he hath covenanted with them" (3 Nephi 5:23, 25). And all the house of Jacob shall "know their Redeemer, who is Jesus Christ, the Son of God" (3 Nephi 5:26).

In the chapters that follow, we will discover ways in which the purposes of the Book of Mormon as generally stated in the title page are shown forth by various literary elements.[22] They correspond with the main genres literary critic Leland Ryken finds in the Bible: "narrative or story, poetry (especially lyric poetry), proverb, and visionary writing (including both prophecy and apocalypse). . . . The letters of the New Testament frequently become literary because of their artistic and poetic style."[23]

Although several aspects of literature are involved in each purpose set forth in the title page, I will emphasize one or two per chapter. Thus, in Chapter 2 the focus is on narrators of the book and on selected narratives. These narratives "show unto the remnant of the House of Israel" the great things done for their fathers—heroic persons such as Nephi, Jacob, Ammon, and Alma.

The next chapter connects epic elements in the Book of Mormon that show "what great things the Lord hath done." The major thousand-year story of the origin, development, and eventual destruction of the Nephite civilization is in its very nature an epic. Contained within this Nephite epic is the story of the

Jaredites, which, Nibley persuasively argues, comes right out of an epic milieu.[24] In the largest sense, the Book of Mormon may also be considered as having the timelessness, sweep of significance, and scope of meaning of cosmic drama.

Chapter 4, "By the Spirit of Prophecy," emphasizes the many instances of Hebraic-like poetry in the Book of Mormon. In it I will point out how a claim David Noel Freedman makes for the Bible often holds for the Book of Mormon as well. Freedman says that "the speeches of angels and other inspired persons are in the form of poetry."[25] The beautiful and sometimes complex poetry of the Book of Mormon is concealed by the English translation's prose format. In passages that I have placed in verse form to reveal their poetry, the manner in which something is said often contains, suggests, and develops its meaning.

The following chapter, "Know the Covenants of the Lord," dwells on sermons. These sermons can be considered belles lettres if they reveal that careful and artistic attention has been paid to form as well as content. Several of the ten sermons we will look at, which often contain poetry and word-play, lend themselves well to rhetorical analysis of the type classics professor George Kennedy applies to the Bible in *New Testament Interpretation through Rhetorical Criticism*.[26] In comparing sermons, we will find that strikingly different approaches are taken with different audiences.

Chapter 6 treats the "fathers" mentioned in the title page of the Book of Mormon as they present themselves in letters and autobiography. We will examine eight letters for contrasting tones and personalities. As with the sermons, I analyze letters for the nature and effectiveness of the message they send. With the Moroni-Ammoron and Moroni-Pahoran correspondence, we will have particular interest in the way the writers respond to each other. Autobiography is connected with letters in revealing personalities. It figures prominently in the book, with Nephi, Enos, Mormon, and others speaking directly about their own experiences.

Chapter 7 picks up on the phrase "not cast off forever" to develop the implications of imagery in the Book of Mormon. A literary approach considers the kinds of images in the Book of Mormon and their relationships and takes the view that the book's truths are approached vitally and vibrantly *through* the imagery. Of principal interest is the polarity in images illustrating the prophet Lehi's understanding that "it must needs be, that there is an opposition in all things" (2 Nephi 2:11). Our study of imagery includes direct imagery as well as figurative devices such as simile and metaphor, and it expands to consider such matters as symbolism and archetypal imagery.

Chapter 8, "That Jesus Is the Christ," deals mainly with typology. As with the Old Testament, the Book of Mormon is filled with types and shadows. Moreover, Book of Mormon prophets make conscious and overt reference to them—especially Abinadi in teaching that all the performances and ordinances of the law of Moses "were types of things to come" (Mosiah 13:31). This chapter considers persons, categories of persons, objects or events, and the Book of Mormon itself as types.

The concluding chapter, "At the Judgment-Seat of Christ," develops the largest implications of a literary approach to the Book of Mormon. Here we will look at the whole book in terms of liminal (threshold) persons, places, and actions, and will review the Book of Mormon as prophecy. Designed for our day, the book points through time to timelessness, through this world to the next, culminating in the last judgment.

CHAPTER 2

"To Show unto the Remnant of the House of Israel"
NARRATORS AND NARRATIVES

One mark of great literature is that it *shows* a concept concretely and avoids telling or explaining it abstractly. Appropriately, then, the Book of Mormon purposes to "show unto the remnant of the House of Israel what great things the Lord hath done for their fathers." In part, this showing comes because the narrators in the Book of Mormon connect actively with their auditors or readers and relate many engaging stories.

Nephi tells his experiences from the first-person point of view, causing the reader to identify with him more fully. Mormon regularly uses *we* in making a point relevant to his latter-day audience, thus immediately engaging the reader. And following the lead of his father, Moroni speaks directly to a latter-day audience throughout his narration.

Mormon is very much aware that his audience is made up of latter-day Lamanites, Jews, and Gentiles; his son, Moroni, also knows his audience (Mormon 8–9). In his closing testimony, Mormon focuses on "the remnant of this people who are spared" to issue a stirring challenge: "Know ye that ye are of the house of Israel. . . . Know ye that ye must come to the knowledge of your fathers, and repent of all your sins and iniquities, and believe in Jesus Christ, that he is the Son of God" (Mormon 7:1–2, 5).

Not only does Mormon speak to a latter-day audience but he counsels with them and personalizes what they learn from his narratives. *"Now we see,"* he emphasizes, "that Ammon could not be slain" (Alma 19:23). Regarding the conversion that follows he says, *"thus we see* that the Lord worketh in many ways to the salvation of his people" (Alma 24:27). Commenting on circumstances of people living at the time of the second Helaman, he confirms, *"Thus we may see* that the Lord is merciful unto all who will, in the sincerity of their hearts, call upon his holy name" (Helaman 3:27).

For his part, Moroni testifies to his audience, "[I shall] meet *you* before the pleasing bar of the great Jehovah, the Eternal Judge of both quick and dead" (Moroni 10:34). Here Moroni brings together past, present, and future. Although he wrote in our past, Moroni speaks to his readers in our present and anticipates meeting them in the future at the judgment bar. Similarly, his references to Jesus Christ combine references to both the past and the future. The title "Jehovah" is associated with the mission of the premortal Savior, the Alpha. The title "the Eternal Judge of both quick and dead" specifies the future mission of Jesus Christ, the Omega. At the judgment bar, we shall acknowledge that his association with the children of men has been timeless.

When we first encounter Mormon, in the Words of Mormon following the books from the small plates of Nephi, we learn a great deal about his narrative approach. He begins at the end of the Nephite drama: "I have witnessed almost all the destruction of my people," he says, and he supposes his son Moroni "will witness the entire destruction of my people" (Words of Mormon 1:1–2). Saying his account is brief, he prays that his brethren, the Lamanites and renegade Nephites, "may once again come to the knowledge of God, yea, the redemption of Christ" (Words of Mormon 1:8). He then focuses on an individual, King Benjamin, in whose experiences we find the repeated dual threats to the Nephites. External opposition is by the Lamanites, who in Benjamin's time are defeated by the Nephites with their king at the fore wielding the sword of Laban (which is inherited by the kings and transferred with the records down to Mormon).

Internal threats come in the form of false Christs, false prophets, and contentions. Benjamin's solution to both problems is to reign in righteousness and to have many holy men "speak the word of God with power and with authority" (Words of Mormon 1:17).

Mormon's methods as an editor-historian are complex, and he masterfully weaves the fabric of his part of the book. His art, though, is unobtrusive. Perhaps that is why relatively little attention has been paid to it.[1] Mormon focuses on individuals, letting them speak for themselves as much as possible through sermons, letters, and dialogues. With the Lord's direction, Mormon selects those experiences that are most important to the book's overall purposes. As Grant Hardy in an essay on Mormon as editor has pointed out, the answer in part to what Mormon includes and excludes "lies in Mormon's purpose, which was not to give an exact historical account of ancient Nephite culture, but rather to turn our hearts to God." Mormon's focus on individuals emphasizes that "those who follow God are blessed, while those who reject him suffer."[2]

REPETITION AND THE BOOK OF MORMON

An important part of Mormon's method is using repetition, parallels, and contrasts to teach, emphasize, and confirm. He clearly knows the ancient principle that repetition can help alert and convince people. That is especially true of threefold repetition. When we knock at a door, we usually do it three times. A typical cheer is repeated three times, with the last cheer being the most emphatic. When we persist in trying something, the third try often produces the desired result. Jesus gives three ascending injunctions to the Nephite people gathered at the temple in Bountiful: "Ask, and it shall be given unto you; seek, and ye shall find; knock, and it shall be opened unto you" (3 Nephi 14:7). They are to speak, then move, then use vigorous action—each operation more intense than the last. On the first level, they are given what they ask for; on the second, they do the finding; on the third and most effectual level, they both receive (the door is opened to them) and act (implicitly, they go through the doorway). In the Old Testament, it is not until the third time Samuel tells about hearing a voice that Eli finally perceives it is the Lord's (1 Samuel 3:8). It is on the third time that the Nephites at the temple in Bountiful finally understand the heavenly voice (3 Nephi 11:5).

Repetition appears purposefully within Book of Mormon narratives; indeed, it seems that every important action, event, or character type is repeated. For instance, two wealthy men (Lehi and Amulek) lose their riches as they pursue prophetic callings. Kings Benjamin and Limhi each assemble their people in order to speak to them. Two sons of kings (Ammon and his brother Aaron) speak with kings (Lamoni and his father). Alma the Younger and Lamoni fall into trances in which they appear to be dead. Two detailed accounts are given of prophets threatened within a prison (Alma and Amulek, Nephi and Lehi). Two Lamanite leaders (who also are brothers) are killed by a spear within their tents. And prophets (Abinadi, Alma, and Samuel) are cast out of cities and then return at the Lord's bidding. Further, prophet-leaders (Lehi, Zeniff, and Mosiah) gather people to read records to them. Antichrists (notably Sherem, Korihor, and Nehor) lead people to follow their iniquities. A man named Ammon, living in the time of King Mosiah, is captured and taken before King Limhi—and ends up helping Limhi's people escape from captivity; Mosiah's son Ammon is captured and taken before the Lamanite king Lamoni and helps save Lamoni's people both spiritually and physically. And three prophets, Alma the Younger, Nephi the son of Helaman, and Samuel the Lamanite, depart out of the land and are "never heard of more," with the implication that Alma is translated and does not taste death (Alma 45:18–19).[3]

Repetitions in the Book of Mormon emphasize the law of witnesses at work within the book. This law is found in Nephi's testimony that he joined Isaiah and his brother Jacob in seeing the Redeemer: "Wherefore, by the words of three, God hath said, I will establish my word. Nevertheless, God sendeth more witnesses, and he proveth all his words" (2 Nephi 11:3). Again, Nephi quotes the Lord as saying, "Know ye not that the testimony of two nations is a witness unto you that I am God, that I remember one nation like unto another?" (2 Nephi 29:8). Near the end of the book, Moroni reaffirms the law of witnesses when he says, "And in the mouth of three witnesses shall these things be established; and the testimony of three, and this work, in the which shall be shown forth the power of God and also his word, of which the Father, and the Son, and the Holy Ghost bear record—and all this shall stand as a testimony against the world at the last day" (Ether 5:4).[4]

Further, the repetitions underscore the relevance of one character or action to people living in a different time. Many persons and actions typify or foreshadow later persons and actions. For example, at one point when his life is threatened, Nephi commands his brothers that they not touch him, for, he says, "I am filled with the power of God, even unto the consuming of my flesh; and whoso shall lay his hands upon me shall wither even as a dried reed" (1 Nephi 17:48). Standing before a hostile king and his court, the prophet Abinadi similarly says, "Touch me not, for God shall smite you if ye lay your hands upon me, for I have not delivered the message which the Lord sent me to deliver" (Mosiah 13:3). Abinadi's face shines "with exceeding luster, even as Moses' did while in the mount of Sinai, while speaking with the Lord" (Mosiah 13:5). This heavenly transfiguration is repeated in the shining faces of the brothers Nephi and Lehi when they are held in prison (Helaman 5:36) and climaxes in the description of the resurrected Jesus: "and the light of his countenance did shine upon them" (3 Nephi 19:25).

This repetition links narratives together in what Robert Alter in *The Art of Biblical Narrative* calls "a kind of rhythm of thematic significance."[5] Alter's point about actions in the Bible is directly relevant to the Book of Mormon parallels I have mentioned. He says: "Recurrence, parallels, analogy are the hall-marks of reported action in the biblical tale. . . . The two most distinctively biblical uses of repeated action are when we are given two versions of the same event and when the same event, with minor variations, occurs at different junctures of the narrative, usually involving different characters or sets of characters."[6]

Alter calls the recurrence of the same event a "type-scene" and considers it "a central organizing convention of biblical narrative."[7] Some examples Alter notes are an annunciation to a barren woman (Sarah, Rebekah, Hannah), an encounter with a future betrothed at a well (Abraham's servant and Rebekah, Jacob and Rachel, Moses and Jethro's daughter), and a life-threatening trial in the wilderness (Ishmael and Isaac).[8] Parallel episodes with their variations or contrasts reinforce and define each other and develop a larger pattern. They bring a narrative intensity as well as a sense of divine direction of events.

Alter notes that type-scenes contrast with each other as well. In the Book of Mormon, we see parallels and a crucial contrast in two scenes in which a very righteous person and a very wicked person put on disguises. Nephi disguises himself as the Jewish ruler Laban to obtain scriptures, which ultimately are for the good of a whole people (1 Nephi 4:19–38). The conspirator Kishkumen disguises himself and murders the chief judge for his own power and gain (Helaman 1:9–12). When we read the account of Kishkumen in the context of the book as a whole, we may well reflect on Nephi's directive from God to kill Laban and take on a disguise to save a nation spiritually (1 Nephi 4:13) and contrast it to the secret combination of robbers and murderers, of which Kishkumen was a part, that eventually caused the destruction of the Nephites (Ether 8:21).

Although it might be argued that some repetition and contrast in the Book of Mormon is accidental, the accumulated evidence is that such narrators as Mormon and Moroni intended parallel materials to instruct and convince. And even if they are not always conscious of the purposes for which they speak, they "write the things which have been commanded . . . of the Lord" (3 Nephi 26:12).

A clear example of a purposeful contrast of persons is that between Benjamin and Noah, a good king and a wicked one.[9] These narratives are presented in significant detail and appear close to each other. King Benjamin is a model of the righteous king. He calls his people together to bless them, affirms that he has labored with his own hands that he might serve them and that they should not be laden with taxes, and humbly confesses his dependence on God (Mosiah 2:14–19; 4:19). King Noah, described soon thereafter, "did cause his people to commit sin, and do that which was abominable in the sight of the Lord" (Mosiah 11:2); he laid a tax of "one fifth part" of all his people possessed to support a luxurious lifestyle for himself, his wives and concubines, his priests, and their wives and concubines (Mosiah 11:3–4). Rather than consider himself a beggar before God, King Noah "placed his heart upon his riches, and he spent his time in riotous living" (Mosiah 11:14). At the time he proposes the institution of judges in place of a king, Benjamin's son Mosiah pointedly tells his people that if they could always have kings like Benjamin, "then it would be expedient that ye should always have kings to rule over you," but one wicked king can cause much iniquity and great destruction (Mosiah 29:13, 17). "Yea, remember king Noah," Mosiah says, "his wickedness and his abominations, and also the wickedness and abominations of his people. Behold what great destruction did come upon them" (Mosiah 29:18).

Finally, repetition intensifies and confirms in memorable ways. Jesus does not simply say that the multitude assembled at Bountiful must "repent, and become as a little child, and be baptized in my name, or ye can in nowise receive these things" (3 Nephi 11:37). He immediately follows this statement with a rearrangement of the three parts and intensifies the result: "And again I say unto you, ye must repent, and be baptized in my name, and become as a little child, or ye can in nowise inherit

25

the kingdom of God" (3 Nephi 11:38). Mormon confirms that Alma repeated elements of his personal experience in counseling his sons. Of his own life, Alma says, "I have been supported under trials and troubles of every kind, yea, and in all manner of afflictions; yea, God has delivered me from prison, and from bonds, and from death; yea, and I do put my trust in him, and he will still deliver me. And I know that he will raise me up at the last day, to dwell with him in glory" (Alma 36:27–28).

Alma then turns around and advises his son Shiblon to "remember, that as much as ye shall put your trust in God even so much ye shall be delivered out of your trials, and your troubles, and your afflictions, and ye shall be lifted up at the last day" (Alma 38:5).

Of the many narratives in the Book of Mormon, we will examine four representative ones developed by repetition and contrast. The first, Nephi's heroic quest to obtain the brass plates from Laban, is intensified and made memorable by events or concerns occurring three times. The second, the account of Ammon and the missionary effort among the Lamanites, builds its meaning with repeated emphasis on power. The remaining two, the encounter between Jacob and Sherem and the conflict between Alma and Korihor, present contrasting persons and world views. In each case, conflicts are resolved dramatically.

Conflict and resolution are found as well in other narratives not analyzed here, such as Abinadi's courageous stand before King Noah; Amulek's confrontation with Zeezrom, "one of the most expert" (Alma 10:31) lawyers in the land of Ammonihah; the showdown between Captain Moroni and the Lamanite chieftain Zerahemnah; the frightening story of the rise to power of the wicked Amalickiah; the experience of the brothers Nephi and Lehi in prison; Nephi the son of Helaman and his detection of the murder of the judge by the judge's brother; the whole drama of the visit of the resurrected Christ; and the fight to the finish between the last two Jaredite kings, Coriantumr and Shiz.

Repetition in Nephi's Quest

There is significant repetition in the hero's task given Nephi and his brothers—retrieving from Laban the scriptural records that would preserve for Lehi and his family "the language of our fathers," the law, and "the words . . . of all the holy prophets . . . since the world began" (1 Nephi 3:19–20). This quest follows what Leland Ryken in *How to Read the Bible as Literature* calls "the storytelling principle of threefold repetition: a given event happens three times, with a crucial change introduced the third time."[10]

In the first of the three visits to Laban, and apparently without a plan, Laman futilely asks Laban to relinquish the records. Next, the brothers follow Nephi's plan to offer their gold, silver, and other precious things for the plates of brass, only to have Laban take all this wealth from them and then try to have them pursued and killed. The third time, Nephi goes alone with no plan: "I was led by the Spirit, not knowing beforehand the things which I should do" (1 Nephi 4:6). Then the Lord's plan goes into effect. This marks the "crucial change" Ryken speaks about.

Each of these efforts is put into motion by a pledge, and the pledges become more and more intense. At the initial request to get the plates, Nephi says to his father, "I will go and do the things which the Lord hath commanded" (1 Nephi 3:7). After Laman's failure, Nephi increases his initial commitment to go and do what the Lord commanded and applies it to all the brothers: "As the Lord liveth, and as we live, we will not go down unto our father in the wilderness until we have accomplished the thing which the Lord hath commanded us" (1 Nephi 3:15). When the next plan fails and the older brothers are reproved by an angel for beating their younger brothers, Nephi calls for them all to "be faithful in keeping the commandments of the Lord" and affirms the power of God by alluding to the great miracle of the Israelites crossing through the Red Sea (1 Nephi 4:1–2). The emphasis has moved from "*I* will go and do," to *we* will not leave until *"we* have accomplished," to *the Lord* is "mightier than Laban and his fifty" and *"the Lord* is able to deliver us, even as our fathers, and to destroy Laban, even as the Egyptians" (1 Nephi 4:1, 3).

Finding Laban drunk in the street, Nephi is three times "constrained by the Spirit" to kill him (1 Nephi 4:10). The first is a simple injunction: Kill Laban. The second is the impression that the Lord has delivered Laban into Nephi's hands. Nephi thinks of three reasons why he could be justified in taking Laban's life: (1) Laban sought to take away Nephi's own life. (2) Laban would not hearken unto the commands of the Lord. (3) He had taken away property belonging to Nephi's family. The third constraint of the Spirit adds the crucial, convincing element: "The Lord slayeth the wicked to bring forth his righteous purposes. It is better that one man should perish than that a nation should dwindle and perish in unbelief" (1 Nephi 4:13).

Nephi then slays Laban, dresses in his clothes and armor, and with the help of Laban's servant Zoram, gets the brass plates and takes them outside the city wall. There, in calling to his frightened brothers, Nephi reveals his identity to Zoram—whom Nephi holds to keep from fleeing. Nephi then makes three levels of appeal to Zoram. These are introduced by a similar formulaic phrase, moving from sparing Zoram's life, to allowing him freedom, to having a place with Lehi's family:

> And it came to pass that I spake with him, that if he would hearken unto my words, as the Lord liveth, and as I live, even so that if he would hearken unto our words, we would spare his life. And I spake unto him, even with an oath, that he need not fear; that he should be a free man like unto us if he would go down in the wilderness with us. And I also spake unto him, saying: Surely the Lord hath commanded us to do this thing; and shall we not be diligent in keeping the commandments of the Lord? Therefore, if thou wilt go down into the wilderness to my father thou shalt have place with us. (1 Nephi 4:32–34)

A three-part pattern is found as well in Sariah's lament to Lehi, with the pattern emphasized by the rhythmical "Behold . . . , and . . . , and . . . ": "Behold thou hast led us forth from the land of our inheritance [as a supposedly visionary man], and my sons are no more, and we perish in the wilderness" (1 Nephi 5:2). This feared decline is counterbalanced by Sariah's three-part praise uttered at the return of her sons. In this utterance she echoes Nephi's initial commitment: "I also know of a surety that the Lord hath protected my sons, and delivered them out of the hands of Laban, and given them power whereby they could accomplish the thing which the Lord hath commanded them" (1 Nephi 5:8). For his part, Nephi affirms that he and his father obtained the records, searched these scriptures, and carried the records with them so the Lord's commandments could be preserved (1 Nephi 5:21–22).

Repetition of Power *as a Narrative Focus*

The missionary endeavor of Ammon with King Lamoni, found in a single chapter in the 1830 edition of the Book of Mormon (Alma 17 through 20 in the current edition), is one of the most interesting stories in the Book of Mormon. By looking at this narrative as a single story, we discover that its center is the kingdom of God in contrast with the kingdom of man, the power of God in contrast with that of man. It shows the ideal power of the missionary. Mormon's headnote regarding the whole mission of the sons of Mosiah underlines this theme: The sons of Mosiah reject their "rights to the kingdom" (an earthly kingdom with its accompanying power) "for the word of God" and go up to the land of Nephi "to preach to the Lamanites." There they experience "sufferings and deliverance." This acceptance of God's power and denial of earthly glory is emphasized in the first paragraph of the 1830 edition. The sons of Mosiah, we are told, "taught with *power* and authority of God. . . . having refused the kingdom which their father was desirous to confer upon them" (Alma 17:3, 6). From this point on, the word *power* becomes a repeated drumbeat throughout the narrative.

Leaving behind a presumably comfortable life in Zarahemla, the sons of Mosiah depart into the wilderness to go among "a wild and a hardened and a ferocious people" (Alma 17:14). Although Aaron appears to have been the eldest of the four, in their journey Ammon is their leader but still their servant—he was "the chief among them, or rather he did administer unto them" (Alma 17:18). On arriving in Lamoni's court, Ammon, a king's son, declares his willingness to leave royalty behind him and "to dwell among this people for a time; yea, and perhaps until the day I die" (Alma 17:23). Offered the possibility of earthly reward (taking one of Lamoni's daughters to wife), Ammon opts instead to be the king's servant.

The story that follows gains dramatic intensity by a greater movement into dialogue and monologue, with the emphatic word being *power*. At the waters of Sebus, the king's servants express their fear of being slain for allowing the flocks to be scattered by robbers. Ammon's interior response is to say, "I will show forth my *power* unto these my fellow-servants, or the *power* which is in me, in restoring these flocks unto the king, that I may win the hearts of these my fellow-servants, that I may lead them to believe in my words" (Alma 17:29). Ammon then serves the servants by being their champion, slinging stones at the bullies: "yea, with mighty *power* he did sling stones amongst them; and thus he slew a certain number of them insomuch that they began to be astonished at his *power*" (Alma 17:36). Later, reporting to the king, the other servants say they "do not believe that a man has such great *power*." The king wants to know, "Where is this man that has such great *power?*" The response is "Behold, he is feeding thy horses" (Alma 18:3, 8–9). This faithfulness elicits even more amazement in King Lamoni, who is now sure Ammon is the Great Spirit. When Ammon enters, the king's servants call him "Rabbanah," which is interpreted as "*powerful* or great king" (Alma 18:13). In this scene of dramatic irony, we know that Ammon has turned down the opportunity to be king in order to be a missionary servant to Lamoni and his people. He, however, never reveals that to Lamoni. Indeed, he maintains the respectful stance of a servant: "What wilt thou that I should do for thee, O king?" (Alma 18:14).

The conversation that ensues revolves around the power question. Lamoni asks: "Tell me by what *power* ye slew and smote off the arms of my brethren that scattered my flocks— . . . if it were needed, I would guard thee with my armies; but I know that thou art more *powerful* than all they." Ammon being "wise, yet harmless," says to Lamoni: "Wilt thou hearken unto my words, if I tell thee by what *power* I do these things?" (Alma 18:20–22).

Lamoni agrees to this missionary opening, and after an exchange of questions and answers in which Ammon teaches Lamoni about God, Lamoni then says: "I believe all these things which thou hast spoken. Art thou sent from God?" Ammon responds: "I am a man; and man in the beginning was created after the image of God, and I am called by his Holy Spirit to teach these things unto this people, that they may be brought to a knowledge of that which is just and true; and a portion of that Spirit dwelleth in me, which giveth me knowledge, and also *power* according to my faith and desires which are in God" (Alma 18:33–35).

Ammon expounds the history of God's dealings unto man, at which the now-believing Lamoni falls into a death-like trance. Ammon recognizes Lamoni's trance as a manifestation of the power of God: "He knew that the dark veil of unbelief was being cast away from his mind" (Alma 19:6).

King Lamoni rises on the third day, bears testimony of the Redeemer, whom he has seen, and then swoons away again, as does the queen, and then Ammon, and then the attending servants. The serving woman Abish, secretly converted earlier, "knew that it was the *power* of God" that made the court swoon. She sees what she thinks is an opportunity, "by making known

31

unto the people what had happened among them, that by beholding this scene it would cause them to believe in the *power* of God, therefore she ran forth from house to house, making it known unto the people" (Alma 19:17).

The action that most miraculously shows forth the power of God is the death of the man who tries to kill the unconscious Ammon—an event that causes great contention among the people as to "the cause of this great *power*" (Alma 19:24). Abish ends the contention when she lifts up the queen, who in turn takes Lamoni by the hand, and he arises. They "declare unto the people the self-same thing—that their hearts had been changed; that they had no more desire to do evil" (Alma 19:33).

Ammon's journey with Lamoni to the land of Middoni to deliver his brother Aaron and two other missionaries from prison brings to a climactic focus the question of power and control (Alma 20). Here, the king over all the land—Lamoni's own father—commands Lamoni to slay Ammon and then tries to kill Ammon himself after Lamoni refuses. But Ammon withstands his assault and immobilizes him; the king then offers Ammon whatever he wants—even up to half the kingdom. For the third time refusing earthly glory or power, Ammon asks only for freedom for his brothers and for Lamoni. This refusal of earthly power opens the way for Ammon to counter a cause of anger held by the Lamanites for centuries: their belief that Nephi had robbed them, that Laman and Lemuel's younger brother had taken over in both land and leadership. Ammon teaches Lamoni, who is a descendant of Ishmael, about the rebellions of Laman, Lemuel, and the sons of Ishmael. Then, before the king over all the land, Ammon responds to the Lamanite view that the Nephites are descendants of a liar and a robber (Alma 20:10–13). By forgoing earthly power, Ammon shows forth God's power and thus opens up the most significant missionary harvest in the Book of Mormon. The editor's (Mormon's) heavily repeated use of the word translated as *power* drives home that point.

JACOB AND SHEREM: A CONFLICT BETWEEN
SPIRIT AND INTELLECT

Nephi's younger brother and spiritual heir, Jacob, also has an overarching view of God's dealings with Israel and a firm spiritual knowledge that comes from "the good word of Christ, and the power of God, and the gift of the Holy Ghost" (Jacob 6:8). They are evident in Jacob's sermons that are quoted at length by Nephi (2 Nephi 6, 9–10) and in the subsequent book of Jacob, which includes his challenging sermonic call to repentance (Jacob 2–3) and his quotation of Zenos's extensive allegory of the tame and wild olive trees. The aged Jacob's dramatic dialogue with the antichrist Sherem is the culmination of his ministry and a fitting close to the book of Jacob.

To this prophet, who has such power of convicting speech and such a comprehensive view of God's dealings with Israel, comes Sherem, described as "learned, that he had a perfect knowledge of the language of the people; wherefore, he could use much flattery, and much power of speech, according to the power of the devil" (Jacob 7:4). Testing his skills on the high priest, Sherem is patronizing and sarcastic as he tries to shake Jacob from the faith and accuses Jacob of the crimes of leading the people into false forms of worship, blasphemy, and false prophecy:

> Brother Jacob, I have sought much opportunity that I might speak unto you; for I have heard and also know that thou goest about much, preaching that which ye call the gospel, or the doctrine of Christ. And ye have led away much of this people that they pervert the right way of God, and keep not the law of Moses which is the right way; and convert the law of Moses into the worship of a being which ye say shall come many hundred years hence. And now behold, I, Sherem, declare unto you that this is blasphemy; for no man knoweth of such things; for he cannot tell of things to come. (Jacob 7:6–7)

Note how Sherem calls Jacob "Brother," portraying himself as a concerned believer trying lovingly to correct a misguided fellow believer. He attempts to undermine Jacob's position by describing his teachings as "that which *ye call* the gospel" and Christ as "a being which *ye say* shall come," as if Jacob had himself fabricated the doctrines he taught.

Sherem challenges here the three central tenets of Jacob's life and teachings. At the beginning of his book, Jacob had accepted Nephi's charge to engrave on the plates *"preaching* which was sacred, or *revelation* which was great, or *prophesying* . . . of Christ and his kingdom, which should come" (Jacob 1:4, 6). Now Sherem disputes Jacob's authority as a prophet who could know by revelation concerning the future. Jacob's recounting of the event shows both the source of his knowledge as well as his ability to counter Sherem.

> But behold, the Lord God poured in his Spirit into my soul, insomuch that I did confound him in all his words. And I said unto him: Deniest thou the Christ who shall come?
>
> And he said: If there should be a Christ, I would not deny him; but I know that there is no Christ, neither has been, nor ever will be.
>
> And I said unto him: Believest thou the scriptures?
>
> And he said, Yea.
>
> And I said unto him: Then ye do not understand them; for they truly testify of Christ. Behold, I say unto you that none of the prophets have written, nor prophesied, save they have spoken concerning this Christ. And this is not all—it has been made manifest unto me, for I have heard and seen; and it also has been made manifest unto me by the power of the Holy Ghost; wherefore, I know if there should be no atonement made all mankind must be lost. (Jacob 7:8–12)

Jacob strikes right at the heart of Sherem's position, challenging him to defend his denial of Christ. Sherem's response is one of intellectual pride, saying he knows there will never be a Christ. In opposing this position, Jacob not only exposes the limitations of Sherem's understanding of the scriptures but also affirms his own knowledge, which has come through divine means. Then with sarcastic scorn, Sherem challenges Jacob to produce a sign: "Show me a sign by this power of the Holy Ghost, in the which ye know so much" (Jacob 7:13).

Here the arrogant Sherem goes one step too far in a conflict of knowing and knowledge. Jacob's response defines the issue and leaves the outcome to God:

> What am I that I should tempt God to show unto thee a sign in the thing which thou knowest to be true? Yet thou wilt deny it, because thou art of the devil. Nevertheless, not my will be done; but if God shall smite thee, let that be a sign unto thee that he has power, both in heaven and in earth; and also, that Christ shall come. And thy will, O Lord, be done, and not mine. (Jacob 7:14)

The humble preacher ("what am I") accepts revelation ("if God shall smite thee") and prophecy ("that Christ shall come"). In response to Jacob's words, Sherem is struck down. Some days later he says to the people:

> Gather together on the morrow, for I shall die; wherefore, I desire to speak unto the people before I shall die. And it came to pass that on the morrow the multitude were gathered together; and he spake plainly unto them and denied the things which he had taught them, and confessed the Christ, and the power of the Holy Ghost, and the ministering of angels. And he spake plainly unto them, that he had been deceived by the power of the devil. And he spake of hell, and of eternity, and of eternal punishment. And he said: I fear lest I have committed the unpardonable sin, for I have lied unto God; for I denied the Christ, and said that I believed the scriptures; and they truly testify of him. And because I have thus lied unto God I greatly fear lest my case shall be awful; but I confess unto God. And it came to pass that when he had said these words he could say no more, and he gave up the ghost. (Jacob 7:16–20)

When Sherem is struck down, he abandons his sophisticated subtlety and assumes, at his death, the position Jacob had taken: He "spake plainly" unto the multitude (the humble preacher, not using much flattery and power of language), he confessed the Christ (prophecy), and he acknowledged the means of acquiring spiritual knowledge, the power of the Holy Ghost (revelation).

35

Both as summarized and then as quoted, Sherem's speech now is plain, not clever, made up of simple sentences and direct declarations. His death seals his confession. This remarkable occurrence initiates a restoration of "peace and the love of God" among the people, and they "hearkened no more to the words of this wicked man" (Jacob 7:23).

ALMA AND KORIHOR: A CONFLICT OF WORLD VIEWS

The conflict between Alma and Korihor echoes the earlier one between Jacob and Sherem. The antichrist Korihor, however, does not seek out Alma but rather is brought before him after other efforts fail to counter Korihor. Analysis of the encounter reveals two opposing manners of communication and two conflicting world views.

Korihor appears on the scene when, in the aftermath of war, the people enjoy "continual peace" and strictly keep the commandments. He violates that peace and harmony by scornfully persuading the people that they are "bound down under a foolish and a vain hope" and asking why they yoke themselves "with such foolish things." His teachings that "every man fared in this life according to the management of the creature; . . . and whatsoever a man did was no crime" are "pleasing unto the carnal mind" (Alma 30:2–3, 13, 17, 53).

This philosophy of Korihor, says Hugh Nibley,

> with its naturalism, materialism, and moral relativism, is the prevailing philosophy of our own day, as was foreseen in the Book of Mormon: "Yea . . . there shall be great pollutions upon the face of the earth . . . when there shall be many who will say, Do this, or do that, and it mattereth not, for the Lord will uphold such at the last day. But wo unto such, for they are in the gall of bitterness and in the bonds of iniquity" (Mormon 8:31).[11]

Chauncey Riddle, in his masterful analysis of Korihor, explores three of Korihor's arguments that continue to seduce people today. The first is that "it is possible to *know* all truth through the senses—by experience and observation." The second is a humanist position that "the solutions to our problems lie in sharp thinking and realistic approaches to life," and success is defined "in terms of wealth, social status, political power, and the glutting of the senses." A third argument is relativist: since so-called commandments and laws "are but social conveniences to give power to priests, the only important thing in life is to do what you want to do—if you can get away with it."[12]

With "great swelling words" (Alma 30:31), Korihor depends on the power of rhetoric and word choice (diction) to cow the church leaders and win over the people. When Giddonah, the high priest of Gideon, asks him why he speaks "against all the prophecies of the holy prophets" (Alma 30:22), Korihor says first it is because of what he does not do: "Because I do not teach the foolish traditions of your fathers, and because I do not teach this people to bind themselves down under the foolish ordinances and performances which are laid down by ancient priests, to usurp power and authority over them, to keep them in ignorance, that they may not lift up their heads, but be brought down according to thy words" (Alma 30:23).

Then he sets up the argument that it is the priest's word against his word. Sarcastically, he uses loaded language that puts down the position of the priests and makes them seem to be the oppressors of the people. If Korihor is allowed to define the terms of the argument and slickly slant his words, his smooth tongue is bound to win:

Ye say that this people is a free people.
Behold, I say they are in *bondage*.
Ye say that those ancient prophecies are true.
Behold, I say that ye do not know that they are true.
Ye say that this people is a guilty and a fallen people, because of the transgression of a parent.
Behold, I say that a child is not guilty because of its parents.
And ye also say that Christ shall come.

But behold, I say that ye do not know that there shall be a
   Christ.
And ye say also that he shall be slain for the sins of the world—
   And thus ye lead away this people after the *foolish* traditions of
your fathers, and according to *your own desires;* and ye *keep them
down,* even as it were in *bondage,* that ye may *glut* yourselves
with the labors of their hands, that they *durst not* look up with
boldness, and that they *durst not* enjoy their rights and privileges.
Yea, they *durst not* make use of that which is their own lest they
should offend their priests, who do *yoke* them according to *their
desires,* and have brought them to believe, by their *traditions* and
their *dreams* and their *whims* and their visions and their *pretended
mysteries,* that they should, if they did not do according to their
words, offend *some unknown being,* who *they say* is God—a
being who never has been seen or known, who never was nor
ever will be. (Alma 30:24–28)

Upon hearing Korihor "revile even against God" (Alma
30:29), Giddonah delivers the antichrist to Alma, who counters
Korihor by affirming the truth in clear tones of authority: "Thou
knowest that we do not glut ourselves upon the labors of this
people" (Alma 30:32). Further, he pointedly challenges Korihor's
lies: "Why sayest thou that we preach unto this people to get
gain, when thou, of thyself, knowest that we receive no gain?"
(Alma 30:35). At almost every point, Alma either anticipates
Korihor's position or gives him a question that calls for a definitive yes or no answer: "Believest thou that there is a God? And
he answered, Nay" (Alma 30:37–38). To counter Korihor's agnos-
ticism, Alma testifies of God and Christ and then asks, "Believest
thou that these things are true? Behold, I know that thou
believest, but thou art possessed with a lying spirit, and ye have
put off the Spirit of God that it may have no place in you; but
the devil has power over you, and he doth carry you about,
working devices that he may destroy the children of God" (Alma
30:41–42).

When Korihor persists in demanding a sign, Alma responds,
"If thou shalt deny again, behold God shall smite thee, that thou

shalt become dumb, that thou shalt never open thy mouth any more, that thou shalt not deceive this people any more" (Alma 30:47). But Korihor's arrogance carries him too far: "I do not deny the existence of a God, but I do not believe that there is a God; and I say also, that ye do not know that there is a God; and except ye show me a sign, I will not believe" (Alma 30:48). In response to that, Alma invokes the power of God to testify of God's existence: "This will I give unto thee for a sign, that thou shalt be struck dumb, according to my words; and I say, that in the name of God, ye shall be struck dumb, that ye shall no more have utterance" (Alma 30:49). The sign takes immediate effect.

There is poetic justice in this consequence: a man whose unrighteous influence depended on his skillful use of words is struck dumb at his own proud insistence. The power of Korihor's language is overcome by the power of God through Alma. To the chief judge's query, "Art thou convinced of the power of God?" (Alma 30:51), Korihor in his extremity writes the truth. In its simplicity and in its emphasis on knowing, Korihor's subdued statement contrasts sharply with his earlier taunting disbelief: "I know that I am dumb, for I cannot speak; and I know that nothing save it were the power of God could bring this upon me; yea, and I always knew that there was a God" (Alma 30:52).

At this point he acknowledges the attractions and yet limitations of the devil's words he has taught:

> But behold, the devil hath deceived me; for he appeared unto me in the form of an angel, and said unto me: Go and reclaim this people, for they have all gone astray after an unknown God. And he said unto me: There is no God; yea, and he taught me that which I should say. And I have taught his words; and I taught them because they were pleasing unto the carnal mind; and I taught them, even until I had much success, insomuch that I verily believed that they were true; and for this cause I withstood the truth, even until I have brought this great curse upon me. (Alma 30:53)

In the aftermath of this conflict, the dumb Korihor is trampled to death by apostate Zoramites. "And thus we see," Mormon says in summation, "the end of him who perverteth the ways of the Lord; and thus we see that the devil will not support his children at the last day, but doth speedily drag them down to hell" (Alma 30:60). Seen from a latter-day perspective, Korihor's appeal to the unwary is highly attractive. On the other hand, by revealing Korihor's character and the aftermath of his fall, Mormon provides a wise warning to those who would follow such appeals.

ENCOUNTERING AN ANTICHRIST

Both Sherem and Korihor could be called antichrists in their opposition to Christ and his servants (Jacob 7:2; Alma 30:6). With *anti-* meaning "against" (as a person's reflection in a mirror is against the real person), an antichrist might also be a counterfeit. That is, the antichrist might act and speak in clever imitation of Christ, as in showing feigned compassion for the multitude. The difference, as in William Blake's etchings of Jesus and Satan, is in the eyes. From this perspective, the men of Christ—Jacob and Alma—are counterfeited by Sherem and Korihor, who make claims to supplant them in the religious leadership of the people. The accounts of these conflicts show the remnant of Israel both the spiritual strength of two of their "fathers," Jacob and Alma, and the personality of the deceiver and how to detect him. Other deceivers in the Book of Mormon are Nehor (Alma 1:2–15), Alma the Younger before his conversion (Mosiah 27), Amlici (Alma 2), Zeezrom (Alma 10 and following), and those belonging to the order of the Nehors (Alma 14).

The main characteristics of the deceiver are that he is learned in all the arts and cunning of the people and has a perfect knowledge of the language; he can use much flattery and much power of speech; he is popular and prominent—a "beautiful person"; he seeks riches and honor and loves the vain things of the world; he is inspired by the devil and deceived by him; and he pretends to believe what he teaches—indeed, he may come to believe that what he teaches is true.

Though he claims to preach truth, the deceiver uses lying and flattering words to lead away the hearts of many. He calls the bad good and the good bad. He makes people think it is all right to do wickedness, appeals to the carnal mind, and attacks the structure and leadership of the church. A clever debater, he challenges leaders boldly and sarcastically denigrates their characters and teachings. He insinuates doubt and makes people feel foolish for believing their leaders. He attributes motives to church leaders that actually he holds himself and, as a last strategy, asks for a sign. His purposes are to overthrow the doctrine of Christ, to lead away the hearts of the people, to gain riches and honor and satisfy pride, and to teach what is pleasing to the carnal mind, with the implication being that what he teaches is appealing to his own carnal mind.

Jacob and Alma show us how to deal with antichrists. Firm in their faith and knowledge, these prophets respond successfully because they are spiritually prepared and open to direction from God. They clarify and expose the nature of the argument the deceiver is using, refer to the established scriptures, and challenge boldly but not contentiously. Essentially, each church leader states the truth and exposes the deceit and then admonishes with the words of God and bears a strong testimony. As directed by the Spirit, he also reveals the thoughts and motives of the deceiver and affirms the power of the devil over the antichrist. Then he assists those who have been deceived to be convinced of the wickedness of the deceiver and to be converted again unto the Lord.

MORMON'S NARRATIVE STANCE

Near the end of his record, Mormon emphasizes the enormous tensions and conflicts under which he is living and writing. Mormon's natural feelings of faith and love (see his sermon on the topic in Moroni 7) are countered by scenes of gross wickedness and destruction. Tragically, he fully recognizes the spiritual disease of which his people are dying but knows that "the day of grace was passed with them" (Mormon 2:15). Prohibited by the Lord from preaching to his own people, Mormon nevertheless finds an outlet for his strong drive to preach by directing the whole of his book to the descendants of those currently trying to destroy him. He looks down through time to his three-part audience: Lamanite, Gentile, and Jew. His purpose is the same as Moroni's, as stated on the title page—to open the eyes of the Lamanites to their origin and destiny and to declare a testimony of Jesus Christ as the Son of the living God (Mormon 5:9–14; 7:1–10). Prevented by their wickedness from helping his own people, Mormon wishes that he "could persuade all ye ends of the earth to repent and prepare to stand before the judgment-seat of Christ" (Mormon 3:22).

Given Mormon's conflicting feelings as he sees his people descend into wickedness, it is understandable that he might wish to take as his own an earlier prophet's desire to "speak with the trump of God . . . and cry repentance unto every people" (Alma 29:1). Throughout the book of Alma, Mormon is generally clear in signaling narrative transitions and personal comments. In abridging Alma's record, he refers to Alma in the third person and marks direct quotations from him in ways like this: "Alma . . . cried, saying: O Lord, have mercy and spare my life" (Alma 2:30). "Alma began to deliver the word of God. . . . And these are the words which he spake" (Alma 5:1–2). In chapter 16, Alma temporarily disappears from the narrative, however, and the last reference to a first-person "I" is to Ammon in chapter 27. In chapter 28, Mormon abridges Alma's record concerning the faithfulness of the people converted through the ministrations of Ammon and his brethren and tells of a subsequent battle that brought great slaughter.

Although the narrator is probably quoting Alma when he employs present tense regarding some events ("many thousands of others truly mourn for the loss of their kindred" [Alma 28:12]), the subsequent attention paid to the lessons of the experience is more typical of Mormon. The narrator says: "And thus we see how great the inequality of man is because of sin and transgression. . . . And thus we see the great call of diligence of men to labor in the vineyards of the Lord" (Alma 28:13–14). In the 1830 edition of the Book of Mormon, these comments are followed immediately in the same paragraph by Alma's well-known words, "O that I were an angel, and could have the wish of mine heart" (Alma 29:1).[13] There is, however, no indication from Mormon that he is here quoting Alma. Someone reading the first edition with no prior knowledge of the speaker might well think it is Mormon. At the least, the presentation of the utterance suggests the extent to which Mormon identifies with Alma's feelings and desires. For his part, Mormon sorrows "because of death and destruction among men" and rejoices "because of the light of Christ unto life" (Alma 28:14). It is only late into the cry of the heart that follows, when Alma refers to his brethren "who have been up to the land of Nephi" (Alma 29:14), that we are certain the speaker is Alma. A parallel instance is Nephi's prophecy that incorporates Isaiah's prophecy (2 Nephi 26–27). In the 1830 edition, one long paragraph contains both Nephi's sayings and his quotations from Isaiah—without any indication as to what has come from Isaiah. The effect is not just that of Nephi's likening Isaiah to himself but more of Nephi's speaking with the voice of Isaiah.

The concerns Alma expresses are fully appropriate to Mormon. Alma desires that people would repent and come unto God so that "there might not be more sorrow upon all the face of the earth." He recognizes nevertheless that men have free agency to choose spiritual death or life. He joys in being "an instrument in the hands of God," and he remembers the captivity of the fathers (Alma 29:2–12). These concerns are repeated in

Mormon's lament at the end of his record: "O ye fair ones, how could ye have rejected that Jesus, who stood with open arms to receive you! . . . But behold, ye are gone, and my sorrows cannot bring your return" (Mormon 6:17, 20). To the remnant who are spared, he exhorts them down through time to know of their fathers, repent, and come unto Christ.

OVERALL NARRATIVE PATTERNS

The larger narratives of the Book of Mormon have many similarities and thus reflect on each other. This repetition serves to emphasize and define the book's major motifs or concerns. The quest theme is introduced with the commission to Lehi to escape from Jerusalem, obtain the scriptural record found on the brass plates, and eventually take his family to the promised land. This pattern of escaping, obtaining spiritual truth, and going to a safe or sanctified land continues in the stories of Nephi, the elder Alma, and Limhi—all of which sustain the Exodus theme of Israel's escape from captivity in Egypt.[14] The story of the Jaredite migration—occurring earlier than the Nephite migration but recounted later as an epitome of the Nephite experience—repeats the Lehite journey to the promised land. The journey is also a spiritual one. As Alma the Younger explains to his son Helaman, just as the "fathers" were directed by the heaven-sent compass to reach the promised land, so "shall the words of Christ, if we follow their course, carry us beyond this vale of sorrow into a far better land of promise" (Alma 37:45). In this respect, the whole Book of Mormon is a Liahona, a guide for escaping from Babylon to the promised land.

Connected to the theme of travel to the promised land (metaphorically, Christ's kingdom) is the pattern of peoples who make a spiritual journey: either they repent and are converted to Christ or they allow themselves to be led by Satan down to destruction. The book has an intensifying pattern of persons choosing good or pridefully turning from it. For example, the people of King Benjamin and the Lamanites taught by Ammon and his brothers accept the gospel and commit themselves to Christ, whereas Laman and Lemuel, Sherem, Korihor, and the Zoramites willfully reject what they know to be the word of God. Frequently, the people move through what has been called a cycle of humility-prosperity-pride-collapse but which might be more vividly seen as a wave that intensifies as the book progresses. The preservation at Christ's coming of the "more righteous part of the people" (3 Nephi 10:12) and at the same time the calamitous destruction of many cities confirms the oft-repeated Book of Mormon motto. Through every major prophet the Lord declares: "Inasmuch as ye shall keep my commandments ye shall prosper in the land; but inasmuch as ye will not keep my commandments ye shall be cut off from my presence" (2 Nephi 1:20).[15] The reality of the second half of the promise is confirmed vividly by Mormon and Moroni, who recount the descent of the Nephites into total destruction.

The nature, rise, and effect of secret combinations is a third significant type of narrative that is reinforced and confirmed by repetition. Jacob anticipates the problem of Gadiantonism when he warns the Nephites about the devil's stirring up secret combinations (2 Nephi 9:9). Likewise, Nephi's prophecies of secret combinations among the Gentiles and Alma's testimony that the Jaredites were destroyed because of their secret works (2 Nephi 26:22; Alma 37:30) prefigure the effect such works of darkness will have on the Nephite nation. The character of secret combinations is presented dramatically and frighteningly in the detailed accounts of Kishkumen and Gadianton and their band (Helaman 2–16) and of Akish's machinations (Ether 8). One account confirms the other. Together they help reinforce Moroni's warning to the latter-day Gentile inhabitants of the promised land:

> And they have caused the destruction of this people of whom I am now speaking [the Jaredites], and also the destruction of the people of Nephi. And whatsoever nation shall uphold such secret

combinations, to get power and gain, until they shall spread over the nation, behold, they shall be destroyed. (Ether 8:21–22)

Countervailing that dismal picture are prophetic challenges to a future audience. "I speak unto you, ye remnant of the house of Israel," Mormon says. "Know ye that ye must come unto repentance, or ye cannot be saved" (Mormon 7:1, 3). Moroni counsels, "Be wise in the days of your probation; . . . and if ye do this, and endure to the end, ye will in nowise be cast out" (Mormon 9:28–29).

Vivid experiences of such "fathers" as Nephi, Ammon, and Alma do indeed show the great things done by the Lord through them—as Mormon and Moroni pointedly emphasize to the "children" of those fathers, the "remnant of the house of Israel" who accept the spiritual fatherhood and leadership of the Nephite prophets. "Another Testament of Jesus Christ" depends especially on recurrence for its witness. Repetition brings conviction, as they say. Repetition also brings conversion, understanding, and commitment. Like Joseph Smith, visited and revisited by Moroni, readers find "the same things as before" (JS–H 1:46) repeated for them so they cannot misunderstand but rather must remember clearly. Most dramatically, repetition in the book purposes to bring an epiphany—a startling awareness of the divine. In a way, readers of the Book of Mormon are put in a position similar to that of the Nephites to whom the resurrected Savior spoke. At first they heard a voice but did not understand it. Again, they heard without understanding. Finally, "they did hear the voice, and did open their ears to hear it. . . . And behold, the third time they did understand the voice which they heard" (3 Nephi 11:5–6).

CHAPTER 3

"Great Things the Lord Hath Done"
EPIC ELEMENTS

When Moroni addresses the Book of Mormon to "a remnant of the house of Israel," he says the book that comes forth to them will show this remnant "what great things the Lord hath done for their fathers." Moroni implies that Lehi's descendants who receive the Book of Mormon will not initially know their complete identity. To truly understand their identity, a people must know who they are, where they come from, and what their destiny is. The Book of Mormon answers those questions for Lehi's descendants. Just as Jacob who became Israel pronounced upon his sons blessings that pertained to his descendants down through the centuries, so Lehi in his patriarchal blessings to his children prophetically foretells what will happen to his descendants. He sees the time when other nations would take away from them "the lands of their possessions" and his people would be "scattered and smitten" (2 Nephi 1:11). Challenging his oldest sons to "Awake! and arise from the dust" (2 Nephi 1:14), Lehi directs his words also to the descendants of Laman and Lemuel in the latter days. While he fears that "a cursing should come upon you for the space of many generations," he hopes that "these things might not come upon you, but that ye might be a choice and a favored people of the Lord" (2 Nephi 1:18–19).

Reiterating his challenge and speaking much more to the descendants of Laman and Lemuel, Lehi implores: "Shake off the chains with which ye are bound, and come forth out of obscurity, and arise from the dust" (2 Nephi 1:23). From this perspective, Lehi's words apply to Lamanites in our time. Lehi commands that Laman and Lemuel "rebel no more" against Nephi and states that "if ye will hearken unto the voice of Nephi ye shall not perish" (2 Nephi 1:24, 28). Modern-day Lamanites can hear the voice of Nephi in the Book of Mormon. They can "arise from the dust" in learning their true identity from the precious record taken from the plates of Nephi. In turn, the record itself is brought forth "out of the dust" (2 Nephi 1:23; Moroni 10:27).

The Book of Mormon is designed to bring the Lamanites to a true knowledge of their relationship to their fathers—and especially to Nephi, their spiritual father. In doing so, the book responds to the Lamanites' false tradition, defined by Zeniff:

> Believing that they were driven out of the land of Jerusalem because of the iniquities of their fathers, and that they were wronged in the wilderness by their brethren, and they were also wronged while crossing the sea; and again, that they were wronged while in the land of their first inheritance, after they had crossed the sea, and all this because that Nephi was more faithful in keeping the commandments of the Lord—therefore he was favored of the Lord, for the Lord heard his prayers and answered them, and he took the lead of their journey in the wilderness. And his brethren were wroth with him because they understood not the dealings of the Lord; they were also wroth with him upon the waters because they hardened their hearts against the Lord. And again, they were wroth with him when they had arrived in the promised land, because they said that he had taken the ruling of the people out of their hands; and they sought to kill him. And again, they were wroth with him because he departed into the wilderness as the Lord had commanded him, and took the records which were engraven on the plates of brass, for they said that he robbed them. And thus they have taught their children that they should hate them, and that they should murder them, and that they should rob and plunder them, and do all they could to destroy them; therefore they have an eternal hatred towards the children of Nephi. (Mosiah 10:12–17)

Just as the brass plates had been essential to the cultural and spiritual preservation of the Nephites, so the Book of Mormon finally is necessary to the spiritual preservation of Lehi's living descendants. They are brought "out of captivity" and "out of obscurity" by being given the Lord's "covenants and his gospel" (1 Nephi 22:11–12) as promised in the title page of the Book of Mormon.

Although readers might not immediately recognize it as such, the Book of Mormon can be considered an epic, and analysis of the elements of this literary form could well assist latter-day Lamanites in a discovery of their origins and history. The great epic of the ancient people of Lehi can show modern Lamanites the possibilities for physical and spiritual fulfillment in the land of promise in which they have been placed. And it informs them of God's relationship with them in times past, present, and future. Especially as we consider the Book of Mormon as a living epic "written to the Lamanites," we can see how the book helps the children of Lehi realize that the "great things" the Lord has done for their fathers are continuing for them today.

The Book of Mormon meets two requirements of an epic: its broad sweep in time and its scope in space and import. Just as the Old Testament has been considered an epic in its character and range of concern, so the Book of Mormon has the breadth and inclusiveness that the British scholar E. M. W. Tillyard considers epic traits.[1] As many classical epics do, the story of father Lehi and his descendants arises out of a crisis: Mormon is abridging the entire history of the Nephite nation at the time when that civilization is being annihilated. And it contains the elements Leland Ryken in his literary introduction to the Bible finds characteristic of an epic: scope; nationalistic emphasis, with narrative motifs including warfare and rulership; a historical impulse, with allusions to key events in the life of a nation; a supernatural context in which the action occurs; and an epic structure of episodic plot with recurrent patterns or situations.[2]

DEFINING THE EPIC

The epic is a literary form that has been defined according to previous examples. Thus, the definition has changed over the years as more works have been considered epics. A generally accepted current definition is that given by M. H. Abrams in *A Glossary of Literary Terms*. In his definition, the epic is

> a long narrative poem on a serious subject, told in a formal and elevated style, and centered on a heroic or quasi-divine figure on whose actions depends the fate of a tribe, a nation, or (in the instance of John Milton's *Paradise Lost*) the human race. . . . The literary epic is certainly the most ambitious of poetic enterprises, making immense demands on a poet's knowledge, invention, and skill to sustain the scope, grandeur, and variety of a poem that tends to encompass the world of its day and a large portion of its learning.[3]

Most of this definition applies to the Book of Mormon, although it is primarily a work of prose, not poetry. Yet, as John McWilliams argues, "Durable and persuasive epics may appear in prose rather than verse," for "the essence of *epos* is heroic narrative."[4]

Abrams notes that literary epics commonly have the following features:

> 1. The hero is a figure of great national or even cosmic importance. In the *Iliad* he is the Greek warrior Achilles, who is the son of the sea-nymph Thetis; and Virgil's Aeneas is the son of the goddess Aphrodite. In *Paradise Lost*, Adam and Eve are the progenitors of the entire human race, or if we regard Christ as the protagonist, He is both God and man. Blake's primal figure is "the Universal Man" Albion, who incorporates, before his fall, humanity and God and the cosmos as well.
> 2. The setting is ample in scale, and may be worldwide, or even larger. Odysseus wanders over the Mediterranean basin (the whole of the world known at the time), and in Book XI he descends into the underworld (as does Virgil's Aeneas). The scope of *Paradise Lost* is the entire universe, for it takes place in heaven, on earth, in hell, and in the cosmic space between. . . .

3. The action involves superhuman deeds in battle, such as Achilles' feats in the Trojan War, or a long, arduous, and dangerous journey intrepidly accomplished, such as the wanderings of Odysseus on his way back to his homeland, despite the opposition of some of the gods. *Paradise Lost* includes the revolt in heaven by the rebel angels against God, the journey of Satan through chaos to discover the newly created world, and his desperately audacious attempt to outwit God by corrupting mankind, in which his success is ultimately frustrated by the sacrificial action of Christ.

4. In these great actions the gods and other supernatural beings take an interest or an active part—the Olympian gods in Homer, and Jehovah . . . and the angels in *Paradise Lost*. . . .

5. An epic poem is a ceremonial performance, and is narrated in a ceremonial style which is deliberately distanced from ordinary speech and proportioned to the grandeur and formality of the heroic subject and epic architecture. Hence Milton's grand style—his diction and elaborate and stylized syntax, which are often modeled on Latin poetry, his sonorous lists of names and wide-ranging allusions, and his imitation of Homer's epic similes and epithets.[5]

There are other generally accepted characteristics of an epic as well. Regarding the style in which an epic is written, McWilliams says, "The language should be as distinct as possible from ordinary speech, and to this end should avail itself of the inversion, compound epithets, and exalted diction of the sublime, as practiced preeminently by John Milton."[6] And whereas such epic poets as Homer invoke a Muse to aid them in their elevated narration, John Milton in *Paradise Lost* invokes the Holy Ghost:

> Sing Heav'nly Muse, that on the secret top
> Of Oreb, or of Sinai, didst inspire
> That Shepherd, who first taught the chosen Seed,
> In the Beginning how the Heav'ns and Earth
> Rose out of Chaos.
>
> (Book I, lines 6–10)

Likewise, Mormon is directed by the Holy Ghost. He writes "for a wise purpose; for thus it whispereth me, according to the workings of the Spirit of the Lord which is in me. And now, I do not know all things; but the Lord knoweth all things which are to come; wherefore, he worketh in me to do according to his will" (Words of Mormon 1:7).

Epics generally begin in the middle of the action, rather than at the beginning or end of the story or journey. Regarding the place in the action an epic starts, however, Gabriel Josipovici says that "epic does not so much tell a story as recount for the community the main features of its world, and it does not therefore much matter where you begin, since any opening will eventually allow you to articulate the whole."[7] As Abrams notes, *Paradise Lost*

> opens with the fallen angels in hell, gathering their forces and determining on revenge. Not until Books V–VII does the angel Raphael relate to Adam the events in heaven which led to this situation; while in Books XI–XII, after the fall, Michael foretells to Adam future events up to Christ's second coming. Thus Milton's epic, although its action focuses on the temptation and fall of man, encompasses all time from the creation to the end of the world.[8]

THE BOOK OF MORMON AS AN EPIC

As we look at the Book of Mormon with the above features in mind, we find that the book is an epic in its own way.

Hero

The Book of Mormon has a number of heroes of national or even cosmic importance, among them the prophet-warriors Nephi, Gideon, Ammon, Captain Moroni, Moronihah, and Mormon. Lehi himself, as Hugh Nibley has shown in *An Approach to the Book of Mormon*, is a product of a Heroic Age.[9] By "Heroic Age," Nibley means a "strange, tense, exciting and very brief moment of history when everything was 'big with the future.' . . . The population squeeze accelerated a world-wide activity in exploration and colonization that . . . reached its peak almost exactly in 600 B.C."[10] The Book of Mormon contains many captivating individual deeds of valor, courage, and strength, such as Nephi's lone quest for wild game, Alma's hand-to-hand combat with Amlici, Ammon's protecting the king's flocks at the waters of Sebus, and Captain Moroni's valiant bearing of his title of liberty at the head of freedom-loving forces. At times these heroes and their deeds appear superhuman—and, indeed, the editor and the writers themselves attribute all heroic successes to the power of God.

In a sense, all the heroic qualities of all the heroes in the Book of Mormon are contained within one hero: Nephi. He, in turn, is a representative of the ultimate hero: Christ. At the fountainhead of his nation and people, Nephi becomes more than an individual hero. He is a prophet-king after whom subsequent kings are titled and for whom the central Book of Mormon people is named. (A parallel is the way *Caesar* became a title for emperors who followed Julius Caesar. Another parallel is Aeneas, back to whom the Romans proudly traced their line.) Further, such leaders as Alma, Amulek, and Mormon claim to be pure descendants of Nephi and identify with him (Mosiah 17:2; Alma 10:2–3; Mormon 1:5).[11]

The original title with which Nephi's record begins, "The First Book of Nephi; His Reign and Ministry," implies that this is the story of a whole people, represented in Nephi. "I, Nephi," the first words of the Book of Mormon, thus suggests not only "I, individual," but also "I, king" and "I, people"—indeed, a whole race of people going down through time. As with Patriarch Jacob's blessing to his beloved son Joseph, Lehi's prophetic blessing to his son refers more to Nephi's "seed," or posterity. For his part, Nephi sees the history of his people down through time, including their destruction as a people (1 Nephi 11–15, 22). In vision he beholds multitudes of people in the land of promise and numberless cities. He sees wars and "great slaughters with the sword" (1 Nephi 12:2), culminating in a great destruction followed by the visit of Christ to the Nephites. After righteousness to the fourth generation, multitudes gather together to a battle in which Nephi's seed are overpowered. Further, he sees the fate of the house of Israel down to the end-time.

Lehi's dream of the tree of life prefigures the epic drama of the entire history of Nephi's people. In the dream, concourses of people move through a mist of darkness, some to catch hold of an iron rod that leads them to a tree laden with precious fruit, others to be lost and drowned or to enter a "great and spacious building" (1 Nephi 8:26) from which they point fingers of scorn at those who partake of the fruit. In the interpretation given to Nephi while he is "caught away . . . into an exceedingly high mountain" (1 Nephi 11:1), the tree represents the love of God, the iron rod is the word of God, and the spacious building is the pride of the world. The dream symbolically sets forth the fate of "numberless concourses of people" (1 Nephi 8:21) as they journey through life, face tests and temptations, and then suffer ignominious death, become haughty in their vanity and pride, or accept God's love.

The last part of the First Book of Nephi and the central section of the Second Book of Nephi put the epic action on a cosmic level. Here the story of the Lehites is linked with Isaiah's prophecies about the scattering and then gathering of the entire house of Israel. Ultimately, the "kingdom of the devil" will tremble and all who belong to it "must be brought low in the dust" (1 Nephi 22:23). Opposed to it will be the kingdom of the Holy One of Israel. Nephi records for his posterity the opposition between "liberty and eternal life" and "the captivity and power of the devil" (2 Nephi 2:27) in a revelation "from the beginning of the world to the ending thereof" (2 Nephi 27:7). Then in his parting testimony, Nephi looks into the past ("I have written [that which is] of great worth"), the present ("I pray continually for [my people]"), and the future—combining both past and present ("I speak unto you as the voice of one crying from the dust") (2 Nephi 33:3, 13). He completes this time cycle by saying that as the head or father of a people, he will meet them at the judgment day. Although the earth shall eventually pass away, his people will be saved by knowing their roots and acting on the prophetic counsel of their fathers. (In this regard, see also Alma 9:8–13.)

In the framework of the book, Mormon becomes in effect the last Nephi, a spokesman for his nation who comments on its main spiritual events and, with his son, concludes its record and preserves it in condensed form for future generations.[12] For his part, Moroni presents a dual epical overview. He closes out the history of the Nephites and surveys the entire history of the Jaredites, who were destroyed about the time the Nephite civilization began. In some parts of the Book of Mormon, "Nephite" is synonymous with "the people of God" (Alma 2:11). The representative of the original Nephi, whether Abinadi, Alma, or Aaron, contains within him some of that quality. He may be strong physically, but his greatest strength is moral. He has power of the sort Abinadi claims before King Noah and his priests: "Touch me not, for God shall smite you if ye lay your hands upon me" (Mosiah 13:3).

In each case, the Book of Mormon hero is an unlikely one. Nephi and Moroni are acutely aware of their weaknesses, King Mosiah's sons Ammon and Aaron are humbly willing to be servants in the missionary cause, and Captain Moroni is reluctant to shed blood unless greatly pressed to it. When the Book of Mormon hero shows great strength or resourcefulness, he invariably gives credit to the Lord. Often that strength is verbal, as in Alma's opposition to Korihor, or quietly courageous, as in Abinadi's return to testify to the people of King Noah despite the threat of death.

The truly central hero of the Book of Mormon is Jesus Christ. It is he who gives direction to the other heroes and whose redeeming power is affirmed throughout the book, culminating in his personal visit. He is the hero whom the others represent. As Ammon declares, "I know that I am nothing; as to my strength I am weak; therefore I will not boast of myself, but I will boast of my God, for in his strength I can do all things" (Alma 26:12). And, as will be developed later, each mortal hero is also a type of Christ. For instance, Nephi prefigures Christ, though not to the extent of commanding the elements himself, when he prays that the storm be stilled. Further, Nephi is like Christ in being an obedient son, a forgiving brother, a skillful carpenter, and a pilot. King Benjamin is a type of Christ as the heavenly King. And Alma comes to new life after being as if dead for three days and three nights, just as Christ rose from the dead after three days. (One of Joseph Campbell's ideas in *Hero with a Thousand Faces* is that all epic heroes have much in common with Christ. It seems that many epic heroes are at base mortal echoes of Christ. Certainly Milton's Adam and the hero Beowulf have been compared to Christ for various reasons, and when Christianity was introduced to the German tribes, they related to Christ primarily as an epic hero.)

Setting

Settings in the Book of Mormon are epic in nature. They are vast and involve large-scale migrations of whole populations across lands and seas. The setting of the main story is implicitly the known mideastern world, the Indian and Pacific oceans, and the promised land of America. The Jaredite story has a similarly vast setting and is a concentrated epic contained within the Nephite story as a second witness to the extremes of the Nephite experience. Both narratives contain the beginning of a vision and an escape to a promised land, a rapid overview of the rise and fall of a civilization, and an end in total collapse and destruction.

Each story also has a spiritual setting: that of God's eternal purposes "prepared from the foundation of the world" and the ultimate destiny of mankind (Alma 42:26). These earthly and spiritual settings are both initially found in Lehi's dream, which tells of mortal members of his family making choices of everlasting import. They may partake of the fruit of the tree of life or choose to join the multitude in a great and spacious building. In another example of dual setting, throughout the book there are frequent reminders that Jerusalem of Judea has a counterpart in the heavenly Jerusalem, that "the kingdom of heaven is soon at hand" (Alma 5:50). At this cosmic level, particular human experience symbolizes man's general destiny.

Action

As there are both physical and spiritual dimensions to the setting, so the action of the Book of Mormon takes place on both the human level and the divine. The human level is mainly a cycle of humbling leading to repentance leading to prosperity leading to pride leading to destruction. This pattern requires a generation or more to complete, guaranteeing that each individual has the opportunity to choose right or wrong. Thus, the action in the Book of Mormon is linear for the individual yet cyclical for the generations of the Nephites. On the divine level, ultimate blessings or punishments are promised, both to the individual and to the group.

On the human plane, for instance, in Alma 16 the Nephites win a physical victory over the desolating Lamanites who have made incursions into the land of the Nephites. But there is another battle as well—the battle of righteousness. First, the wicked people of Ammonihah, who had imprisoned Alma and Amulek and burned the wives and children of their followers, are destroyed at the hands of the Lamanites; second, Alma and Amulek go forth to preach the word throughout all the land and get "the victory over the devil" (Alma 16:21).

Both of these cycles, physical and spiritual, illustrate the repeated statement by the Lord: "Inasmuch as ye shall keep my commandments ye shall prosper in the land; but inasmuch as ye will not keep my commandments ye shall be cut off from my presence" (2 Nephi 1:20).[13] This blessing or curse provides an epic rhythm in the Book of Mormon because it applies to all people living in the promised land, whether in the past, present, or future. The firm connection between righteousness and existence as a nation is evident on a large scale with the Nephite civilization. In a relatively brief example, it is shown in the fate of the Jaredites, who "did not repent; therefore they have been destroyed" (Alma 37:26). The Jaredite and Nephite civilizations, because they refused to repent, both experienced the annihilation of their earthly societies. Against that, however, is juxtaposed the continuation of a divine society: Ether and Moroni, whose records are the final two in the Book of Mormon, conclude with references to being "saved in the kingdom of God" (Ether 15:34) and having "rest in the paradise of God" (Moroni 10:34).

Northrop Frye in *Anatomy of Criticism* finds in the Bible two epic frameworks, "the epic of return and the epic of wrath." In the first, "the movement is first down and then up to a permanently redeemed world." The "epic of wrath" is the "cycle of human life without redemptive assistance," ending with "bondage, exile, continuing war, or destruction by fire (Sodom, Babylon) or water (the flood)."[14] In the Book of Mormon, the end of an epic of wrath, or what Frye calls the "all too human" cycle, is the destruction of the unrepentant Nephites (and, in a parallel, of the wicked Jaredites). The conclusion of an epic of return, or what Frye calls the divine cycle, is found in Moroni's last words, in which he says he will meet his readers at the bar of God. He speaks to them, he says, "out of the dust" (Moroni 10:27).

Supernatural Beings

As with ancient poetic epics, a hallmark of the Book of Mormon is the way supernatural beings are involved in events, from Lehi's initial vision of God's dealings with man in the duration of the earth's existence to Moroni's declaration that at the judgment bar God will affirm the truth of his writings.

There is hardly a page of the Book of Mormon that does not contain some reference to divine intervention or revelation. In the opening pages we are told of Lehi's vision of God on his throne and see the angel protecting Nephi against the physical abuse of Laman and Lemuel; we learn of Alma the Elder's people fleeing their captors during the day while their guards were in a profound sleep caused by the Lord; and we read of Alma the Younger being confronted by a chastising angel. Most noteworthy are the appearances of Jesus Christ.

Supernatural powers in the Book of Mormon are not directed by whim, as might be found in a Greek epic. Rather, they function in accordance with people's faith. For example, after Nephi incurs the wrath of his brothers when he breaks his steel bow, he is directed by means of a brass ball, the Liahona, to a mountaintop where he slays wild beasts for food. After the rebellious brothers bind up Nephi and cause the Liahona (the ship's navigation system) to fail, the ship is kept from going down only by their untying Nephi. (In an interesting turn on the Jonah story, the main company is at fault, and it is the loosing of a righteous man—not the casting away of an unrighteous one—that brings calm.) An agent of divine powers, the Liahona thus functions strictly according to the "faith and diligence" of the people (Alma 37:41).

Overarching all the interrelationships of heavenly powers and humankind are revelations given to Lehi, Nephi, Mormon, and others, showing conditions of the world from the beginning to the end. One effect of this is to extend the epic scope of the Book of Mormon to include all humankind; another is to illustrate that past, present, and future are one eternal round with the Lord.

Ceremonial Performance

At first glance, the Book of Mormon is hardly a poem, let alone a ceremonial performance. But as will be demonstrated later, divine revelations, as well as prayers and many other impassioned declarations or appeals, are actually related to Hebraic poetry.

The ceremonial quality of the book is supported, too, by the numerous formal occasions on which people are taught, such as Lehi's last injunctions to his sons, King Benjamin's address, and the parting testimonies of Nephi, Mormon, and Moroni. In the incident of Mosiah's reading the record of the people of Zeniff to those gathered at Zarahemla, we see a parallel with the Book of Mormon as a whole: they (and thus the reader) learn about a people through their records. Mosiah's audience rejoice over those Zeniffites who have been delivered out of bondage and shed tears of sorrow over their brethren slain by the Lamanites; they are grateful for God's power in behalf of Alma and his people, and are pained for the plight of the sinful Lamanites. In the same way, we may read the records of the peoples of Nephi and Jared and rejoice over their triumphs and sorrow over their ultimate destruction—and, if we are perceptive enough, apply the lessons of their records to our own lives and civilization.

Middle of the Action

The literary convention called beginning *in medias res,* or "in the middle of things," is a standard characteristic of an epic. As is typical of epics, many narratives in the Book of Mormon begin in the middle of the action, with the interest being on *why* something happens rather than on *what* happens. We know the ending of the Nephite story from the beginning. Lehi recounts to his children the Babylonian captivity, the coming of the Messiah, the travels of his people to the land of promise, the time when the Gentiles would receive the fulness of the gospel, and the final return of the remnants of the house of Israel to the Messiah (1 Nephi 10). Nephi's revelation of the implications of Lehi's vision of the tree of life gives in brief the whole of the Nephite experience, down to the final devastation in the fourth generation after the coming of Christ (1 Nephi 12).

Likewise, Mormon introduces his abridgment by confirming Nephi's prophecies. Yet the real end is still to come: Mormon supposes that his son Moroni "will witness the entire destruction of my people" (Words of Mormon 1:2). Thus we read the rest of the Book of Mormon knowing all the while the outcome of the story but still wanting to know the final details. In the Words of Mormon near the beginning of his record, Mormon prepares us to focus on *why* the Nephites were destroyed. He then asks the larger question about the eventual eternal destiny of his people and prays that a remnant of them will receive the life-giving message of his sacred record.

So that we recognize the sweep of history throughout the Book of Mormon, we are told what will happen before we get the details of such major events as the annihilation of the Jaredites, the coming of Christ to the Nephites, the destruction of the wicked city Ammonihah, and the success of the sons of Mosiah. The last is a representative example of this foretelling: At the very beginning of the extensive account of their missionary journey, we learn that the sons of Mosiah "had been teaching the word of God for the space of fourteen years among the Lamanites, having had much success in bringing many to the knowledge of the truth" (Alma 17:4).

This pattern of anticipation is also illustrated in the story of the people of Zeniff, which is recounted in Mosiah 7 through 25. We begin the story with Zeniff's grandson, Limhi, and his people in bondage to the Lamanites. Then in Limhi's discourse to his people we learn what has led up to that bondage. He tells of Zeniff's migration, refers to the trickery of the Lamanite king, and alludes to a slain prophet of the Lord (Abinadi). We thus learn the fate of the people and get something of an overview of their story, although we do not know exactly how it will end. Then Limhi has Ammon the explorer read the plates containing the record of Zeniff's people from the time they left Zarahemla, and excerpts from the record of Zeniff and the story of the people of Alma are inserted into the text of the book of Mosiah. From that we learn the *why* and *how* of *what* we already knew. The story of the Zeniffites is completed when Ammon assists Limhi and his people in their escape from bondage back to Zarahemla and as the people of Alma are also led back to Zarahemla.

The same pattern occurs in the account of the Jaredites. At several points before the book of Ether we are informed that a great people has been completely destroyed, leaving behind twenty-four gold plates. We also learn as early as the book of Omni about Coriantumr, the last survivor of this people. We are kept in anticipation by Mormon's promise that the account would be written "hereafter; for behold, it is expedient that all people should know the things which are written in this account" (Mosiah 28:19)—a promise fulfilled by Moroni with the book of Ether. Knowing all this, the reader, along with Limhi, is eager to know the contents of those twenty-four engraved gold plates: "Perhaps, they will give us a knowledge of a remnant of the people who have been destroyed, from whence these records came" (Mosiah 8:12). Again, the reader's concern is with knowing *why* the people have been destroyed and what the lesson is in that destruction.

This "middle of the action" structure in the Book of Mormon is paralleled and reinforced by prophetic structure. Before going sequentially through the story of the sons of Mosiah, for example, the narrator gives us Alma's report that they are alive and well, that they had "much success in bringing many to the knowledge of the truth," and that they had suffered much in both body and mind (Alma 17:1–5). Soon after this report we are told that at the beginning of their dangerous missionary venture, the sons of Mosiah learned through the Spirit that they should be patient in afflictions and would be instruments in the Lord's hands for the salvation of many souls (Alma 17:11). Thus the essential events are known ahead of time—both by the narrator's foretelling and by prophecy.

The Book of Mormon epic provides, if you will, a "backward" story. Jaredite records seen by King Mosiah give "an account of the people who were destroyed, from the time that they were destroyed *back* to the building of the great tower, . . . yea, and even from that time back until the creation of Adam" (Mosiah 28:17). Whether or not the record progressed this way, the interest was from the foregone event (the destruction) *back* to its origins (the time they were scattered at the building of the great tower) and then back to the very beginning (the creation of Adam). The interest thus is different from that of a regular story: we care much more about knowing the whys than the whats.

The "middle of the action" structure also allows for an ironic dimension. For example, King Noah's people tell him: "We are strong, we shall not come into bondage, or be taken captive by our enemies" (Mosiah 12:15). Yet at that point we already know wicked King Noah and his people were brought into bondage. Indeed, from our frame of reference as we read the Book of Mormon, we think of the people as still in bondage and wonder how they are going to get out of it.

Finally, this structure underlines the constant relation of past, present, and future in the Book of Mormon. In his parting testimony, Nephi speaks of great worth in that which he has written, prays continually for his people, and speaks to a future audience "as the voice of one crying from the dust" (2 Nephi 33:13). Alma, too, considers both past and future from his present: He always remembers the captivity and the deliverance of his fathers, he rejoices in the present repentance of many of his brethren, and he looks forward to bringing some soul to repentance, with the hope that his redeemed brethren will enter the timeless state of the heavenly kingdom of God to "go no more out" (Alma 29:17).

In this respect, Isaiah is particularly important in providing prophetic texts that present the judgments of God upon Israel in the sweep of time. A voice out of Israel's past, Isaiah establishes the grand connection with the house of Israel in the Old World, the remnant of Israel in the New World, and modern-day Israel— with many of his prophecies yet to be fulfilled.

A LIVING EPIC

The record brought forth "out of the dust" (Moroni 10:27) of centuries past becomes a living epic in claiming to speak to descendants of the people treated in the record. It gives them their origins, presents the truth about the heroic Nephi (the people as well as the man and his subsequent representatives), shows God's dealings with their ancestors over a millennium of time, and challenges them to come forth out of an obscurity caused by disobedience and by the repression of latter-day Gentiles.

The Book of Mormon is an active epic. Its story of a people has yet to be completed; it is both history and prophecy. Told in plainness and high seriousness, it says to Lehi's living descendants that they are a part of an illustrious covenant people. Like their fathers the Anti-Nephi-Lehies, they can repent, receive the gospel, and not only prosper in the land temporally but, what is more important, be rewarded with life everlasting in the eternal promised land.

As Alma instructed his son Helaman, the Book of Mormon plates were destined to "retain their brightness" (Alma 37:4–5; see also 1 Nephi 5:18–19). And how do they retain their brightness? They come alive for the audience that receives them. They are a continuing epic of Lehi's people. On an even larger scale, they give meaning to humankind's general destiny.

CHAPTER 4

"By the Spirit of Prophecy"

POETRY

Because "the testimony of Jesus is the spirit of prophecy" (Revelation 19:10), a book subtitled "Another Testament of Jesus Christ" would be expected to contain much prophecy. As Susan Easton Black has affirmed in *Finding Christ through the Book of Mormon,* the book is indeed "Christ-centered."[1] But because the Book of Mormon is published wholly as prose, we may not recognize that much of the prophecy in the book actually is poetry.[2]

It has long been known that about a third of the Old Testament, especially Psalms, Job, and the prophetic books, is poetry; what is just being discovered is that a significant portion of the Book of Mormon is poetry as well.[3] Although Book of Mormon poetry appears in many places of elevated discourse, such as sermons and instructions, a close examination of the text will show that often when a Book of Mormon prophet says or implies, "Thus saith the Lord," the passages that follow will be poetic.[4]

Prophesy means "to utter by divine interpretation," and so we would expect the prophetic message to be of an elevated nature. Poetry helps the message reach beyond the surface by adding rhythmical repetitions that touch the soul. That accords with David Noel Freedman's view of the correlation between poetry and prophecy: In "communication or action between heaven and earth, the appropriate language is that of poetry. Prose may be adequate to describe setting and circumstances and to sketch historical effects and residues; only poetry can convey the mystery of the miraculous and its meaning for those present."[5] Robert Alter agrees: "Since poetry is our best human model of intricately rich communication, not only solemn, weighty, and forceful but also densely woven with complex internal connections, meanings, and implications, it makes sense that divine speech should be represented as poetry."[6] Latter-day Saint poet Orson F. Whitney put it simply, "The highest poetry is prophetic; there is always in it a suggestion of infinity."[7] Through poetry, according to T. R. Henn, prophecies exalt the heart; both words and imagery acquire depth by repetition, and there is a peculiar exaltation proper to the chant.[8] Or as Edgar Allan Poe put it in another context: "Without a certain continuity of effort—without a certain duration or repetition of purpose—the soul is never deeply moved. There must be the dropping of the water upon the rock."[9]

In any language, the appeal of poetry is similar to the appeal of music. Through its rhythms, sounds, and images, poetry touches our feelings and enlightens our understanding. It is no wonder, then, that the first use of language was poetic ("Every word was once a poem," Emerson says.[10]) and that many of the world's greatest writers, such as Homer, Virgil, Sophocles, Dante, Petrarch, Chaucer, Shakespeare, and Milton, should have chosen poetry as their primary medium of imaginative expression.

A simple but effective instance of poetry in the Book of Mormon is Lehi's memorable teaching:

> Adam fell that men might be;
> and men are, that they might have joy.
> (2 Nephi 2:25)

Here the second line repeats the word *men* and shows that the fall of man actually allows for joy.

Another poetic passage is the beginning of Nephi's parting testimony in which he repeats the phrase "I glory" in building one affirmation upon another:

I glory in plainness;
I glory in truth;
I glory in my Jesus,
for he hath redeemed my soul from hell.

(2 Nephi 33:6)[11]

Though lacking regular line length and rhyme (such as is found in much English-language poetry), these passages do have a rhythmical development of ideas. In this respect, they are akin to the poetic writings of Isaiah, one of the great poets of the Old Testament whom Nephi and Jacob admired so much. ("My soul delighteth in the words of Isaiah," Nephi declares in 2 Nephi 25:5.) Although there is more to Isaiah's poetry than parallelism, a main characteristic of his poetry is the repetition of an idea.[12] Usually, the second line of a Hebraic poem *repeats,* with some intensification or amplification, the thought of the first line; *contrasts* an opposing idea to the first line; *completes* the idea; or repeats the idea in a *reverse* order.[13] We find both completion and repetition of an idea in this well-known passage from Isaiah:

But they that wait upon the Lord shall renew their strength;
they shall mount up with wings as eagles;
they shall run, and not be weary;
and they shall walk, and not faint.

(Isaiah 40:31)

The next example, which is also from Isaiah and quoted in the Book of Mormon, reveals in an almost self-evident fashion the rhythm of ideas and the great poetic power of Isaiah. It also allows us to see a number of the principal characteristics of Hebraic poetry.

My righteousness is near;
my salvation is gone forth,
and mine arm shall judge the people.
The isles shall wait upon me,
and on mine arm shall they trust.
Lift up your eyes to the heavens,
and look upon the earth beneath;

5

for the heavens shall vanish away like smoke,
and the earth shall wax old like a garment;
and they that dwell therein shall die in like manner.   10
But my salvation shall be forever,
and my righteousness shall not be abolished.

                                        (2 Nephi 8:5–6; compare Isaiah 51:5–6)

The main characteristic of Isaiah's poetry is what Ruth apRoberts calls "a rhyme of thoughts, or a music of ideas" or what Robert Alter speaks of as semantic parallelism.[14] The second and third ideas in the passage from Isaiah, "my salvation is gone forth" and "mine arm shall judge the people," are parallel to the first idea, "My righteousness is near." They are not simply synonymous, though, but amplify the nature of God's righteousness. The idea of the fourth line is repeated in the fifth line, with the passivity of "wait upon me" changed to the action of "trust on mine arm."

Lines 6 and 7 give us a parallel pair of antonyms: Look up to the heavens; look down to the earth. This type of parallelism continues in the next two lines, in which the destinies of the heavens and the earth are set next to each other, with line 10 applying the destiny of the earth to its inhabitants.

The last two lines repeat, in reverse order, the subjects of righteousness and salvation found in the first two lines. In this inverted parallelism, or *chiasmus* (literally, a "crossing"),[15] the subject of the first line is mirrored in the last line, with that of the second found in the next-to-last line. Whereas in the beginning salvation is in motion, going forth to the people of the earth, in the end its eternal duration is emphasized—as is that of righteousness, in an inverse way (it shall not be abolished). The last lines also sustain the two overall ideas of the passage: the first, that God's people should trust him and his salvation; and the second, that they should not put their trust in the heavens and the earth because they are temporary—whereas the Lord's righteousness will not die.

As with the poetry of the Old Testament, Book of Mormon poetry helps give emphasis, unity, and memorability to the utterances in which it is found. Further, in Robert Alter's words, the "poetic vehicle of parallelistic verse offered a particularly effective way of imaginatively realizing inevitability, of making powerfully manifest to the listener the idea that consequences he might choose not to contemplate could happen, would happen, would happen without fail."[16] We should also keep in mind the virtues of poetry in the world from which Lehi and his family came. According to Moshe Greenberg,

> Poetry was the form taken by sapiential observation and speculation throughout the ancient Near East. With its engagement of the emotions and the imagination, it was the usual mode of persuasive discourse. Through its compression, poetry allows stark, untempered expression that, while powerful in impact, awakens the kind of careful reflection that leads to the fuller apprehension of a subject. Moreover, the density of poetic language, compelling the reader to complement, to fill in gaps, fits it peculiarly for representing impassioned discourse, which by nature proceeds in associative leaps rather than by logical development.[17]

Having just quoted from Isaiah (in the passage from 2 Nephi 8:5–6, which we analyzed above), Jacob employs poetry himself to help sustain the high level of the previous discourse (consider especially 2 Nephi 9:17–18, 41–43). Though Jacob's poetry may not be as vivid as Isaiah's, it contains some of the same elevation of expression and richness of comparison. In the example that follows, Jacob integrates Isaiah effectively into his own sermon.

Behold, my soul abhorreth sin,
and my heart delighteth in righteousness;
and I will praise the holy name of my God.

Come, my brethren, every one that thirsteth, come ye to the
waters;
and he that hath no money, come buy and eat;   5
yea, come buy wine and milk without money and without price.

Wherefore, do not spend money for that which is of no worth,
nor your labor for that which cannot satisfy.
Hearken diligently unto me,
and remember the words which I have spoken;   10
and come unto the Holy One of Israel,
and feast upon that which perisheth not, neither can be
    corrupted,
and let your soul delight in fatness.

Behold, my beloved brethren,
remember the words of your God;   15
pray unto him continually by day,
and give thanks unto his holy name by night.
Let your hearts rejoice.

              (2 Nephi 9:49–52; compare Isaiah 55:1–2)[18]

The Hebraic parallelism in Jacob's poetry is clear. Jacob's
soul abhors sin, and his heart, a synonym for soul, positively
delights in righteousness. At the end of the passage, Jacob uses
parallel ideas that contain both synonyms ("pray unto him" and
"give thanks unto his holy name") and antonyms ("day" and
"night").

Parallelism is the dominant characteristic of poetry in the
Bible and Book of Mormon, but it is not the only one. In the last
stanza above, for example, a poetic element is the rhythmic
intensity of the action Jacob calls for. First, he simply asks his listeners to behold—that is, hear him. Then he wants them to
remember, followed by the actions of praying and giving thanks
(the humble and grateful element of prayer). For its part, parallelism is not only a poetic element; it can be found as well in
prose passages. Further, there are no sharp distinctions between
scriptural prose and poetry.[19] Rather, one can flow into and out
of the other. Preceding the passage quoted above, Jacob speaks
in prose but sets up two opposite situations, holiness and unho-
liness: "Behold, if ye were holy I would speak unto you of holiness; but as ye are not holy, and ye look upon me as a teacher,
it must needs be expedient that I teach you the consequences of
sin" (2 Nephi 9:48). Then he moves into a more rhythmic and

exalted expression with "Behold, my soul abhorreth sin, / and my heart delighteth in righteousness."

NEPHI'S PSALM

For his part, Nephi expresses some of the most powerful poetry in the Book of Mormon in what has been called the psalm of Nephi (2 Nephi 4:15–35), a title given prominence by Sidney B. Sperry.[20] The psalm presents feelingly the conflicting emotions Nephi experienced after the death of his father, Lehi. He responds to the anger directed against him by his brothers Laman and Lemuel and their families—an animosity that soon after causes Nephi and his people to flee into the wilderness to escape destruction. On the other hand, Nephi expresses the joyful intensity of his trust in the Lord. His psalm is both a supplication ("a poetic cry of distress to the Lord in time of critical need"[21]) and a psalm of praise:

> For my soul delighteth in the scriptures,
> and my heart pondereth them,
> and writeth them for the learning and the profit of my children.
> Behold, my soul delighteth in the things of the Lord;
> and my heart pondereth continually upon the things which I
>   have seen and heard.   5
> Nevertheless, notwithstanding the great goodness of the Lord,
> in showing me his great and marvelous works,
> my heart exclaimeth: O wretched man that I am!
> Yea, my heart sorroweth because of my flesh;
> my soul grieveth because of mine iniquities.   10
> I am encompassed about, because of the temptations and the
>   sins which do so easily beset me.
> And when I desire to rejoice, my heart groaneth because of
>   my sins;
> nevertheless, I know in whom I have trusted.
> My God hath been my support;
> he hath led me through mine afflictions in the wilderness;   15
> and he hath preserved me upon the waters of the great deep.
> He hath filled me with his love,
> even unto the consuming of my flesh.

He hath confounded mine enemies,
unto the causing of them to quake before me.   20
Behold, he hath heard my cry by day,
and he hath given me knowledge by visions in the nighttime.
And by day have I waxed bold in mighty prayer before him;
yea, my voice have I sent up on high;
and angels came down and ministered unto me.   25
And upon the wings of his Spirit hath my body been carried
    away upon exceedingly high mountains.
And mine eyes have beheld great things,
yea, even too great for man;
therefore I was bidden that I should not write them.
O then, if I have seen so great things,   30
if the Lord in his condescension unto the children of men
    hath visited men in so much mercy,
why should my heart weep and my soul linger in the valley
    of sorrow,
and my flesh waste away, and my strength slacken,
because of mine afflictions?
And why should I yield to sin, because of my flesh?   35
Yea, why should I give way to temptations,
that the evil one have place in my heart to destroy my peace
    and afflict my soul?
Why am I angry because of mine enemy?
Awake, my soul! No longer droop in sin.
Rejoice, O my heart, and give place no more for the enemy
    of my soul.   40
Do not anger again because of mine enemies.
Do not slacken my strength because of mine afflictions.
Rejoice, O my heart, and cry unto the Lord, and say:
O Lord, I will praise thee forever;
yea, my soul will rejoice in thee, my God, and the
    rock of my salvation.   45
O Lord, wilt thou redeem my soul?
Wilt thou deliver me out of the hands of mine enemies?
Wilt thou make me that I may shake at the appearance of sin?
May the gates of hell be shut continually before me,
because that my heart is broken and my spirit is
    contrite!   50

O Lord, wilt thou not shut the gates of thy righteousness
    before me,
that I may walk in the path of the low valley,
that I may be strict in the plain road!
O Lord, wilt thou encircle me around in the robe of thy
    righteousness!
O Lord, wilt thou make a way for mine escape before mine
    enemies!   55
Wilt thou make my path straight before me!
Wilt thou not place a stumbling block in my way—
but that thou wouldst clear my way before me,
and hedge not up my way, but the ways of mine enemy.
O Lord, I have trusted in thee, and I will trust in thee forever. 60
I will not put my trust in the arm of flesh;
for I know that cursed is he that putteth his trust in the arm
    of flesh.
Yea, cursed is he that putteth his trust in man or maketh flesh
    his arm.
Yea, I know that God will give liberally to him that asketh.
Yea, my God will give me, if I ask not amiss;   65
therefore I will lift up my voice unto thee;
yea, I will cry unto thee,
my God, the rock of my righteousness.
Behold, my voice shall forever ascend up unto thee,
my rock and mine everlasting God.   70
    (2 Nephi 4:15–35)

As with the passages from Isaiah and Jacob, the dominant poetic feature of the psalm of Nephi is parallelism. An idea expressed in one line is completed, amplified, contrasted, or reversed in the subsequent line or lines. Both completion and contrast are evident in lines 17 through 20:

> He hath filled me with his love,
> even unto the consuming of my flesh.
> He hath confounded mine enemies,
> unto the causing of them to quake before me.

The second line completes the thought begun in the first line; similarly, the fourth line completes the third. Taken together, the third and fourth lines contrast with the first two lines.

Contrast with intensification is found in lines 21 and 22:

Behold, he hath heard my cry by day,
and he hath given me knowledge by visions in the nighttime.

"Nighttime" contrasts with "day"; the intensification comes in the greater detail of the second line.

Both the opposition and the repetition of an idea in a reverse order are found in these lines:

Wilt thou *make my path straight* before me!
Wilt thou not place a *stumbling block* in my way—
but that thou wouldst *clear my way* before me,
and *hedge not up my way,* but the ways of mine enemy.

Intensification of thought and feeling are especially evident in lines 14 through 16. Here there is movement through space, first through the wilderness and then over the ocean. That is joined with divine aid, which increases from support through guidance to preservation:

My God hath been my support;
he hath led me through mine afflictions in the wilderness;
and he hath preserved me upon the waters of the great deep.

A more intricate intensification is found in lines 39 through 45:

Awake, my *soul!* No longer droop in sin.
Rejoice, O my *heart,* and give place no more for the enemy of
my soul.
Do not anger again because of mine enemies.
Do not slacken my strength because of mine afflictions.
Rejoice, O my *heart,* and cry unto the Lord, and say:
O Lord, I will praise thee forever;
yea, my *soul* will rejoice in thee, my God, and the rock of my
salvation.

The powerful effect of the first line is amplified in the second; the last expands the significance of both preceding lines. The appeals to the soul and heart say what not to do ("no longer droop," "give place no more"), the mirror use of *heart* and *soul* affirms what to do: "praise" and "rejoice."

This and essentially all of the poetry in the Book of Mormon testifies of Jesus Christ, the rock of salvation. It helps invite and entice the reader to Christ[22] by appealing to him or her on many levels. It especially reaches both the mind and the heart of the Lamanite who reads or hears it in the right spirit. That is in harmony with the purpose of the Book of Mormon as set forth in the third section of the Doctrine and Covenants:

> For inasmuch as the knowledge of a Savior has come unto the world, through the testimony of the Jews, even so shall the knowledge of a Savior come unto my people— . . . And for this very purpose are these plates preserved, which contain these records—that the promises of the Lord might be fulfilled, which he made to his people; and that the Lamanites might come to the knowledge of their fathers, and that they might know the promises of the Lord, and that they may believe the gospel and rely upon the merits of Jesus Christ, and be glorified through faith in his name, and that through their repentance they might be saved. (D&C 3:16, 19–20)

AMMON'S SPEECH

Poetic structure may be seen in Ammon's impassioned response to criticism by the other sons of Mosiah regarding his apparent boasting about the conversion of Lamanites:

I do not boast in my own strength,
    nor in my own wisdom;
but behold, my joy is full,
    yea, my heart is brim with joy,
    and I will rejoice in my God.   5

Yea, I know that I am nothing;
    as to my strength I am weak;
therefore I will not boast of myself,

but I will boast of my God,
for in his strength I can do all things;   10
   yea, behold, many mighty miracles we have wrought in
this land,
   for which we will praise his name forever. . . .

Yea, we have reason to praise him forever,
   for he is the Most High God,
   and has loosed our brethren from the chains of hell.   15

Yea, they were encircled about with everlasting darkness and
   destruction;
but behold, he has brought them into his everlasting light,
   yea, into everlasting salvation;
and they are encircled about with the matchless bounty of his
   love;
yea, and we have been instruments in his hands of doing this
   great and marvelous work.   20

Therefore, let us glory, yea, we will glory in the Lord;
yea, we will rejoice, for our joy is full;
yea, we will praise our God forever.
Behold, who can glory too much in the Lord?
Yea, who can say too much of his great power,   25
   and of his mercy,
   and of his long-suffering towards the children of men?
Behold, I say unto you, I cannot say the smallest part which I
   feel.

                     (Alma 26:11–12, 14–16)

Recognized both visually and aurally, the dominant poetic feature in Ammon's defense is parallelism. For example, the denial of boasting in line 1 is completed in line 2; the declaration of joy in line 3 is amplified in lines 4 and 5; not boasting of self in line 8 is reversed in line 9 to boasting of God; the affirmation of God's strength in line 10 is specified in line 11; and everlasting darkness and everlasting light are contrasted in lines 16 and 17.

In each of the three stanzas is an intensification and expansion of feeling. In the first stanza, denial of boasting in his own strength and wisdom is turned into Ammon's emphasis on joy and rejoicing in God. The second stanza moves from limitations of self to praise for the strength of God and exemplification of his miraculous power. The third stanza builds from the simple "let us glory" to "we will glory in the Lord" to "we will praise our God forever." The climax comes in "who can glory too much" being amplified by "who can say too much," followed by the three parallel "of his" phrases. This climax is appropriately concluded with the quietly understated reversal, "I say unto you, I cannot say the smallest part which I feel." In tone, this reversal confirms his earlier confession that "I am nothing" and leaves ringing the repeated words of praise to God while acknowledging the limitations of man in treating spiritual matters in language.

THE POETRY OF PROPHECY

As prophecy, Book of Mormon poetry gains power through repeated words as well as through parallel ideas. The following prophecy by Abinadi illustrates this power:

Behold, thus saith the Lord, and thus hath he commanded me,
    saying, Go forth, and say unto this people, thus saith the
    Lord—

Wo be unto this people, for I have seen their abominations,
and their wickedness, and their whoredoms;
and *except they repent* I will visit them in mine anger.
And *except they repent* and turn to the Lord their God,
behold, I will *deliver* them into the hands of their enemies;
yea, and they shall be *brought into bondage;*
and they shall be *afflicted* by the hand of their enemies.
And it shall come to pass that they shall know that I am the Lord
    their God,
and am a jealous God, visiting the iniquities of my people.
And it shall come to pass that *except this people repent* and turn
    unto the Lord their God,
they shall be *brought into bondage;*

and none shall *deliver* them, except it be the Lord the Almighty
    God.
Yea, and it shall come to pass that when they shall *cry* unto me
I will be slow to hear their *cries;*
yea, and I will suffer them that they be smitten by their enemies.
And *except they repent* in sackcloth and ashes,
and *cry* mightily to the Lord their God,
I will not hear their prayers,
neither will I *deliver* them out of their *afflictions;*
and thus saith the Lord, and thus hath he commanded me.
(Mosiah 11:20–25)

Abinadi, like Nephi and Jacob, has a love for the greatness
of Isaiah's poetry and makes it part of his thinking and feeling.
Like Old Testament poet-prophets, Abinadi is not concerned
with originality; indeed, variation on a familiar theme or phrase
was part of the beauty of the matter. One of King Noah's priests
asks the meaning of Isaiah's words:

How beautiful upon the mountains are the feet of him that
    bringeth good tidings;
that publisheth peace;
that bringeth good tidings of good;
that publisheth salvation;
that saith unto Zion, Thy God reigneth;
Thy watchmen shall lift up the voice;
with the voice together shall they sing;
for they shall see eye to eye when the Lord shall bring again
    Zion.
(Mosiah 12:21–22; cf. Isaiah 52:7–8)

In his response, Abinadi shows the meaning of Isaiah
through his poetic variations. Having assimilated Isaiah, Abinadi
says regarding the prophets of old, "And O how beautiful upon
the mountains were their feet!" He then implicitly applies Isaiah's
words to himself: "And again, how beautiful upon the mountains
are the feet of those that are still publishing peace!" (Mosiah
15:15–16). In tribute to the greatest Prophet of all, Abinadi says:

And behold, I say unto you, this is not all.

For O how beautiful upon the mountains are the feet of him that
    bringeth good tidings,
that is the founder of peace,
yea, even the Lord, who has redeemed his people;
yea, him who has granted salvation unto his people.
                                   (Mosiah 15:18)

The Savior, when he comes to the New World, again quotes this idea from Isaiah (3 Nephi 20:40). Like Nephi, Jacob, and Abinadi, Jesus loves the writings of Isaiah and incorporates Isaiah's words as his words (which indeed they are, since Isaiah in essence had them from the Lord). His variation on Isaiah refers to the time when the gospel will be preached to the covenant people in Jerusalem and the Lord at last establishes Zion:

And they shall believe in me, that I am Jesus Christ, the Son of
    God,
and shall pray unto the Father in my name.
Then shall their watchmen lift up their voice,
and with the voice together shall they sing;
for they shall see eye to eye.
                                (3 Nephi 20:31–32)

Because the Book of Mormon is printed as prose, the full power of numerous testimonies of Jesus Christ has been obscured. When arranged as verse, these testimonies reveal their poetic nature. They "soar" in a manner similar to that attributed by William Everson to Walt Whitman's original preface to *Leaves of Grass:* "Long celebrated among Whitman's prose pieces for its vigor, [the 1855 preface] resists assimilation into that genre. Arranged as prose, its inversions clog, its rhythms fight themselves. Arranged as verse, they soar, proclaiming the presence of an unacknowledged masterpiece of American poetry."[23] Just so do we see the true power of the Book of Mormon when we read some of its most important passages as poetry instead of prose.

In the following prophetic statement found early in the Book of Mormon, we hear a shift from Nephi's prose to the Lord's poetry. There is a rhythm of cause-and-effect relationships ("inasmuch as . . . ye/they shall"), the order is of ascending significance ("land of promise" becomes "land which is choice above all other lands"), and the conclusion shows contrast between punishment and blessing:

> But, behold, Laman and Lemuel would not hearken unto my words; and being grieved because of the hardness of their hearts I cried unto the Lord for them. And it came to pass that the Lord spake unto me, saying:
>
> Blessed art thou, Nephi, because of thy faith,
> for thou hast sought me diligently, with lowliness of heart.
> And inasmuch as ye shall keep my commandments,
> ye shall prosper,
> and shall be led to a land of promise;
> yea, even a land which I have prepared for you;
> yea, a land which is choice above all other lands.
> And inasmuch as thy brethren shall rebel against thee,
> they shall be cut off from the presence of the Lord.
> And inasmuch as thou shalt keep my commandments,
> thou shalt be made a ruler and a teacher over thy brethren.
> (1 Nephi 2:18–22)

Again, we find a similar shift in Alma 7:8–9:

> Now as to this thing I do not know; but this much I do know, that the Lord God hath power to do all things which are according to his word. But behold, the Spirit hath said this much unto me, saying: Cry unto this people, saying—
>
> Repent ye, and prepare the way of the Lord,
> and walk in his paths, which are straight;
> for behold, the kingdom of heaven is at hand,
> and the Son of God cometh upon the face of the earth.

In the last passage, one idea builds on another. Personal repentance is a foundation for preparing the way of the Lord, and in turn, planning ("prepare") leads to action ("walk in his paths"). Following this pattern, the personal is a basis for the universal, which is presented first as general anticipation of the kingdom of heaven and then specified and intensified as the actual second coming of Christ.

CONNECTING HEAVEN AND EARTH

Analysis of several additional poetic passages from the Book of Mormon reveals their intricate artistry, heightening features, unity, memorability, and vigor in reaching the heart as well as the mind. Their exalted poetic language acts as a means of connecting earth and heaven.

When God endows Nephi the son of Helaman with power, He speaks poetically. He first defines the power He is giving Nephi through increasing levels of physical power (famine to pestilence to destruction), but then He gives it spiritual significance as well (sealed/loosed in heaven). The intensity of destructive power builds from rending the temple to leveling a mountain to the climax of smiting the people. With the confidence that comes from this vision of God's power given to him, Nephi is now ready to declare to the people the simple but meaningful message: "Except ye repent ye shall be smitten, even unto destruction." In lines 2 through 7 God is explaining the power to Nephi, in lines 8 through 11 God is actually giving Nephi the power, and in lines 12 through 20 God is again explaining the power to Nephi—thus creating a physical-spiritual-physical structure to Nephi's experience.

> And it came to pass as he was thus pondering . . . the wickedness of the people of the Nephites, . . . a voice came unto him saying:
> . . .
>
> Behold, thou art Nephi, and I am God.
> Behold, I declare it unto thee in the presence of mine angels,
> that ye shall have power over this people,
> and shall smite the earth with famine,
> and with pestilence,   5
> and destruction,
> according to the wickedness of this people.

Behold, I give unto you power,
that whatsoever ye shall seal on earth shall be sealed in heaven;
and whatsoever ye shall loose on earth shall be loosed in
    heaven; 10
and thus shall ye have power among this people.
And thus, if ye shall say unto this temple
it shall be rent in twain,
it shall be done.
And if ye shall say unto this mountain, 15
Be thou cast down and become smooth,
it shall be done.
And behold, if ye shall say that
God shall smite this people,
it shall come to pass. 20
And now behold, I command you,
that ye shall go and declare unto this people,
that thus saith the Lord God, who is the Almighty:
Except ye repent ye shall be smitten,
even unto destruction. 25

And behold, now it came to pass that when the Lord had spoken these words unto Nephi, he did stop and did not go unto his own house, but did return unto the multitudes who were scattered about upon the face of the land, and began to declare unto them the word of the Lord which had been spoken unto him, concerning their destruction if they did not repent. (Helaman 10:3, 6–12)

Nephi's final testimony at the end of the Second Book of Nephi also provides an example of the poetic artistry found in the Book of Mormon:

I glory in plainness; [stanza 1]
I glory in truth;
I glory in my Jesus,
for he hath redeemed my soul from hell.

I have charity for my people, [stanza 2]
and great faith in Christ that I shall meet many souls spotless at
    his judgment-seat.
I have charity for the Jew—

I say Jew, because I mean them from whence I came.
I also have charity for the Gentiles.

But behold, for none of these can I hope   [stanza 3]
except they shall be reconciled unto Christ,
and enter into the narrow gate,
and walk in the strait path which leads to life,
and continue in the path until the end of the day of probation.

And now, my beloved brethren,   [stanza 4]
and also Jew,
and all ye ends of the earth,
hearken unto these words and believe in Christ;
and if ye believe not in these words believe in Christ.
And if ye shall believe in Christ ye will believe in these words,
for they are the words of Christ,
and he hath given them unto me;
and they teach all men that they should do good.

And if they are not the words of Christ, judge ye—   [stanza 5]
for Christ will show unto you, with power and great glory,
that they are his words, at the last day;
and you and I shall stand face to face before his bar;
and ye shall know that I have been commanded of him to write
    these things,
notwithstanding my weakness.
And I pray the Father in the name of Christ that many of us,
if not all,
may be saved in his kingdom at that great and last day.

And now, my beloved brethren,   [stanza 6]
all those who are of the house of Israel,
and all ye ends of the earth,
I speak unto you as the voice of one crying from the dust:
Farewell until that great day shall come.
                    (2 Nephi 33:6–13)

Overall, this poetic conclusion to the two books of Nephi is
at once Nephi's personal testimony and his solemn admonition
to future generations. The resonating word in the first stanza
is *glory* as the parallelism moves in a staircase, or climactic,
manner. Personal redemption is followed by charity for others

(second stanza). Then, in the beginning of the third stanza, the qualification of hope—tying in with the charity and faith of the preceding stanza—links back with Nephi's own reconciliation with Christ ("he hath redeemed my soul"). The motion intensifies in a dynamic way from "enter" to "walk" to "continue," with the long last line also suggesting continuity.

The fourth stanza speaks of the audience in a heightened manner: "my people" becomes "my beloved brethren," and "the Gentiles" becomes "all ye ends of the earth." The echoing word here is "believe," with the simple admonition to "hearken unto these words and believe in Christ" moving to a more complex response to the relationship of "these words" and Christ. In the fifth stanza, the emphasis has shifted from belief in Christ to Christ's own demonstration of his words—with Nephi as witness. The sixth stanza confirms that witness with Nephi's distant yet vital "crying from the dust" to his tripartite audience.

Considering the context of all of Nephi's writings, with special emphasis on his interpretation of Lehi's vision of the tree of life, Clinton F. Larson says of Nephi's farewell: The "spirit of the Lord tells him to speak no more—no more will he be stirred to poetic expression. In his humility, he claims that what he has spoken is not poetic, but it is, with the substantive qualities of the best literature."[24]

ZENOS'S PRAYER OF WORSHIP

The prayer of worship by Zenos in Alma 33 is marked by simplicity and clarity. Its power is developed by repetition that varies slightly but meaningfully.

Thou art merciful, O God,   [stanza 1]
for thou hast heard my prayer,
    even when I was in the wilderness;
yea, thou wast merciful
    when I prayed concerning those who were mine enemies,
      and thou didst turn them to me.
Yea, O God, and thou wast merciful unto me

when I did cry unto thee in my field;
    when I did cry unto thee in my prayer,
        and thou didst hear me.
And again, O God, when I did turn to my house
    thou didst hear me in my prayer.
And when I did turn unto my closet,
O Lord, and prayed unto thee,
        thou didst hear me.

Yea, thou art merciful unto thy children   [stanza 2]
        when they cry unto thee,
        to be heard of thee and not of men,
            and thou wilt hear them.

Yea, O God, thou hast been merciful unto me,   [stanza 3]
        and heard my cries in the midst of thy congregations.
Yea, and thou hast also heard me when I have been cast out
        and have been despised by mine enemies;
yea, thou didst hear my cries,
        and wast angry with mine enemies,
        and thou didst visit them in thine anger with speedy
            destruction.

And thou didst hear me because of mine afflictions and my
        sincerity;   [stanza 4]
and it is because of thy Son that thou hast been thus merciful
    unto me,
        therefore I will cry unto thee in all mine afflictions,
for in thee is my joy;
for thou hast turned thy judgments away from me,
because of thy Son.
                    (Alma 33:4–11)

In the first stanza the imagery changes the location from the
dangerous exterior wilderness—a place where one encounters
enemies—to the cultivated exterior ("field") to the safe interior
("house") to the even more secure interior ("closet"). The second
stanza serves as a transition, moving the focus from place (stanza
1) to human environment (stanza 3). In either case, however,
whether with fellow Saints ("thy congregations") or with foes

("mine enemies"), Zenos is confident in the integrity of his direct relationship with God ("to be heard of thee and not of men").

The third stanza contains a striking variation from the first. In the first stanza, Zenos expresses gratitude that his enemies were turned to him (that is, their hearts were softened toward him). But in the third stanza, when they renewed their unkindness to him (casting him out and despising him), the prophet cried to God over his afflictions, until God chose to punish Zenos's enemies.

The concluding stanza links Christ with the mercy referred to earlier—bringing to a climactic close the intensified power created throughout the poem by the repetition of "merciful." This stanza moves from past ("thou didst hear me") to future ("I will cry unto thee") to present ("thou hast turned thy judgments away"), closing with the powerful and final repeated phrase: "because of thy Son."

The poem builds intensity with variations on "hear," "cry," and "merciful." These three words are developed in the first stanza, with "thou didst hear" being intensified through repetition. They are interlinked in stanza 2, with the principle of prayer being applied to all of God's prayerful children. Then in stanza 3, when we come to "thou didst hear my cries," we feel the emotional shrillness of "cries" in the context of Zenos's being "despised by mine enemies"; here the tension is increased as well. The fourth and last stanza resolves the problem and has a calming effect. The preceding stanza repeats the expressions "enemies," "angry/anger," and "destruction"; in contrast, the last stanza emphasizes "sincerity," "joy," and especially the repeated phrase "because of thy Son."

ALMA'S INSTRUCTIONS TO HELAMAN

Alma's guidance to his son Helaman contains this elevated poetic exhortation, given memorability by its structure:

O, remember, my son, and *learn* wisdom in thy youth;

86

yea, *learn* in thy youth to keep the commandments of God.
Yea, and *cry unto God* for all thy support;
yea, let all thy *doings* be *unto the Lord,*
and whithersoever thou *goest* let it be *in the Lord;*   5
yea, let all thy *thoughts* be directed *unto the Lord;*
yea, let the *affections* of thy heart be placed *upon the Lord*
     forever.

Counsel with the Lord in all thy doings,
and he will direct thee for good;
yea, when thou liest down at *night* lie down unto the Lord,   10
that he may watch over you in your sleep;
and when thou risest in the *morning*
let thy heart be full of thanks unto God;
and if ye do these things,
ye shall be lifted up at the *last day.*   15
                    (Alma 37:35–37)

The second line adds to the kind of learning found in the
first. Line 3 sets up a relationship with God that in the next four
lines intensifies in importance and emphasis, moving from crying to doing to going and, in lines 6 and 7, from thoughts to
affections. The relationship between Helaman and the Lord
advocated in the second half of the poem is more intimate, starting with "counsel with the Lord" (contrast with the more distant
"cry unto God" in the first half). The paired opposites of times
of day are used in the climax of the poem. The actions of lying
down at night unto the Lord and rising in the morning with
thanks unto God are followed by being lifted up at the last day.

HELAMAN 12

Alma's poetic exhortation is contained within essentially
prose instructions to his son. In a similar manner, Mormon in
Helaman 12 progresses from prose to poetry as he waxes elo-
quent regarding the increasing wickedness of the Nephites:

At the very time when [the Lord] doth prosper his people, . . . then
is the time that they do harden their hearts. . . . And thus we see

that except the Lord doth chasten his people with many afflictions, yea, except he doth visit them with death and with terror, and with famine and with all manner of pestilence, they will not remember him.

O how foolish, and how vain,   [stanza 1]
and how evil, and devilish,
and how *quick* to do iniquity, and how *slow* to do good,
are the children of men;
yea, how *quick* to hearken unto the words of the evil one,   5
and to set their hearts upon the vain things of the world!
Yea, how *quick* to be lifted up in pride;
yea, how *quick* to boast,
and do all manner of that which is iniquity;
and how *slow* are they to remember the Lord their God,   10
and to give ear unto his counsels,
yea, how *slow* to walk in wisdom's paths!

Behold, they do not desire that the Lord their God,   [stanza 2]
who hath created them, should rule and reign over them;
notwithstanding his great goodness and his mercy
        towards them,   15
they do set at naught his counsels,
and they will not that he should be their guide.

O how great is the nothingness of the children of men; [stanza 3]
yea, even they are less than the dust of the earth.
For behold, the dust of the earth moveth hither and thither,   20
to the dividing asunder, at the command of our great and
        everlasting God.
Yea, behold at his voice do the hills and the mountains
        tremble and quake.
And by the power of his voice they are broken up, and
        become smooth,
yea, even like unto a valley.
Yea, by the power of his voice doth the whole earth shake;   25
Yea, by the power of his voice, do the foundations rock,
even to the very center.
Yea, and if he say unto the earth—Move—it is moved.
Yea, if he say unto the earth—

Thou shalt go back, that it lengthen out the day for many
    hours— 30
it is done;
And thus, according to his word the earth goeth back,
and it appeareth unto man that the sun standeth still;
yea, and behold, this is so;
for surely it is the earth that moveth and not the sun. 35
And behold, also, if he say unto the waters of the great deep—
Be thou dried up—it is done.
Behold, if he say unto this mountain—
Be thou raised up, and come over and fall upon that city,
that it be buried up—behold it is done. 40

And behold, if a man hide up a treasure in the earth, [stanza 4]
and the Lord shall say—Let it be accursed,
because of the iniquity of him who hath hid it up—
behold, it shall be accursed.
And if the Lord shall say—Be thou accursed, that no man
    shall find thee from this time henceforth and forever— 45
behold, no man getteth it henceforth and forever.

And behold, if the Lord shall say unto a man— [stanza 5]
Because of thine iniquities, thou shalt be accursed forever—
it shall be done.
And if the Lord shall say— 50
Because of thine iniquities thou shalt be cut off from my
    presence—
he will cause that it shall be so.
And wo unto him to whom he shall say this,
for it shall be unto him that will do iniquity,
and he cannot be saved; 55
therefore, for this cause, that men might be saved,
hath repentance been declared.

Therefore, blessed are they who will repent and hearken
    unto the voice of the Lord their God; [stanza 6]
for these are they that shall be saved.
And may God grant, in his great fulness, 60
that men might be brought unto repentance and good works,
that they might be restored unto grace for grace,
according to their works.

And I would that all men might be saved.

But we read that in the great and last day there are some who
    shall be cast out,   65
yea, who shall be cast off from the presence of the Lord;

Yea, who shall be consigned to a state of endless
    misery,   [stanza 7]
fulfilling the words which say:
They that have done good shall have everlasting life;
and they that have done evil shall have everlasting
    damnation.   70
And thus it is. Amen.

                    (Helaman 12:2–26)[25]

This powerful and sweeping poetry is designed to stir its auditors to profit from Mormon's triple perspective. Mormon responds to the situation of the Nephites whom he has just described, implicitly he is stirred by the iniquity of degenerating Nephites of his own time, and he looks down through time to the audience who will receive his words. Mormon's scope is vast; he presents the power of God to effect cataclysmic changes in the earth. He personalizes God's power to an individual ("if the Lord shall say unto a man—Because of thine iniquities, thou shalt be accursed forever—it shall be done"). He then closes by moving out in his thoughts to the dual possibilities for all humankind, to have everlasting life or to have everlasting damnation.

The first two lines set up the concentrated concern found throughout the remainder of the poem. There is a progression from "foolish" to "vain" to "evil" to "devilish." This culminates in the balance of opposites: "quick to do iniquity" and "slow to do good." The remainder of the stanza builds on the alternation of "quick" and "slow."

Stanza 2 summarizes the position of the unfaithful children of men. In stanza 3, the vanity of man lifted up in pride is put into perspective: man is actually less than the dust. Then follows an ascending action upon physical things. The "dust of the earth" is divided asunder by the command of God; hills and mountains tremble and quake and then are broken up; the whole earth shakes; the foundations rock to the center; the earth moves, and then it goes back—all showing the power of God. Following this action of the "dust of the earth" is another buildup with the potential for even greater miracles: waters of the great deep would be dried up and, instead, a great wave of the earth itself—a mountain—would engulf a city, demonstrating God's total command over the physical world.

References to the physical power of the Lord prepare for specific and intensifying application to potential distress of the people. If a wicked man hide a treasure, the Lord will curse it that it cannot be found; a wicked man will be cursed forever; a wicked man will be cut off from God's presence (lines 41–46).

Finally, there comes an appeal to iniquitous persons who have been stirred by this progression to repent (stanza 5). If they hearken to the voice of the Lord, they shall be saved (stanza 6). The simple but effective conclusion, contained in paired opposite lines, specifies the everlasting judgments to those who have done good and those who have done evil. "And thus it is," Mormon says, quietly and briefly affirming the truth of the whirlwind experience through which he has taken his auditors—and his readers.

MORMON'S LAMENTATION

In what Sidney B. Sperry calls a lamentation, Mormon responds in a poignant and lyrical manner to the destruction of his people:

And my soul was rent with anguish, because of the slain of my people, and I cried:

O ye fair ones, how could ye have departed from the ways of
　　the Lord! [stanza 7]
O ye fair ones, how could ye have rejected that Jesus, who stood
　　with open arms to receive you!
Behold, if ye had not done this, ye would not have fallen.
But behold, ye are fallen, and I mourn your loss.

O ye fair sons and daughters,
    ye fathers and mothers,   [stanza 2]
ye husbands and wives, ye fair ones,
how is it that ye could have fallen!
But behold, ye are gone, and my sorrows cannot bring your
    return.

And the day soon cometh that your mortal must put on
    immortality,   [stanza 3]
and these bodies which are now moldering in corruption must
    soon become
incorruptible bodies;
and then ye must stand before the judgment-seat of Christ, to be
    judged according
to your works;
and if it so be that ye are righteous, then are ye blessed with
    your fathers who
have gone before you.

O that ye had repented before this great destruction had come
    upon you.   [stanza 4]
But behold, ye are gone,
and the Father, yea, the Eternal Father of heaven, knoweth your
    state;
and he doeth with you according to his justice and mercy.
                  (Mormon 6:16–22)

In the first stanza, a more general departure from the ways
of the Lord is portrayed as both absolute and tenderly specific:
Mormon's people have rejected Jesus, who stood with open
arms to receive them. The same sorrowful finality is contained
in the subsequent parallel lines, with the echoed word "fallen"
providing the anguished climax of the second stanza.

In keeping with references to the future, the tone of the third
stanza is calmer. In the first line of the fourth and last stanza,
though, the tone again becomes emotional. Mormon cries from
his soul, "O that ye had repented before this great destruction had
come upon you." This last part of the lament is linked by the initial "O" with earlier declarations. Most powerfully connecting
them is Mormon's simple but profound sense of loss. "But behold,

ye are fallen," Mormon says in the first stanza. "But behold, ye are gone," he says in the next. And again in the last, "But behold, ye are gone." This quietly states the finality of their fate. The final paired lines affirm God's knowledge and then his action. The last word, "mercy," befits Mormon's feelings for his people.[26]

POETIC ENTICINGS TO "COME UNTO CHRIST"

Scores of other passages in the Book of Mormon can properly be identified and analyzed as poetry. These range from Lehi's brief desert poems (a form Hugh Nibley identifies as a *QasÉida*[27]) to the extensive poetic sermons of Jacob (as in 2 Nephi 9), of Abinadi (as in Mosiah 12), and of Christ (as in 3 Nephi 27). Some representative excerpts reveal the character and variety of this poetry.

Lehi's desert poems consist of similes:

And when my father saw that the waters of the river emptied into the fountain of the Red Sea, he spake unto Laman, saying:

O that thou mightest be like unto this river,
continually running into the fountain of all righteousness!

And he also spake unto Lemuel:

O that thou mightest be like unto this valley,
firm and steadfast,
and immovable in keeping the commandments of the Lord!
(1 Nephi 2:9–10)

The next poetic excerpt, one of Lehi's exhortations to his sons, begins with a terrace pattern—that is, the key word at the end of the first line is repeated and built upon at the beginning of the next line:

O that ye would awake;
awake from a deep sleep,
yea, even from the sleep of hell,
and shake off the awful chains by which ye are bound,
which are the chains which bind the children of men,

that they are carried away captive
down to the eternal gulf of misery and woe.
          (2 Nephi 1:13)

The first simple "awake" is intensified to "awake from a deep sleep"; then the "deep" part of the sleep is defined as the sleep of "hell." By association, being in "hell" is being bound by "chains," universalized in the next line to apply to the "children of men." The passage ends with "carried away" being a motion contrasting with "shake off," with "bind" being intensified to "captive," and "hell" expanded into "the eternal gulf of misery and woe."

Chiasmus in the following passage, from one of Nephi's sermons in 2 Nephi, was first noticed by John W. Welch, who called this example "relatively lyrical in character."[28]

And others will he pacify,
and lull *them away* into carnal security,
    that they will say:
    All is well in *Zion;*
    yea, *Zion* prospereth,
    all is well—
and thus the devil cheateth their souls,
and leadeth *them away* carefully down to hell.
          (2 Nephi 28:21)

The next example, taken from Jacob's sermon, builds intensity through movement from "marvelous" to "mysteries" and from "unsearchable" to "impossible." It also builds logically in its connection between the greatness of the works of the Lord, the limitations of man, and the necessity of revelation in knowing God's ways:

Behold, great and marvelous are the works of the Lord.
How unsearchable are the depths of the mysteries of him;
and it is impossible that man should find out all his ways.
And no man knoweth of his ways save it be revealed unto him;
wherefore, brethren, despise not the revelations of God.
          (Jacob 4:8)

In Abinadi's instructions to visit the court of the wicked King
Noah, we find this example of intensification:

> Thus has the Lord commanded me, saying—
> Abinadi, go and prophesy unto this my people,
> for they have hardened their hearts against my words;
> they have repented not of their evil doings;
> therefore, I will visit them in my anger,
> yea, in my fierce anger will I visit them in their iniquities and
>   abominations.
> Yea, wo be unto this generation!
> (Mosiah 12:1–2)

The people are indicted first for preventing the good (hardened against "my words") and performing the bad. Anger
becomes "fierce anger" and the evil doings of the people build
up from "iniquities" to "abominations." In sum, the Lord is saying, "The people are wicked; I will punish; wo to them."

In the following poetic passage, the Lord is responding to
Alma's fervent prayer. The focus first alternates between Alma
and the people he baptized. Then the concern moves increasingly outward to "whoever is baptized." In the third stanza, the
focus turns to the Lord and then back to the believer. The subsequent part of the Lord's poetic instruction, not given here,
develops potential punishments or rewards.

> And it came to pass that after he had poured out his whole soul
> to God, the voice of the Lord came to him, saying:

> Blessed art thou, Alma,
>   and blessed are they who were baptized in the waters of
>   Mormon.
> Thou art blessed because of thy exceeding faith in the words
>   alone of my servant Abinadi.
>   And blessed are they because of their exceeding faith in
>   the words alone which thou hast spoken unto them.
> And blessed art thou because thou hast established a church
>   among this people;
>   and they shall be established,

and they shall be my people.
   Yea, blessed is this people who are willing to bear my
   name;
      for in my name shall they be called; and they are mine.
And because thou hast inquired of me concerning the
   transgressor,
thou art blessed.
Thou art my servant;
and I covenant with thee that thou shalt have eternal life;
and thou shalt serve me and go forth in my name,
and shalt gather together my sheep.

And he that will hear my voice shall be my sheep;
and him shall ye receive into the church,
and him will I also receive.
For behold, this is my church;
whosoever is baptized shall be baptized unto repentance.
And whomsoever ye receive shall believe in my name;
and him will I freely forgive.

For it is I that taketh upon me the sins of the world;
for it is I that hath created them;
and it is I that granteth unto him that believeth unto the end a
place at my right hand.
For behold, in my name are they called;
and if they know me they shall come forth,
and shall have a place eternally at my right hand.
                          (Mosiah 26:14–24)

This segment from Alma's sermon builds on images of nour-
ishment:

Yea, he saith:
Come unto me and ye shall partake of the fruit of the tree of life;
yea, ye shall eat and drink of the bread and the waters of life
   freely;
Yea, come unto me and bring forth works of righteousness,
and ye shall not be hewn down and cast into the fire—
                    (Alma 5:34–35)

Amulek's instructions on prayer are made memorable by the
anaphora (initial repetition) of "cry," by frequent amplification,

as in lines 9 through 12, and by the progressive development of prayer from "call" to "cry" to "pour out your souls":

> Therefore may God grant unto you, my brethren,
> that ye may begin to exercise your faith unto repentance,
> that ye begin to call upon his holy name,
> that he would have mercy upon you;
>
> Yea, cry unto him for mercy;   5
> for he is mighty to save.
> Yea, humble yourselves,
> and continue in prayer unto him.
> Cry unto him when ye are in your fields,
> yea, over all your flocks.   10
> Cry unto him in your houses,
> yea, over all your household,
> both morning, mid-day, and evening.
> Yea, cry unto him against the power of your enemies.
> Yea, cry unto him against the devil,   15
> who is an enemy to all righteousness.
> Cry unto him over the crops of your fields,
> that ye may prosper in them.
> Cry over the flocks of your fields,
> that they may increase.   20
>
> But this is not all;
> ye must pour out your souls in your closets,
> and your secret places,
> and in your wilderness.
> Yea, and when you do not cry unto the Lord,   25
> let your hearts be full,
> drawn out in prayer unto him continually for your welfare,
> and also for the welfare of those who are around you.
>   (Alma 34:17–27)

The following passage, from Christ's sermon to the Nephites at the temple in Bountiful, is part of a larger declaration that builds power through use of the refrain, "O house of Israel":

> And then will I remember my covenant which I have made unto
>   *my people, O house of Israel,*
> and I will bring my gospel unto them.

And I will show unto thee, *O house of Israel,*
that the Gentiles shall not have power over you;
but I will remember my covenant unto you, *O house of Israel,*
and ye shall come unto the knowledge of the fulness of my
  gospel.
But if the Gentiles will repent and return unto me, saith the
  Father,
behold they shall be numbered among *my people, O house of*
  Israel.

(3 Nephi 16:11–13)

In the next example we notice poetic repetitions in Moroni's account of the song of the Jaredites and then in his narrative "hymn" describing their preservation.

And they did *sing praises unto the Lord;* yea,
the brother of Jared did *sing praises unto the Lord,*
and he did thank and *praise the Lord* all the *day* long;
and when the *night* came, they did not cease to *praise the Lord.*

And thus they were driven forth;
and no *monster* of the sea could break them,
neither *whale* that could mar them;
and they did have light continually,
whether it was *above the water* or *under the water.*
And thus they were driven forth,
three hundred and forty and four days *upon the water.*

And they did *land upon the shore of the promised land.*
And when they had *set their feet upon the shores of the*
  promised land
they *bowed themselves* down upon the face of the *land,*
and did *humble themselves before the Lord,*
and did *shed tears of joy before the Lord,*
because of the multitude of his tender mercies over them.

(Ether 6:9–12)

Poetry of the sort Moroni and others write is designed to convince "the Jew and Gentile that Jesus is the Christ" and to help them come unto Christ. In his final appeal, Moroni urges his audience to

come unto Christ,
and lay hold upon every good gift,
and touch not the evil gift,
nor the unclean thing.
And awake, and arise from the dust, O Jerusalem;
yea, and put on thy beautiful garments, O daughter of Zion;
and strengthen thy stakes and enlarge thy borders forever,
that thou mayest no more be confounded,
that the covenants of the Eternal Father which he hath made
    unto thee, O house of Israel, may be fulfilled.
Yea, come unto Christ,
and be perfected in him,
and deny yourselves of all ungodliness;
and if ye shall deny yourselves of all ungodliness,
and love God with all your might, mind and strength,
then is his grace sufficient for you,
that by his grace ye may be perfect in Christ;
and if by the grace of God ye are perfect in Christ,
ye can in nowise deny the power of God.
                                (Moroni 10:30–32)

This poetic challenge incorporates poetry by Isaiah, whom Victor L. Ludlow in *Isaiah: Prophet, Seer, and Poet* says "delivered his prophetic messages in such sophisticated and exalted poetry that his writings attain heights of spiritual, intellectual, and artistic expression almost unparalleled in world literature."[29] Moroni is not simply quoting Isaiah, though. He has made Isaiah's writings so much a fabric of his thinking and feeling that at this point Isaiah's words have become Moroni's. Further, Moroni's poetry here is on the high level of Isaiah's, producing a seamless garment.

Isaiah wrote:

Awake, awake; put on thy strength, O Zion;
put on thy beautiful garments, O Jerusalem, the holy city:
for henceforth there shall no more come into thee the
    uncircumcised
and the unclean.
Shake thyself from the dust;
arise, and sit down, O Jerusalem:

loose thyself from the bands of thy neck,
O captive daughter of Zion.

(Isaiah 52:1–2)

Enlarge the place of thy tent,
and let them stretch forth the curtains of thine habitations:
spare not, lengthen thy cords, and strengthen thy stakes.

(Isaiah 54:2)

In his inspired understanding, Moroni calls for Jerusalem first to arise from the dust and then to put on her beautiful garments. From that will come a strengthening of her stakes. And then will come enlargement of Zion's borders and a perfection of Zion as its people come unto Christ in faith, repentance, and love. Moroni says this fully in the spirit of Isaiah, a great prophet of all Israel.

Thus with its penetrating power, stirring rhythms of ideas, and rich texture of striking words and memorable images, poetry in the Book of Mormon is indeed an appropriate medium through which "the spirit of prophecy" can be conveyed. It persuades and stirs the honest in heart to come feelingly to Christ.

Poetry in the Book of Mormon is best appreciated when listened to. We are to *hear* prophets such as Moroni "crying from the dead" and "speaking out of the dust" (Moroni 10:27). Read aloud, exalted Book of Mormon passages will resonate, touching us as beautiful music does. Responding to the Christ-centered poetry of the book, we may well be stirred to join Abinadi in his poetic praise of the Savior:

He is the *light* and the *life* of the world;
yea, a *light* that is endless,
that can never be darkened;
yea, and also a *life* which is endless,
that there can be no more death.

(Mosiah 16:9)

CHAPTER 5

"Know the Covenants of the Lord"
SERMONS

King Benjamin may have given the most effective sermon ever recorded. We are told that *all* the people listening to him, except for the little children, who were not accountable, were so moved by his sermon that they "entered into a covenant with God to keep his commandments" and took "upon them the name of Christ" (Mosiah 6:1–2). The effectiveness of this sermon continues with those who experience it today. King Benjamin's address, together with other sermons selected by inspired writers of the Book of Mormon, helps the "remnant of the House of Israel . . . know the covenants of the Lord" (title page). Some other noteworthy prophetic discourses that provide knowledge of the covenants and stir people to accept them (or challenge people who are unwilling to accept them) are Jacob's sermon in 2 Nephi 6–10; Alma's sermon to the people of Zarahemla (Alma 5); Alma's contrasting sermon (in Alma 7) to the people in Gideon; Alma's challenge to the people of Ammonihah (Alma 9:8–30); Alma's impromptu follow-up to Amulek's response to Zeezrom (Alma 12:3–13:30); the words of King Anti-Nephi-Lehi (Alma 24:7–16); Alma's discourse on faith to the poor Zoramites (Alma 32:8–33:23); the Savior's sermon on Israel found in 3 Nephi 20–23;[1] and Mormon's sermon on faith, hope, and charity (Moroni 7).[2]

The power of a Book of Mormon sermon comes from a combination of all its elements. The prophetic discourse is designed to appeal to the spirit, the mind, and the emotions. Close analysis of the nine sermons mentioned above will show how they are crafted artistically to have great rhetorical effectiveness.

Before looking at these sermons for content regarding covenants, however, we need to know what Moroni in the title page might have meant by "covenants of the Lord." The covenant had many dimensions, promises, and obligations, including the following: Lehi and his family brought with them knowledge of the Lord's covenant that through Abraham's seed "shall all the kindreds of the earth be blessed" (1 Nephi 15:18). As Nephi taught so powerfully (2 Nephi 31:10–20), they covenanted by baptism to keep the commandments—which were the "words of the covenant, the ten commandments" (Exodus 34:28) as well as the rites and observances of the law of Moses. Although as Jacob put it, the Nephites saw themselves as "a lonesome and a solemn people, wanderers . . . in a wilderness" (Jacob 7:26), they were comforted by covenants that they would inherit a land "choice above all other lands" (1 Nephi 13:30; 2 Nephi 1:5). As "the covenant people of the Lord" (1 Nephi 15:14), they were entitled to the promises made to the house of Israel. Especially, they fulfilled the promise made to Joseph the patriarch that a remnant of his seed would be a "righteous branch unto the house of Israel" (2 Nephi 3:5) and that his descendants would not be completely destroyed (2 Nephi 3:23; 9:53). The promise is that after a period of spiritual darkness, when they come to believe in Christ, they shall be restored "unto the lands of their inheritance" (2 Nephi 10:7). In sum,

> at that day shall the remnant of our seed know that they are of the house of Israel, and that they are the covenant people of the Lord; and then shall they know and come to the knowledge of their forefathers, and also to the knowledge of the gospel of their Redeemer, which was ministered unto their fathers by him; wherefore, they shall come to the knowledge of their Redeemer and the

very points of his doctrine, that they may know how to come unto him and be saved. (1 Nephi 15:14)

The reward to an individual who serves God and keeps his commandments "in all things" is eternal life (Mosiah 5:5, 15). According to the words of Jesus Christ recorded by Mormon, if Gentiles covenant by baptism, they "may receive a remission of [their] sins, and be filled with the Holy Ghost, that [they] may be numbered with my people who are of the house of Israel" (3 Nephi 30:2). Those who "by the grace of God are perfect in Christ, and deny not his power," Moroni says, are "sanctified in Christ by the grace of God, through the shedding of the blood of Christ, which is in the covenant of the Father unto the remission of your sins, that ye become holy, without spot" (Moroni 10:33). The covenanted descendants of those whom the resurrected Savior addressed will reside in a New Jerusalem. "And the powers of heaven shall be in the midst of this people; yea, even I will be in the midst of you" (3 Nephi 20:22).

KING BENJAMIN'S ADDRESS

Though King Benjamin wants his people to transfer their allegiance to their new king, his son Mosiah, his main purpose in gathering his people and speaking to them is to cement their allegiance to their heavenly king.[3] He desires that his people covenant to keep all of God's commandments and take upon them a new name: They "shall be called the children of Christ, his sons, and his daughters; for behold, this day he hath spiritually begotten you." Then if they are obedient unto the end of their lives, they are promised they "shall be found at the right hand of God" (Mosiah 5:7, 9).[4]

Apparently all of King Benjamin's people have come together on short notice, eager to listen to their beloved king (Mosiah 2:1).[5] Reading between the lines, we assume that the people are previously baptized church members who are confident they are righteous (King Benjamin says "they have been a diligent people in keeping the commandments of the Lord" [Mosiah 1:11]); they observe the law of Moses (Mosiah 2:3); and they have come "that they might give thanks to the Lord their God" for actions on the part of the Lord and others (Mosiah 2:4). What they do not realize, though, is that this type of observance, including their prayers of gratitude, is passive and low-level obedience. Indeed, the assembled people may have been self-satisfied in thinking they were keeping all God's commandments by avoiding such sins as theft and murder (Mosiah 2:13). Further, they have a tendency to be proud; the king asks, "Of what have ye to boast?" (Mosiah 2:24). Given their self-satisfaction, we may imagine the people's shock in hearing their kind old king say, "I have caused that ye should assemble yourselves together that I might rid my garments of your blood" (Mosiah 2:28), and to say that the unrepentant person among them is "in open rebellion against God" (Mosiah 2:37).

King Benjamin's last address to his people is carefully structured into four main parts. Besides teaching his people humility, King Benjamin initially tries to move them beyond passive obedience to active involvement and higher levels of perception. He calls for action in saying, "Hearken unto me, and open your ears that ye may hear, and your hearts that ye may understand, and your minds that the mysteries of God may be unfolded to your view" (Mosiah 2:9). He teaches them by both precept and example to render unselfish service—by which they serve God. The second part of his address pertains to the atonement of Jesus Christ. Then, after the people manifest their repentance, King Benjamin develops the application of his speech, calling on the people continually to have faith, repent, and be merciful and righteous. The fourth part of King Benjamin's religious instruction begins with his request to know if the people believe his words. Their affirmation shows they have now reached the final stage King Benjamin desired.

The speech combines rhetorical forms George Kennedy finds in both the Old Testament and New Testament. "In the Old Testament," Kennedy says,

> the most characteristic form of speech to an audience already disposed to believe is the "covenant speech," an address built on the assumption of a covenant between God and the people of Israel. The general pattern of a covenant speech is, first, to strengthen the authority of the Lord by reminding the audience of what he has done; second, to add new commandments; and third, to conclude with a warning of what will happen if the commandments are disregarded. . . . A second form of rhetoric in the Old Testament is that of prophecy. If the covenant speech deals with the past, and thus has resemblance to classical judicial oratory, prophecy looks to the future and adapts the message of the covenant to future circumstances, thus resembling deliberative oratory.[6]

In the New Testament, Kennedy says, preaching is "not persuasion, but proclamation, and is based on authority and grace, not on proof."[7] Combining these forms, King Benjamin reminds the people what the Lord has done, refers to new commandments that will be delivered to them by his son Mosiah, and reminds them of "the awful situation of those that have fallen into transgression" (Mosiah 2:40). He prophesies of Christ's coming, and he proclaims by authority, speaking "the words which the Lord God hath commanded" him (Mosiah 3:20, 23). The people are thus awakened to a sense of their nothingness by a knowledge of the goodness, power, and wisdom of God.

Taking Kennedy's *New Testament Interpretation through Rhetorical Criticism* as a guide, we can see how King Benjamin's covenant speech first persuades the audience to reaffirm a present point of view and then becomes deliberative rhetoric aimed "at effecting a decision about future action, often the very immediate future."[8] (Kennedy's philosophical justification for approaching the New Testament through classical rhetoric is applicable as well to the Book of Mormon: "Though rhetoric is colored by the traditions and conventions of the society in which it is applied, it is also a universal phenomenon which is conditioned by basic workings of the human mind and heart and by the nature of all human society."[9])

King Benjamin begins his address with an exordium, or preface, "which seeks to obtain the attention of the audience and goodwill or sympathy toward the speaker."[10] The preface extends from verse 9 to verse 16 of Mosiah 2, with verse 17 functioning as a transition: "when ye are in the service of your fellow beings ye are only in the service of your God." The people are already favorably disposed toward King Benjamin, believing they have "a just man to be their king" (Mosiah 2:4). Nevertheless, he has an important strategy in reminding the people at length that he has not sought riches or imposed high taxes on them but rather has labored to serve them. He has not imprisoned them or allowed them to enslave and persecute each other but has taught them to keep the Lord's commandments. Having stirred up their feelings of gratitude for him, he then transfers that gratitude to God, declaring, "And behold also, if I, whom ye call your king, who has spent his days in your service, and yet has been in the service of God, do merit any thanks from you, O how you ought to thank your heavenly King!" (Mosiah 2:19).

Thanks, though, are not enough. Benjamin clarifies the people's true relationship to God in a series of "if . . . then" statements, saying, for example, "If ye should serve him with all your whole souls yet ye would be unprofitable servants" (Mosiah 2:21). That leads to the proposition about covenant making that Benjamin wishes to elaborate: "And behold, all that he requires of you is to keep his commandments" (Mosiah 2:22). Benjamin ends his proposition with a summary statement that he has served his people with a clear conscience. He is then ready to stir them to repent.

The three modes of artistic proof Kennedy details are evident in King Benjamin's address: ethos, "the credibility that the author or speaker is able to establish in his work"; pathos, the appeal to emotions; and logos, "the logical argument found within the discourse."[11] Those elements correspond incompletely to terms that Kennedy in *Classical Rhetoric* considers to be more appropriate to Judeo-Christian rhetoric: "grace, authority, and logos, the divine message which can be understood by man."[12] Benjamin's long service as a just and beloved king is sufficient to establish his credibility, and he builds upon it by reminding them that he has been chosen by the people, consecrated by his father, and permitted by the Lord to be a ruler and king over the people. His statements gain integrity and power by their being the last words of a dying king: "And ye behold that I am old, and am about to yield up this mortal frame to its mother earth" (Mosiah 2:26).[13]

The greatest authority, though, comes in what Kennedy calls "radical Christian rhetoric," in which the speaker is a vehicle of God's will.[14] King Benjamin affirms that authority by quoting the words given him by an angel from God (Mosiah 3:2–27). That is the central part of King Benjamin's address. Quoting the angel, this humble king teaches concerning the coming Messiah and the atonement He offers. He calls the people to repentance— which is both a turning away from the "natural man" and turning toward Christian living with childlike humility. He explains the purpose of the law of Moses, and he clarifies the judgment of Christ. In concluding his quotation from the angel, King Benjamin evokes a portrait of evil people who are "consigned to an awful view of their own guilt and abominations, which doth cause them to shrink from the presence of the Lord into a state of misery and endless torment." They have "drunk out of the cup of the wrath of God" and their torment "is as a lake of fire and brimstone, whose flames are unquenchable, and whose smoke ascendeth up forever and ever" (Mosiah 3:25–27).

Both in their attitudes and their words, the people respond immediately to each of the main points King Benjamin has made. They had been passively sitting in their tents so that they might "hear the words which king Benjamin should speak unto them" (Mosiah 2:6). When Benjamin finishes speaking, the multitude fall to the earth as though they were shrinking from the presence of the Lord, "for the fear of the Lord had come upon them" (Mosiah 4:1). This physical falling is emblematic of what King Benjamin calls their "worthless and fallen state" (Mosiah 4:5). He has taught them that they are not "even as much as the dust of the earth" and urged them to put off worldliness and become sanctified "through the atonement of Christ the Lord" (Mosiah 2:25; 3:19). In response, they view themselves "in their own carnal state, even less than the dust of the earth" and pray for mercy through the atonement of Christ, after which they receive a remission of their sins and are filled with joy (Mosiah 4:2–3).

After that response, King Benjamin reiterates all the main points of his sermon, including those of the angel's message:

> If the knowledge of the goodness of God at this time has awakened you to a sense of your nothingness, and . . . if ye have come to a knowledge of . . . the atonement which has been prepared from the foundation of the world, that thereby salvation might come to him that should put his trust in the Lord, and should be diligent in keeping his commandments, and continue in the faith even unto the end of his life, I mean the life of the mortal body—I say, that this is the man who receiveth salvation. (Mosiah 4:5–7)

The diligence in keeping God's commandments includes imparting "your substance to the poor, every man according to that which he hath, such as feeding the hungry, clothing the naked, visiting the sick and administering to their relief, both spiritually and temporally, according to their wants" (Mosiah 4:26). This physically trembling but spiritually strong old man is a premier example of continuing in faith until the end of life. His own manifest purity of soul supports his injunction to "always retain a remission of your sins" (Mosiah 4:12).

At the end of this part of the sermon, King Benjamin specifically reaffirms his ethos (his credibility): he sends among the people desiring to know if they believe his words. As they had done before in praying for mercy, they make their response "with one voice" (Mosiah 5:1–2). They confess the "mighty change" which has been wrought in them and say they have "no more disposition to do evil, but to do good continually" (Mosiah 5:2). They are "willing to enter into a covenant with our God to do his will, and to be obedient to his commandments in all things that he shall command us, all the remainder of our days" (Mosiah 5:5). For his part, King Benjamin approves the covenant and gives them a new name—that of Jesus Christ—which seals the covenant they have made. Finally, he takes down the names of those who had covenanted with God to keep his commandments.[15]

King Benjamin develops logos (the logical argument) by frequent use of the *enthymeme*, a syllogistic argument in which one of the premises is often suppressed. For example, Benjamin says, "As ye have kept my commandments . . . and have prospered, . . . even so if ye shall keep the commandments of my son, or the commandments of God which shall be delivered unto you by him, ye shall prosper in the land" (Mosiah 2:31). Again, "If God, who has created you, . . . doth grant unto you whatsoever ye ask that is right, . . . O then, how ye ought to impart of the substance that ye have one to another" (Mosiah 4:21).

Although King Benjamin uses logic, he is most compelling in employing what Kennedy calls "radical Christian rhetoric." That is, King Benjamin solemnly affirms repeatedly that his message comes from God by using such phrases as "spoken the words which the Lord gave," "thus saith the Lord," and "thus hath the Lord commanded me."

A figure of speech King Benjamin uses effectively is to begin a series of clauses with the same word, a device called *anaphora*, as in this passage:

Believe in God;
believe that he is, and that he created all things, both in heaven and in earth;
believe that he has all wisdom, and all power, both in heaven and in earth;

109

believe that man doth not comprehend all the things which the
    Lord can comprehend.
And again, *believe* that ye must repent of your sins and forsake
    them, and humble yourselves before God;
    and ask in sincerity of heart that he would forgive you;
      and now, if you *believe* all these things see that ye do them.
(Mosiah 4:9–10)

The cumulative power of this figure is the climactic shift from
believe to the injunction "see that ye *do* them."

King Benjamin uses several other thought-provoking figures
of speech. He employs antithesis by juxtaposing positives and
negatives throughout; for example, "putteth off the natural man
and becometh a saint" and "always retain in remembrance, the
greatness of God, and your own nothingness" (Mosiah 3:19;
4:11). He poses rhetorical questions, such as, "Can ye say aught
of yourselves? I answer you, Nay. Ye cannot say that ye are even
as much as the dust of the earth" (Mosiah 2:25). He constructs
analogies to teach his point vividly: "Doth a man take an ass
which belongeth to his neighbor, and keep him? I say unto you,
Nay; he will not even suffer that he shall feed among his flocks,
but will drive him away, and cast him out. I say unto you, that
even so shall it be among you if ye know not the name by
which ye are called" (Mosiah 5:14). He employs comparison to
help his people relate to his words: "Ye will not suffer that the
beggar putteth up his petition to you in vain, and turn him out to
perish. . . . For behold, are we not all beggars? Do we not all
depend upon the same Being, even God, for all the substance
which we have?" (Mosiah 4:16, 19). And he uses the ancient
Hebrew device of chiasmus, or inversion.

As John Welch has demonstrated, "Chiastic repetitions occur
frequently in Benjamin's rhetoric."[16] His coronation proclamation
is balanced by a later covenant proclamation (Mosiah 5:1–5). The
subsequent call for obedience to divine laws the people have
been taught (Mosiah 2:31–41) is repeated in specific admonitions
to keep the laws of love and service (Mosiah 4:13–30). The

angel's declaration of Christ's atoning mission for the salvation of mankind (Mosiah 3:2–10) is balanced by Benjamin's later testimony of the goodness and glory of God and his salvation (Mosiah 4:4–12). The chiasm is bracketed by the opening instructions regarding physical creation, a covenant people, and exaltation, and the closing references to the people being spiritually begotten and knowing God by serving him as a covenant people.[17] Welch further points out that the central statement of the speech—the need for atonement and purification—is constructed as an elaborate chiasm. The crossing point, or center, is the possibility of reconciliation or the alternative of damnation found in Mosiah 3:11–27, focused precisely on the chiastic centerpiece in Mosiah 3:18–19. "Benjamin tells his nation that they will be lost unless:

a) They *humble* themselves
  b) and become as little *children*
    c) believing that salvation is in the *atoning blood of Christ;*
      d) for the *natural man*
        e) is an enemy to *God*
          f) and *has been* from the fall of Adam
          f') and *will be* forever and ever
        e') unless he yieldeth to the *Holy Spirit*
      d') and putteth off the *natural man*
    c') and becometh a saint through the *atonement of Christ*
  b') and becometh as a *child*
a') submissive, meek and *humble*
               (Mosiah 3:18–19)".[18]

The power of this figure is both its memorability and its intense focus on the center of the chiasm. Itself found in the center of the angel's message, this chiasm turns on the larger concern with the atonement of Christ and shows how that atonement can be accepted. The two central phrases emphasize what is true for all past history and for the future unless one immediately follows the steps in the second part of the chiasm.

Welch also reveals the following chiasm near the end of Benjamin's speech in which the repetition is precise and meaningful:

> a) And . . . whosoever shall not take upon him the *name of Christ*
> > b) must be *called* by some other name;
> > > c) therefore, he findeth himself *on the left hand of God.*
> > > > d) And I would that ye should *remember* also, that this is *the name* that I said I should give unto you
> > > > > e) that never should be *blotted out,*
> > > > > > f) except it be through *transgression;*
> > > > > > f') therefore, take heed that ye do not *transgress,*
> > > > > e') that the name be not *blotted out* of your hearts.
> > > > d') I say unto you, I would that ye should *remember* to retain *the name* written always in your hearts,
> > > c') that ye are not found *on the left hand of God,*
> > b') but that ye hear and know the voice by which ye shall be *called,*
> a') and also, the *name* by which he shall call you.
> (Mosiah 5:10–12)[19]

Again, the crossing point of the chiasm emphasizes the central point: to take heed not to transgress and then to do what is necessary to be called by the name of Christ.

The last chiasm is also part of the epilogue, or peroration—King Benjamin's final words to his audience. He concludes his intricately prepared address with a clear yet elevated appeal. His injunction achieves its effect through rhythmic intensification of words or phrases. The final plea is both overarching and quietly simple:

> Therefore, I would that ye should be steadfast and immovable, always abounding in good works,
> that Christ, the Lord God Omnipotent, may seal you his,
> that you may be brought to heaven,

that ye may have everlasting salvation and eternal life,
through the wisdom,
and power,
and justice,
and mercy
of him who created all things,
in heaven and in earth,
who is God above all.

(Mosiah 5:15)

JACOB'S SERMON

In his sermon in 2 Nephi 6 through 10, Jacob has a purpose similar to Benjamin's. He wants to stir his people to repentance, confirm covenants with them, and rid himself of their blood (sins). But Jacob differs strikingly from King Benjamin, showing forth his unique personality.[20] King Benjamin is calm and deliberate in his sermon; Jacob exhibits an exclamatory style. For instance, he says "How great . . . !" five times, in addition to "O the greatness . . . !" twice. (King Benjamin does not use this expression at all.) Jacob says to his people that his "anxiety is great" (2 Nephi 6:3) for them. In showing this anxiety, Jacob makes a personal appeal—indicated in part by his referring to his "beloved brethren" thirteen times. Too, while King Benjamin four times says, "I would that ye should remember," Jacob more directly (and more frequently—eleven times) urges his people to "remember."

Jacob's sermon develops poetically from his consideration of Isaiah's prophecies about the destiny of Israel and the Lord's promises that Israel will be restored. Jacob introduces his remarks by saying he will read the words of Isaiah, which "may be likened unto you" (2 Nephi 6:5)—meaning his "beloved brethren" and their descendants. Then he reads aloud and applies scriptures found in Isaiah 49, 50, 51, 52, and 55.

Jacob's sermon is carefully elaborated and rhetorically powerful.[21] It moves from the rational to the emotive in what

Kennedy in *New Testament Interpretation through Rhetorical Criticism* would classify as a deliberative sermon—one designed to persuade an audience "to take some action in the future."[22] The action is primarily remembering and reaffirming covenants, while the context may well be, as John Lundquist and John Welch persuasively argue, a coronation.[23]

Jacob begins by firmly establishing his authority. He has been called of God and ordained after his holy order, he was consecrated by his brother Nephi the king, and he speaks the words his brother desired he should speak. This is not Jacob's first sermon to the people (2 Nephi 6:2), but it is the first one Nephi reports. It follows Nephi's telling us that he consecrated Jacob and Joseph to be "priests and teachers over the land" (2 Nephi 6:2; 5:26). Nephi may have selected this sermon because it so thoroughly expounds on the implications of Isaiah's prophecies regarding the fulfilling of God's covenants with the house of Israel (1 Nephi 14:17). The sermon centers on the mission of Jesus Christ, identified as the person Isaiah frequently calls the Holy One of Israel, and testifies that the Messiah, the Holy One of Israel, is Jesus. It also serves well as an introduction to the selections from Isaiah that eventually follow (2 Nephi 12–24).

Jacob's initial purpose is that his "beloved brethren" may "learn and glorify the name of [their] God" (2 Nephi 6:4). The first part of his sermon therefore contains extensive readings from Isaiah in presenting the sweep of the history of God's dealings with Israel; it emphasizes especially God as their deliverer.

The main weight of the sermon is found in 2 Nephi 9. Jacob follows the presentation of his text—Isaiah's prophecies—with what in a Puritan sermon would be called the doctrine.[24] His purpose in reading Isaiah, Jacob affirms, is so that his people "might know concerning the covenants of the Lord that he has covenanted with all the house of Israel" (2 Nephi 9:1). Then he explains step by step the relationship of the Fall and the Redemption. In doing so, he builds upon what Isaiah had taught

(Isaiah 50:1–52:2) about the Messiah's sufferings in the meridian of time and the Lord's gathering of Israel in the last days.

> For as death hath passed upon all men, to fulfil the merciful plan of the great Creator, there must needs be a power of resurrection, and the resurrection must needs come unto man by reason of the fall; and the fall came by reason of transgression; and because man became fallen they were cut off from the presence of the Lord. Wherefore, it must needs be an infinite atonement—save it should be an infinite atonement this corruption could not put on incorruption. (2 Nephi 9:6–7)

What follows is praise for the great plan of God, developed in declarations mostly beginning with *O* on this pattern: "O the wisdom of God, his mercy and grace!" "O how great the goodness of our God," "O how great the plan of our God!" (2 Nephi 9:8, 10, 13).

After explaining the Atonement and clarifying the rewards of the righteous and unrighteous, Jacob gives a catalog of ten woes (and an eleventh implied woe) that come unto the disobedient and the sinner (2 Nephi 9:27–38). With increasing weight of repetition on the word *wo,* and with the balanced clauses that set forth actions and consequences, Jacob says:

> But wo unto him that has the law given . . . and that wasteth the days of his probation, for awful is his state! . . .
> [Wo unto the learned who] think they are wise, and they hearken not unto the counsel of God. . . .
> But wo unto the rich, who are rich as to the things of the world. For because they are rich they despise the poor, and they persecute the meek, and their hearts are upon their treasures; wherefore, their treasure is their god. And behold, their treasure shall perish with them also.
> And wo unto the deaf that will not hear; for they shall perish.
> Wo unto the blind that will not see; for they shall perish also.
> Wo unto the uncircumcised of heart, for a knowledge of their iniquities shall smite them at the last day.
> Wo unto the liar, for he shall be thrust down to hell.
> Wo unto the murderer who deliberately killeth, for he shall die.

115

Wo unto them who commit whoredoms, for they shall be thrust
down to hell.
Yea, wo unto those that worship idols, for the devil of all devils
delighteth in them.
And, in fine, wo unto all those who die in their sins; for they
shall return to God, and behold his face, and remain in their
sins.[25]

(2 Nephi 9:27–38)

Jacob ends his sermon with application to his auditors, calling on them to free themselves from iniquity and prepare their
souls for God's judgments. In a vivid symbolic gesture, Jacob
says, "Behold, I take off my garments, and I shake them before
you; I pray the God of my salvation that he view me with his all-
searching eye; wherefore, ye shall know at the last day, when all
men shall be judged of their works, that the God of Israel did
witness that I shook your iniquities from my soul, and that
I stand with brightness before him, and am rid of your blood"
(2 Nephi 9:44).[26] With a turn on the action of shaking, Jacob then
pleads poetically:

O, my beloved brethren, turn away from your sins;
shake off the chains of him that would bind you fast;
come unto that God who is the rock of your salvation.
(2 Nephi 9:45)

We can imagine Jacob continuing to shake his garments as he
admonishes his listeners to shake off their chains of iniquity.
Rather than be bound passively, they are to take action in attach-
ing themselves to the rock of their salvation.

Jacob is aware of the power of his sermon—which with the
"plainness of the truth" is awakening his brethren "to an awful
reality of these things" and is harrowing up their souls (2 Nephi
9:47). Pressing for action, he quotes Isaiah about buying "wine
and milk without money and without price" (2 Nephi 9:50) and
calls for an ascending order of involvement:

Hearken diligently unto me,

and *remember* the words which I have spoken;
and *come* unto the Holy One of Israel,
and feast upon that which perisheth not, neither can be
    corrupted,
and let your soul delight in fatness.

                        (2 Nephi 9:51)

After a sermon filled with pronouncements of woe upon specific sinners and a plain setting forth of the "awful reality" of their sinfulness, Jacob reverses his focus and gently leads his auditors to "come" and "feast" in "delight."

The beautiful structure of this sermon is more apparent in the 1830 edition of the Book of Mormon. In that edition, the sixteen paragraphs of the sermon flow in this manner (the paragraph numbers in the 1830 edition are followed by those of the 1981 edition verses in parentheses):

1 (1–2) *Past covenants.* Jacob affirms God's covenants made with the house of Israel through time.

2 (3–7) *The resurrection.* While recognizing death, Jacob gives his witness of the promise of the resurrection.

3–5 (8–14) *Gratitude for the plan of salvation.* The prophet expresses gratitude for God's mercy and grace, his goodness, and his plan of resurrection. Each utterance begins in a similar manner: "O the wisdom of God, his mercy and grace!" "O how great the goodness of our God," "O how great the plan of our God!" (2 Nephi 9:8, 10, 13).

6 (15–16) *Judgment.* He explains the nature of the last judgment.

7–9 (17–26) *Atonement and way to accept it.* Jacob gives an ascending description of God's great justice (reward to Saints), mercy (deliverance of Saints), and holiness (atonement and requirements of faith, repentance, baptism, or claim of mercy where no law is given). Each paragraph begins with recognition of the greatness of God: "O the greatness and the justice of our God!" "O the greatness of the mercy of our God, the Holy One of Israel!" "O how great the holiness of our God!" (2 Nephi 9:17, 19, 20).

10–12 (27–38) *Woes to the disobedient.* He pronounces woes upon those who have the law and transgress it, such as the rich who despise the poor.

13–16 (39–53) *Exhortation to Christian living.* In paragraphs beginning with a call to his "beloved brethren," Jacob warns them to remember the awfulness in transgressing against God and then pleads with them to "remember the greatness of the Holy One of Israel," to "come unto the Lord," and to "turn away from [their] sins" (2 Nephi 9:40, 41, 45). Jacob closes with an injunction and testimony that link back to his initial concern with covenants and the house of Israel:

> Behold, my beloved brethren, remember the words of your God;
> pray unto him continually by day,
> and give thanks unto his holy name by night.
> Let your hearts rejoice.
> And behold how great the covenants of the Lord,
> and how great his condescensions unto the children of men;
> and because of his greatness,
> and his grace and mercy,
> he has promised unto us that our seed shall not utterly be
>   destroyed,
> according to the flesh,
> but that he would preserve them;
> and in future generations they shall become
> a righteous branch unto the house of Israel.
>   (2 Nephi 9:52–53)

Jacob seeks to persuade his audience to take action. He starts with a rational prophetic exposition and moves to the poetic oppositions of the central part of his sermon. He then calls for repentance and ends by beckoning to the people with such comforting words as *beloved, thanks, rejoice, condescensions, grace, mercy, preserve,* and *righteous.*

Promising to declare the remainder of his words the next day, Jacob dismisses his brethren. Then in the night, something dramatic happens: Jacob is visited by an angel who gives him a message that provides the climax to close Jacob's sermon. The angel tells Jacob—and this is the first time in the Book of Mormon that this information is presented—that the name of the Redeemer who should come is Christ. That information is part of a revelation about important events in the history of Israel from the time of Christ's first coming until the gathering of Israel in the last days. Deriving his authority from an angel of God, Jacob declares directly, "Thus saith the Lord God" (2 Nephi 10:7). (That is another example of what Kennedy calls "radical Christian rhetoric.")

With language echoing Isaiah's, Jacob quotes the Lord in telling how he will fulfill his promises. Speaking of the Jews, the Lord says: "When the day cometh that they shall believe in me, that I am Christ, then have I covenanted with their fathers that they shall be restored in the flesh, upon the earth, unto the lands of their inheritance" (2 Nephi 10:7). As for evildoers, "That my covenants may be fulfilled which I have made unto the children of men," the Lord says, "I must needs destroy the secret works of darkness" (2 Nephi 10:15). The Lord's covenant with the descendants of Lehi is that he will consecrate the land to them (2 Nephi 10:19). After setting forth the covenants in this manner, Jacob encourages his "beloved brethren" to "cheer up [their] hearts, and remember that [they] are free to act for [themselves]—to choose the way of everlasting death or the way of eternal life" (2 Nephi 10:23).

ALMA THE YOUNGER

Contrasting with the ceremonial style of King Benjamin and the highly poetic style of Jacob is the impassioned personal style of Alma, the son of Alma. Speaking out of his experience of conversion from being a "very wicked and an idolatrous man" who misled the people by "much flattery," Alma reclaims others by "bearing down in pure testimony against them" (Mosiah 27:8;

Alma 4:19). It might be said that Alma is beyond eloquence in that he strives for directness and simplicity.

Sermon at Zarahemla

Alma's first recorded sermon is directed to the inhabitants of the capital city, Zarahemla. In calling the covenant-breaking church members of Zarahemla to repentance, Alma develops powerful images by appealing first to his father's and then to his own experience. Alma the Elder and his converts (the "fathers" of Alma's listeners) were in bondage to the Lamanites but because of their faith were miraculously delivered out of captivity. Alma asks, Do you today have a similar faith? The implicit answer is no. The captivity of his audience is a spiritual one, similar to that experienced by their fathers before they were converted. His appeal is that they likewise seek freedom from bondage: "Behold, [God] changed their hearts; yea, he awakened them out of a deep sleep, and they awoke unto God. Behold, they were in the midst of darkness; nevertheless, their souls were illuminated by the light of the everlasting word; yea, they were encircled about by the bands of death, and the chains of hell, and an everlasting destruction did await them" (Alma 5:7). This type of awakening is like Alma's own conversion. Earlier, after being struck down, he had testified: "My soul hath been redeemed from the gall of bitterness and bonds of iniquity. I was in the darkest abyss; but now I behold the marvelous light of God. My soul was racked with eternal torment; but I am snatched, and my soul is pained no more" (Mosiah 27:29; see also Alma 36:18–20, 27).

Regarding the experience of "the fathers," Alma concludes, there was a mighty change wrought in their hearts; consequently, "they were faithful until the end; therefore they were saved" (Alma 5:13). From that climax comes a long series of searching questions calling for self-examination. The first question is "I ask of you, my brethren of the church, have ye spiritually been born of God? Have ye received his image in your countenances? Have ye experienced this mighty change in your hearts?" (Alma 5:14). Additional questions build to the ironic question, "I say unto you, can you imagine to yourselves that ye hear the voice of the Lord, saying unto you, in that day: Come unto me ye blessed, for behold, your works have been the works of righteousness upon the face of the earth?" (Alma 5:16). The ironic content is exposed by the following question: "Or do ye imagine to yourselves that ye can lie unto the Lord in that day, and say—Lord, our works have been righteous works upon the face of the earth—and that he will save you?" (Alma 5:17). Probing more deeply with each rhetorical question, Alma eventually asks, "I say unto you, can ye think of being saved when you have yielded yourselves to become subjects to the devil?" (Alma 5:20).

He answers his own question: "I say unto you, ye will know at that day that ye cannot be saved; for there can no man be saved except his garments are washed white; yea, his garments must be purified until they are cleansed from all stain, through the blood of him of whom it has been spoken by our fathers, who should come to redeem his people from their sins" (Alma 5:21). To a people whose pride is often manifest in their clothes, Alma challenges them to be "stripped" of pride. "I say unto you, if ye are not ye are not prepared to meet God. . . . Behold, I say, is there one among you who is not stripped of envy? I say unto you that such an one is not prepared" (Alma 5:28–29). The dramatic summary of this phase of the sermon is "Yea, even wo unto all ye workers of iniquity; repent, repent, for the Lord God hath spoken it!" (Alma 5:32). In reaching this point, Alma has stressed the urgency of his message with references to "quickly" or "at hand" and has built it up rhythmically with such repeated phrases as "I say unto you" and "Wo unto."

Alma then changes the nature of his appeal. Drawing on a series of common yet powerful metaphors, he presents the Lord as saying to the repentant: "Come unto me and ye shall partake of the fruit of the tree of life; yea, ye shall eat and drink of the bread and the waters of life freely; yea, come unto me and bring forth works of righteousness, and ye shall not be hewn down and cast into the fire. . . . Behold, I say unto you, that the good shepherd doth call you; yea, and in his own name he doth call you, which is the name of Christ" (Alma 5:34–35, 38). These become controlling metaphors to the end of the sermon, with the metaphor of the shepherd amplified and exemplified:

> For what shepherd is there among you having many sheep doth not watch over them, that the wolves enter not and devour his flock? And behold, if a wolf enter his flock doth he not drive him out? Yea, and at the last, if he can, he will destroy him. And now I say unto you that the good shepherd doth call after you; and if you will hearken unto his voice he will bring you into his fold, and ye are his sheep; and he commandeth you that ye suffer no ravenous wolf to enter among you, that ye may not be destroyed. (Alma 5:59–60)

After the initial amplification of the central metaphors, Alma presents a strong and moving claim to authority. He declares that he speaks in the energy of his soul, he is called to speak after this manner, he is commanded to stand and testify, and he knows the things he has spoken are true because they were revealed to him by the Spirit of God (Alma 5:43–48). In a message frequently personalized by reference to "you," Alma also amplifies his audience from "my beloved brethren" to everyone in the land—from "you the aged, and also the middle aged, and the rising generation" to "all ye ends of the earth" (Alma 5:49–50). The effect is the one achieved in essentially every Book of Mormon sermon—an immediate application to the modern-day reader.

Then quoting the highest authority ("thus saith the Spirit" [Alma 5:50]), Alma repeats in an intensified way the appeals he had used earlier: He asks soul-probing questions such as, "Will you persist in turning your backs upon the poor, and the needy, and in withholding your substance from them?" (Alma 5:55). He gives his words vividness and immediacy with extensive comparisons involving the ax, tree, fruit, fire, clothing, sheep, and shepherd. These are used to develop both threats and promises. On the one hand, "the ax is laid at the root of the tree; therefore every tree that bringeth not forth good fruit shall be hewn down and cast into the fire" (Alma 5:52). On the other hand, Alma says that "the good shepherd doth call after you; and if you will hearken unto his voice he will bring you into his fold" (Alma 5:60). And he ends with both a stern directive and a tender invitation: "And now I, Alma, do command you in the language of him who hath commanded me, that ye observe to do the words which I have spoken unto you. I speak by way of command unto you that belong to the church; and unto those who do not belong to the church I speak by way of invitation, saying: Come and be baptized unto repentance, that ye also may be partakers of the fruit of the tree of life" (Alma 5:61–62).

The effect of the sermon is reported later to the people in Gideon: God has given Alma great joy in knowing that his brethren at Zarahemla are "established again in the way of his righteousness" (Alma 7:4).

Sermon at Gideon

The address Alma gives to the righteous people of Gideon—the city named after a martyred hero—is strikingly different from the one he gave to the worldly people of Zarahemla. It is a low-key, loving, and sensitive sermon, with each of the four main sections beginning "my beloved brethren."

The structure is effective in its simplicity. Alma begins with his hope and expectation that he will find the Gideonites faithful and not "in the awful dilemma that our brethren were in at Zarahemla" (Alma 7:3). The key word in his expression is *trust,* spoken five times in such phrases as, "I trust that ye are not lifted up in the pride of your hearts" (Alma 7:6). Better than hope, trust emphasizes the confidence Alma has in this expectation.

The central message, to be given to all the Nephites, is of repentance and belief in the Son of God, who will "take upon

123

him the pains and the sicknesses of his people. And he will take upon him death, that he may loose the bands of death which bind his people" (Alma 7:11–12). Alma's desire is similar to King Benjamin's (whom Alma quotes): to stir his people to make a binding covenant with the Lord. "Show unto your God that ye are willing to repent of your sins," Alma urges, "and enter into a covenant with him to keep his commandments, and witness it unto him this day by going into the waters of baptism" (Alma 7:15). The person who does "shall have eternal life" (Alma 7:16).

This prompting is followed by the question, "And now my beloved brethren, do you believe these things?"—to which Alma immediately responds, "Behold, I say unto you, yea, I know that ye believe them; and the way that I know that ye believe them is by the manifestation of the Spirit which is in me" (Alma 7:17). The subsequent repeated word is *perceive,* as in "I perceive that ye are in the path which leads to the kingdom of God" (Alma 7:19). It is the perfect word here, for the literal meaning of *perceive* is "to take in thoroughly."

Then follows a statement of the applicability of Alma's message to the Gideonites: "And now my beloved brethren, I have said these things unto you that I might awaken you to a sense of your duty to God, that ye may walk blameless before him, that ye may walk after the holy order of God, after which ye have been received" (Alma 7:22). Unlike the people of Zarahemla who unless they repented had, figuratively, "garments stained with blood and all manner of filthiness" (Alma 5:22), the people of Gideon receive Alma's prayer that the Lord may keep their garments spotless (Alma 7:25).

After further words of encouragement and counsel, Alma closes with a warm expression of his joy and a tender benediction: "My soul doth exceedingly rejoice, because of the exceeding diligence and heed which ye have given unto my word. And now, may the peace of God rest upon you, and upon your houses and lands, and upon your flocks and herds, and all that you possess, your women and your children, according to your faith and good works, from this time forth and forever" (Alma 7:26–27). If Alma were counseling us today, he would undoubtedly urge us to give similar "diligence and heed" to the words of the Book of Mormon.

First Sermon at Ammonihah

The third in this series of sermons by the head of the church and the former judge over all the land is to the people of Ammonihah. Unlike the people of Zarahemla or Gideon, however, the people of Ammonihah reject Alma's exhortations and remain unregenerate. As with the sermon to the people of Zarahemla, Alma emphasizes deliverance, this time reflecting on how God brought Lehi and his family out of Jerusalem. Yet Alma declares that the people of Ammonihah are in danger of being cut off and destroyed.

Rather than calling them his "beloved brethren" (Alma 7:1), he designates these people a "wicked and perverse generation" (Alma 9:8). Implicitly, he seems to have little hope for reform but desires, if at all possible, to shake them into awareness and action. Alma then details blessings the people are not acknowledging, bracketing their ingratitude with warnings of their destruction by the Lamanites—who are morally better off than the people of Ammonihah. The core of the sermon builds with Alma's repetition of the past participle (italicized below) to emphasize the weight of God's blessings in the past. By implication, that emphasis also marks the absence of blessings in the present because of the people's unrighteousness. The Lord

> would rather suffer that the Lamanites might destroy all his people who are called the people of Nephi, if it were possible that they could fall into sins and transgressions, after *having had* so much light and so much knowledge given unto them of the Lord their God; yea, after *having been* such a highly favored people of the Lord; yea, after *having been favored* above every other nation, kindred, tongue, or people; . . . *having been visited* by the Spirit of God; *having conversed* with angels, and *having been spoken unto*

by the voice of the Lord; and *having* the spirit of prophecy, and the spirit of revelation, and also many gifts, the gift of speaking with tongues, and the gift of preaching, and the gift of the Holy Ghost, and the gift of translation; yea, and after *having been delivered* of God out of the land of Jerusalem, by the hand of the Lord; *having been saved* from famine, and from sickness, and all manner of diseases of every kind; and they *having waxed* strong in battle, that they might not be destroyed; *having been brought* out of bondage time after time, and *having been kept* and *preserved* until now; and they have *been prospered* until they are rich in all manner of things—And now behold I say unto you, that if this people, who have received so many blessings from the hand of the Lord, should transgress contrary to the light and knowledge which they do have, I say unto you that if this be the case, that if they should fall into transgression, it would be far more tolerable for the Lamanites than for them. (Alma 9:19–23)

Alma's closing plea lapses into resignation as his words fail to move the people of Ammonihah away from their path of self-destruction: "And now, my beloved brethren, for ye are my brethren, and ye ought to be beloved, and ye ought to bring forth works which are meet for repentance, seeing that your hearts have been grossly hardened against the word of God, and seeing that ye are a lost and a fallen people" (Alma 9:30).

Given the people's earlier reactions and Alma's resignation about their fate, it is no surprise that the people of Ammonihah become angry and attempt to cast Alma into prison. From the first, these people deny and mock Alma's claims to authority. At the beginning of his attempted ministry to them, they revile him, saying that while he was high priest over the church, they did not acknowledge him, and that since he has delivered up the judgment seat to another, he has no authority over them. As he begins to preach to them, they challenge him with cries such as, "Who art thou? Suppose ye that we shall believe the testimony of one man, although he should preach unto us that the earth should pass away? . . . Who is God, that sendeth no more authority than one man among this people, to declare unto them the truth of such great and marvelous things?" (Alma 9:2, 6). Finally, to Alma's claim that his words are those of an angel (Alma 9:29), they respond with angry violence (Alma 9:32). We see here the limit of a sermon, no matter how powerful. The only message that has any effect on the leaders of the people of Ammonihah is the collapse of the prison walls upon them (Alma 14:27).

Second Sermon at Ammonihah

In Alma 12 and 13, Alma establishes the words of Amulek, his missionary companion, and explains "things beyond" in an impromptu sermon that leads some people of Ammonihah to repentance and baptism and others to vilification and murder.[27] This sermon is striking in respect to the multiple audiences it addresses. Further, it develops important meanings around the words *order, ordain,* and *ordinance.*

Amulek has just contended with Zeezrom, an expert lawyer, who is caught in his "lying and deceiving to destroy" Amulek (Alma 12:1). Alma steps forth and speaks to Zeezrom, his first audience, in words that are "heard by the people round about; for the multitude was great" (Alma 12:2). Two groups emerge in this multitude. The first group, after Alma's sermon, "did believe on his words, and began to repent, and to search the scriptures" (Alma 14:1). The "more part of them," however, "were desirous that they might destroy Alma and Amulek; for they were angry with Alma, because of the plainness of his words unto Zeezrom" (Alma 14:2). A fourth audience—whom we can imagine standing at the head of the group of people who desire to destroy Alma and Amulek—is Antionah, "a chief ruler among them" (Alma 12:20).

Alma first shows Zeezrom that his plan comes from the devil. A humbled and shaken Zeezrom then inquires diligently to know about the resurrection and the plan of redemption. Alma teaches him about this plan, emphasizing the need to soften one's heart and repent. Though Zeezrom is now receptive to Alma's teachings, Antionah, a chief judge, tries to trap Alma with a question about death and immortality. Alma responds brilliantly, but he does so not as much to persuade Antionah as to reach the multitude listening attentively (especially, we can imagine, because Antionah is clearly a learned adversary to Alma and represents the rulers of the people). Expounding more thoroughly the plan of salvation, Alma addresses his audience in the plural, speaking of them as his brethren and pleading with them, "And now, my brethren, seeing we know these things, and they are true, let us repent, and harden not our hearts" (Alma 12:37).

After that appeal and challenge, Alma expounds on the Melchizedek Priesthood. He emphasizes the righteousness of the high priests who chose good rather than evil, exercised great faith, and did good works, "they choosing to repent and work righteousness rather than to perish" and consequently being sanctified by the Holy Ghost and entering "into the rest of the Lord their God" (Alma 13:10, 12). He ends by affirming the God-directed authority of his message: "Now is the time to repent, for the day of salvation draweth nigh; yea, and the voice of the Lord, by the mouth of angels, doth declare it unto all nations" (Alma 13:21–22). Three more times he speaks of the "glad tidings" declared by angels and ends with an appeal, "from the inmost part of [his] heart," that his brethren humble themselves, have faith, and repent, "having the love of God always in [their] hearts, that [they] may be lifted up at the last day and enter into his rest" (Alma 13:27, 29).

Some of the people believe Alma's impassioned sermon, but most join in binding Alma and Amulek with cords and taking them before the chief judge to be accused of reviling against the law and the lawyers and judges. Subsequently, the people, under the leadership of judges like Antionah, cast out the believing men and put their wives and children to death by fire. Then they imprison Alma and Amulek and threaten to put them to death, only to have the prison collapse upon themselves. The climax of the scene is described this way:

And Alma cried, saying: How long shall we suffer these great afflictions, O Lord? O Lord, give us strength according to our faith which is in Christ, even unto deliverance. And they broke the cords with which they were bound; and when the people saw this, they began to flee, for the fear of destruction had come upon them.

And it came to pass that so great was their fear that they fell to the earth, and did not obtain the outer door of the prison; and the earth shook mightily, and the walls of the prison were rent in twain, so that they fell to the earth; and the chief judge, and the lawyers, and priests, and teachers, who smote upon Alma and Amulek, were slain by the fall thereof. (Alma 14:26–27)

In the conflict with Zeezrom and then with Antionah, Alma asserts his authority: he holds the higher priesthood and has received his message from God by the mouths of angels. He is opposed by the lawyers "learned in all the arts and cunning of the people" (Alma 10:15). The corrupt lawyers and judges are eager to accuse and punish Alma and Amulek for reviling against their law (Alma 14:2–5). They are, however, exposed by this Book of Mormon narrative to be false and corrupt.

Alma's teachings about the Melchizedek Priesthood are in part a response to this unjust exercise of authority. The Lord God, Alma says, "ordained priests, after his holy order, which was after the order of his Son" (Alma 13:1). This order is implicitly set against the unrighteous dominion of the lawyers and judges.

The word *order* appears fourteen times in Alma's teachings about the priesthood in Alma 13; forms of *ordain* appear seven times; and *ordinance* or *ordinances* appears three times. The English words *order, ordain,* and *ordinances* all stem from the same root: Latin *ordo,* which means literally a straight row or regular series. To ordain originally meant "to put in order" and still has the force of that meaning. Having put the church in order elsewhere (Alma 5–8), Alma here teaches the principles of order according to God's economy. Those holding the Melchizedek Priesthood, Alma says, "were ordained after this manner—being called with a holy calling, and ordained with a holy ordinance, and taking upon them the high priesthood of the holy order, which calling, and ordinance, and high priesthood, is without beginning or end" (Alma 13:8). From this order comes redemption, sanctification, and the rest of the Lord.

Conversely, those who harden their hearts (*harden* appears eight times in Alma's sermon) experience the opposite of order. They are "taken captive by the devil, and led by his will down to destruction," and, the Lord swears in his wrath, they "shall not enter into my rest" but shall be condemned to the "everlasting destruction" of their souls (Alma 12:11, 35, 36).

The chief judge who opposes the holy order of the Son of God belongs to a radically different kind of order—"the order and faith of Nehor, who slew Gideon" (Alma 14:16). Chief among those who have hardened their hearts against the gospel taught by Alma and Amulek, he experiences a physical destruction that typifies the spiritual destruction Alma has been teaching about. In the collapse of the prison, "nature and history conform to the will of one God, and each forms the counterpart and complement of the other."[28] Alma had taught that the consequence of evildoing was everlasting destruction and captivity, that at the bar of God those who have done wickedly would "fain be glad if [they] could command the rocks and the mountains to fall upon [them] to hide [them] from his presence" (Alma 12:14). At the climax of their wickedness, the persecutors of Alma and Amulek do have rocks—the broken walls of the prison—fall upon them, bringing them to physical destruction and implicitly marking their spiritual destruction as well.

There is one more audience to be accounted for: Zeezrom. In Alma 15 we learn that he is "scorched with a burning heat" as his once-hardened mind is harrowed up (Alma 15:3). Calling on the priesthood power of Alma and Amulek, Zeezrom is healed of his burning fever as he believes "in the power of Christ unto salvation" (Alma 15:6). Subsequently, Zeezrom is baptized and begins "from that time forth to preach unto the people" (Alma 15:12).

Alma's sermon thus brings blessings to those who believe it and cursings to those who do not. In this regard, it is like the Book of Mormon as a whole. Speaking of the Lehite record as well as other scriptures, the Lord through Nephi says: "Out of the books which shall be written I will judge the world, every man according to their works, according to that which is written" (2 Nephi 29:11). When the children of God have the truth as found in the scriptures, they can accept it and act on it or reject it. Those "who live without God in the world" shall, at the last judgment, "quake, and tremble, and shrink beneath the glance of his all-searching eye" (Mosiah 27:31).

As a type of this, what could be called Amulek's "all-searching eye" reveals "the thoughts and intents of [Zeezrom's] heart" (Alma 12:7). And when Alma portrays Satan's intent to chain Zeezrom "down to everlasting destruction," Zeezrom begins "to tremble more exceedingly" (Alma 12:6–7). On the other hand, Antionah is one of those whose words and works condemn them to destruction (Alma 12:14). A judge himself, in teaching about judgment Alma repeatedly sets forth alternatives: Give heed and diligence to the word and eventually know the mysteries of God; or harden your heart and be taken captive by the devil (Alma 12:9–11). Believe, repent, and be saved; or die in your sins and then die a spiritual death (Alma 12:15–17). Do not provoke the Lord to "pull down his wrath"; but rather, "enter into the rest of God" (Alma 12:37). Repent and have the "love of God always in your hearts, that ye may be lifted up at the last day"; or "be bound down by the chains of hell" (Alma 13:29–30).

WORDS OF KING ANTI-NEPHI-LEHI

As with his brother, Lamoni, and his father, the king of all the Lamanites, King Anti-Nephi-Lehi has gained through Ammon and his brothers an understanding of the true nature of God and his relationship to man (see the dialogue between Aaron and Lamoni's father in Alma 22). This understanding accounts for the king's repeated references to his great God. These references are effectively developed in King Anti-Nephi-Lehi's speech to his people through the rhetorical figure of climax, the ladderlike building up of elements:

> *I thank my God,* my beloved people, that *our great God* has in goodness sent *these our brethren, the Nephites,* unto us to preach unto us, and to convince us of the traditions of our wicked fathers.
>
> And behold, *I thank my great God* that he has given us a portion of his Spirit to soften our hearts, that we have opened a *correspondence* with *these brethren, the Nephites.*
>
> And behold, *I also thank my God,* that by opening this *correspondence* we have been convinced of our *sins,* and of the many *murders which we have committed.*
>
> And *I also thank my God, yea, my great God,* that he hath granted unto us that we might repent of these things, and also that he hath forgiven us of those our many *sins* and *murders which we have committed,* and taken away the guilt from our hearts, through the merits of his Son. (Alma 24:7–10)

In this passage we immediately note the repeated expressions of gratitude toward God, and we see the force of "my God" and "great God" in the first sentence becoming "my great God" in the second, moving again from "my God" in the third sentence to an intensified "my God, yea, my great God" in the fourth. Likewise, there is a progression from the preaching to its immediate effect, a softening of hearts, to its more important effect, being convinced of sins, to its greatest effect, forgiveness following repentance.

The rest of King Anti-Nephi-Lehi's brief exhortation builds through a series of compelling paradoxes and wordplay to a call to pacifism. Because God has taken away our *stains* of sin, he argues, "and our swords have become bright, then let us *stain* our swords no more with the blood of our brethren" (Alma 24:11–12). For perhaps, he goes on, "if we should stain our swords again they can no more be *washed bright through the blood* of the Son of our great God, which shall be shed for the atonement of our sins" (Alma 24:13). Symbolically, the blood of Christ has removed the blood from their swords, thus cleansing the repentant Lamanites. By fully accepting Christ's shedding his blood for them, they no longer will shed the blood of their brethren. The token of that pledge, the king proposes, is to bury their swords deep in the earth as a testimony at the last day that they have never used them. The people make this covenant with God by assembling "all the weapons which were used for the shedding of man's blood" and burying them deep in the earth (Alma 24:17). The figurative power of the sermon finds completion in symbolic action by a converted people.

ALMA'S SERMON TO THE ZORAMITES

Alma's stirring sermon to the poor of the Zoramites on the topic of faith occurs in the middle of one long chapter in the 1830 edition of the Book of Mormon, most of which might be called the Zoramite unit (chapters 31–35 in the 1981 edition). In this context, we are first shown the antichrist Korihor, who preached his own sermons on disbelief in Christ and on hedonism: "whatsoever a man did was no crime" (Alma 30:17). Although the continuity from Korihor to the Zoramites initially seems tenuous (Korihor is killed by a Zoramite), a much tighter connection is observable below the surface. Mormon dismisses Korihor by saying, "And thus we see the end of him who *perverteth the ways of the Lord*"; in the next sentence, he writes that after the end of Korihor, Alma "received tidings that the Zoramites were *perverting the ways of the Lord*" (Alma 30:60; 31:1). In their behavior and creed, the Zoramites reflect point for point the anti-Christian religion of Korihor. Like him, they say there shall be no Christ, they are materialists, and they speak of foolish traditions of the Nephites. Their proud form-prayer is contrasted by the sincere and humble prayer of Alma, which brings results "because he prayed in faith" (Alma 31:38).

In brief, here are the contrasts between the two types of prayer (from Alma 31:15–35):[29]

Zoramites' prayer	Alma's prayer
Proud (on Rameumptum)	Humble (pleads for power and wisdom)
Exalt themselves	Confesses his infirmities
Say the elect (i.e., the Zoramites) shall be saved	Sorrow regarding wickedness of Zoramites
Seemingly exult that others will be damned to hell	Says Zoramite "souls are precious"
Call themselves a chosen and holy people	Recognizes the Zoramites' wickedness
Materialists: love gold and silver, wear costly apparel	Opposed to materialism; calls it to the Lord's attention
Lift up their hearts unto great boasting	Lifts up his voice to heaven

Immediately after the reference in the narrative to his prayer of faith, Alma is led to preach to the people about faith. Following this sermon, Amulek rises to reiterate Alma's main points and to amplify his teachings on the atonement of Christ. Thus the Korihor-Zoramite disbelief in Christ is answered by the Alma-Amulek witness of Christ. This Zoramite unit ends with a narrative of the outcome: although many of the Zoramites, especially the poor, were brought to repentance, "the more popular part of the Zoramites" (Alma 35:3)—that is, their rulers and teachers—identified believers and then cast them out. Ironically, the charity of the people of Ammon in receiving these cast-out Zoramites stirs the Zoramite leaders to so much anger that they incite the Lamanites to prepare for war against the Nephites.

Alma's sermon is interactive. While speaking to the people on the hill Onidah, he is approached by a multitude of poor people whose spokesman asks how they can worship God, because they have been cast out of their synagogues on account of their "exceeding poverty" (Alma 32:5). Alma immediately turns around, finds "that their afflictions had truly humbled them, and that they were in a preparation to hear the word" (Alma 32:6). Speaking no more to the other multitude, he begins his masterful sermon.

Alma's text is the people themselves: "I behold that ye are lowly in heart. . . . It is well that ye are cast out of your synagogues, that ye may be humble, and that ye may learn wisdom" (Alma 32:8, 12). The logical structure of his argument is cause and effect: (1) Their coarse apparel caused the poor Zoramites to be cast out of the synagogues they had helped build. (2) That expulsion leads to their being outside at the hill Onidah, feeling that they have no place to worship. (3) Because the poor Zoramites are thus humbled, they are prepared to hear the word. (4) Hearing the word can lead them to salvation. Alma puts it this way: "And now, because ye are compelled to be humble blessed are ye; for a man sometimes, if he is compelled to be humble, seeketh repentance; and now surely, whosoever repenteth shall find mercy; and he that findeth mercy and endureth to the end the same shall be saved" (Alma 32:13).

As in his previous sermons, Alma speaks out of the depths of his own experience. His series of sermons is bracketed by the account in Mosiah 27 of his own dramatic conversion and his retelling of that conversion in Alma 36 to his son Helaman. Alma knows from personal experience what apostasy is like; he knows how important it is to acknowledge the relationship of God with the fathers (compare Alma 9:9–22; 36:28–29); and here, in his appeal to persons compelled to be humble, he recognizes the preferred condition of being humbled without compulsion. Likewise, he knows from his own experience the risk of witnessing a sign from heaven as well as the more secure position of having only faith—to "hope for things which are not seen, which are true" (Alma 32:21). Finally, he employs figurative language from his conversion experience of having tasted "of the exceeding joy of which I did taste" (Alma 36:24). Alma had earlier appealed to the people of Zarahemla to accept the Lord's invitation to partake of the fruit of the tree of life (Alma 5:34). Now to the humble Zoramites, Alma shows the process by which the fruit can be nourished and obtained.

Indeed, Alma's sermon appeals directly to the people's agricultural experiences. Choosing the natural metaphor that compares his word to a seed, Alma leads the people step by step through the process of faith.

> If ye give place, that a seed may be planted in your heart, behold, if it be a true seed, or a good seed, if ye do not cast it out by your unbelief, that ye will resist the Spirit of the Lord, behold, it will begin to swell within your breasts; and when you feel these swelling motions, ye will begin to say within yourselves—It must needs be that this is a good seed, or that the word is good, for it beginneth to enlarge my soul; yea, it beginneth to enlighten my understanding, yea, it beginneth to be delicious to me. (Alma 32:28)

The progression continues from swelling to sprouting to growing rapidly. With nourishing, the plant puts down roots and grows up to bring forth fruit. Neglect of the tree (lack of nourishing by faith), on the other hand, keeps it from getting roots, "and when the heat of the sun cometh and scorcheth it, because it hath no root it withers away, and ye pluck it up and cast it out" (Alma 32:38). But if you nourish the word by faith with great diligence, Alma says, "it shall take root; and behold it shall be a tree springing up unto everlasting life" (Alma 32:41). The reward comes in plucking the fruit of the tree of life,

> which is sweet above all that is sweet,
> and which is white above all that is white,
> yea, and pure above all that is pure;
> and ye shall feast upon this fruit even until ye are filled,
> that ye hunger not, neither shall ye thirst.
> (Alma 32:42)

After this poetic and persuasive close to Alma's sermon, his auditors ask what they should believe and how they should plant the seed he has spoken of. Alma's response is to give them three main categories of means of belief as presented by three ancient prophet-witnesses: The first is prayer, as recalled by the poetic words of Zenos—whose main point is that one can pray anywhere and be heard (Alma 33:3–11). Second is the scriptures, as evidenced by the prophet Zenock's teaching found in the brass plates that witness to the truth of the teachings of Zenos (Alma 33:15–16). Third is the testimony of Jesus found in types, specifically here the brazen serpent that Moses raised in the wilderness as a type of Christ (Alma 33:19–22).

Alma desires the poor Zoramites to be like the believing Israelites who looked on the brazen serpent, to have faith in the word—which is simultaneously Christ, the truth of Christ, and faith in Christ. Alma sums up the first half of his sermon: "I desire that ye shall plant this word in your hearts, and as it beginneth to swell even so nourish it by your faith. And behold, it will become a tree, springing up in you unto everlasting life. And then may God grant unto you that your burdens may be light, through the joy of his Son. And even all this can ye do if ye will" (Alma 33:23).

The result of Alma's sermon is spelled out after the record of Amulek's testimony: many of the poor of the Zoramites are brought to repentance, but the rulers and the priests "[find] out privily the minds of all the people" (Alma 35:5) concerning Alma's and Amulek's teachings and then cast the believers out of the land.

JESUS' SERMON ON ISRAEL

The resurrected Jesus' actions and words described in 3 Nephi 20 through 23 are the culmination of teachings about covenants in the Book of Mormon. Participating in the miraculously provided sacrament, the people renew their baptismal covenants and are filled with the Spirit. Then they are prepared for the greatest sermon ever given on covenants, one that binds together the covenantal relationship of the Lord with the three-part audience of the Book of Mormon—the Lamanites, the Gentiles, and the Jews.

Jesus' sermon integrates Isaiah's teachings on covenants with the Savior and his covenantal relationship. It bears a powerful witness through Isaiah that Jesus Christ is the God with whom ancient Israel made covenants. A complex sermon, it works through a subtle relationship between Isaiah's and Micah's sayings and the redemptive role of Jesus Christ.

The text, in effect, is the sacramental experience of the people. Jesus promises, "He that eateth this bread eateth of my body to his soul; and he that drinketh of this wine drinketh of my blood to his soul; and his soul shall never hunger nor thirst, but shall be filled" (3 Nephi 20:8). The people respond by giving "glory to Jesus, whom they both saw and heard" (3 Nephi 20:9). Because the members of Jesus' audience have been commanded to pray in their hearts, their giving glory to Jesus is a prayer of thanksgiving. In response, he speaks to them in what becomes a dialogue between God and man, an answer to the people's prayers.[30]

The people are now prepared to be enlightened about the covenants they have made. This enlightenment, though, is not only for them, "a remnant of the house of Israel" (3 Nephi 20:10), but for all Israel as well as for the Gentiles, especially in the time of "the fulfilling of the covenant which the Father hath made unto his people" (3 Nephi 20:12).

Jesus opens up to both his immediate and his distant audience the meaning of the words of Isaiah at the time when they "should be fulfilled" (3 Nephi 20:11) and concludes by enjoining his people to "search these things diligently; for great are the words of Isaiah" (3 Nephi 23:1). He uses parallels, repetitions, and reversals as literary techniques on a large scale, just as Isaiah used those elements in the smaller units of his poetry.

Jesus also prophesies the gathering of the remnants of Israel. This is especially a spiritual gathering: they are "brought to the knowledge of the Lord their God" (3 Nephi 20:13). Then he prophesies that a curse will befall the Gentiles if they do not repent and that the people of Lehi will be blessed. He will fulfill "the covenant which [he] made with [their] father Jacob" in establishing these people in a New Jerusalem (3 Nephi 20:15–22).

Identifying himself as the prophet who is like Moses and affirming that all the prophets have testified of him, Jesus confirms that the blessing upon the children of Lehi fulfills the covenant with Abraham (3 Nephi 20:23–27). For their part, the Gentiles will be blessed, as will the Jews, who are to be gathered to the land of Jerusalem (3 Nephi 20:17–29). That will bring fulfillment of Isaiah's poetic declaration: "Sing together, ye waste places of Jerusalem; for the Father hath comforted his people, he hath redeemed Jerusalem" (3 Nephi 20:34). In the last days, the Jews will acknowledge Jesus as their God, and then "shall this covenant which the Father hath covenanted with his people be fulfilled; and then shall Jerusalem be inhabited again with my people, and it shall be the land of their inheritance" (3 Nephi 20:46).

The emergence of the Book of Mormon is the sign of when these things will take place. It will be when the Gentiles learn about the Lamanites through the Book of Mormon and when the Book of Mormon is brought to the Lamanites from the Gentiles. Through this, "the covenant of the Father may be fulfilled which he hath covenanted with his people" (3 Nephi 21:4).

Earlier, Jesus quoted Isaiah regarding the marred servant (3 Nephi 20:43–44); now he affirms the marred servant will be healed (3 Nephi 21:10). This kind of repetition and reversal continues, knitting together the complex of prophecies from Micah and Isaiah: In the last days, Jews "shall believe in me, that I am Jesus Christ, the Son of God" (3 Nephi 20:31); conversely, those who do not believe in Jesus Christ "shall be cut off from among my people who are of the covenant" (3 Nephi 21:11). The first time the Savior speaks of Jacob as a lion, he emphasizes how his people are strengthened (3 Nephi 20:16–19); the second time, he stresses the effects on the lion's adversaries, the unrepentant

Gentiles. Except the Gentiles repent, he says, the "sword of [the Father's] justice shall hang over them" (3 Nephi 20:20); but if they repent, then the Gentiles shall "come in unto the covenant and be numbered among this the remnant of Jacob" (3 Nephi 21:22).

Jesus promises that the gospel will be preached to the Lamanites, the lost ten tribes, and all the dispersed of his people, and then the work will commence in gathering people home to the lands of their inheritance. At the heart of this establishment of Zion in the last days is a reminder of the covenant made with Noah. Jesus quotes the words of the Lord through Isaiah: "For as I have sworn that the waters of Noah should no more go over the earth, so have I sworn that I would not be wroth with thee. For the mountains shall depart and the hills be removed, but my kindness shall not depart from thee, neither shall the covenant of my peace be removed" (3 Nephi 22:9–10).

In closing, Jesus gives the people a new understanding of familiar words of Old Testament prophets, especially of Isaiah. He admonishes all of Israel and the Gentiles to "give heed to [his] words" (3 Nephi 23:4) and ends with a reference to the baptismal covenant. Earlier, Jesus said to the Nephites: "And whoso believeth in me, and is baptized, the same shall be saved; and they are they who shall inherit the kingdom of God" (3 Nephi 11:33). He now concludes his sermon on covenants with the same simple counsel: "And whosoever will hearken unto my words and repenteth and is baptized, the same shall be saved" (3 Nephi 23:5).

MORMON'S SERMON

One of the most tightly woven and forceful sermons in the Book of Mormon is that recorded by Moroni as given by his father, Mormon, on faith, hope, and charity. The topic is particularly poignant in its context: Mormon has been killed by the Lamanites, and Moroni is the solitary survivor, recording these words out of his own generosity of spirit. We can also imagine that Moroni is rereading this sermon to strengthen his own faith, hope, and charity—a topic Moroni addresses in his concluding words in the Book of Mormon.

Mormon's sermon is designed to strengthen and reconfirm the "peaceable followers of Christ" (Moroni 7:3), and it begins with a gracious but clear affirmation of Mormon's authority—it is, Mormon says, because of the gift of the Lord's calling that he is permitted to speak unto them. Then he wins the favorable attention of those followers by affirming that by their "peaceable walk with the children of men" he judges they have obtained a sufficient hope to "enter into the rest of the Lord" (Moroni 7:4, 3).

In speaking of his calling as a gift, Mormon establishes a thread that takes on significance as the sermon continues. His is a good gift; later he speaks of the impossibility of a hypocrite's offering a gift and having it acceptable to God: "Wherefore, a man being evil cannot do that which is good; neither will he give a good gift" (Moroni 7:6–10). On the other hand, "every thing which inviteth to do good, and to persuade to believe in Christ, is sent forth by the power and gift of Christ" (Moroni 7:16). Then Mormon teaches about faith, hope, and charity, which are gifts of the Spirit. The metaphor of the gift is especially appropriate in a sermon about love presented in love: something precious is offered without compulsion, yet it will be efficacious only if accepted.

The sermon progresses in a simple yet subtle interlocking of parts. Mormon's initial discourse on works and their derivation from good or evil leads to analysis of principles on how to judge whether something is of Christ or of the devil. The counsel stemming from this knowledge is "See that ye do not judge wrongfully; for with that same judgment which ye judge ye shall also be judged" (Moroni 7:18). The earlier counsel "If ye will lay hold upon every good thing, and condemn it not, ye certainly will be a child of Christ" is turned into the leading question "And now, my brethren, how is it possible that ye can lay hold upon every

141

good thing?" (Moroni 7:19–20). This question leads to the presentation and analysis of the answer: faith. On a continuum from God to man, faith is created by ministrations of angels, by teachings of prophets, and by various other ways (Moroni 7:22–25). There is also a temporal progression in the exercise of faith from before the coming of Christ to the present, with an amplification of the missions of angels and prophets (Moroni 7:25–32). At this point, Mormon gives his interim conclusion: "And Christ hath said: If ye will have faith in me ye shall have power to do whatsoever thing is expedient in me. And he hath said: Repent all ye ends of the earth, and come unto me, and be baptized in my name, and have faith in me, that ye may be saved" (Moroni 7:33–34).

Mormon establishes the intimacy of his relationship with his audience by repeatedly speaking of them as "my beloved brethren" and then asks a conditional rhetorical question with a parenthetical testimony: "If this be the case that these things are true which I have spoken unto you, and God will show unto you, with power and great glory at the last day, that they are true, and if they are true has the day of miracles ceased?" (Moroni 7:35). His question, with related questions about the ministration of angels and the power of the Holy Ghost, relates back to the latter half of the preceding section on faith. His own answer to the question is "Nay; for it is by faith that miracles are wrought; . . . wherefore, if these things have ceased wo be unto the children of men, for it is because of unbelief, and all is vain" (Moroni 7:37). Linking faith with redemption, Mormon then confidently affirms, "I judge better things of you, for I judge that ye have faith in Christ because of your meekness" (Moroni 7:39).

This treatise on faith naturally leads to analysis of hope, a necessary result of faith. Mormon shows the root of faith to be hope; of hope, meekness; and of meekness, lowliness of heart (Moroni 7:42–43). If the latter two are lacking, then faith is vain. Put in the positive, if one is meek and lowly in heart and confesses that Jesus is the Christ, he must needs have charity, "for if he have not charity he is nothing" (Moroni 7:44). This declaration leads to a definition of charity comparable to the one in 1 Corinthians 13, with the summation being that "charity is the pure love of Christ, and . . . whoso is found possessed of it at the last day, it shall be well with him" (Moroni 7:47).

In his conclusion, Mormon admonishes his "beloved brethren" to "pray unto the Father with all the energy of heart, that ye may be filled with this love, which he hath bestowed upon all who are true followers of his Son, Jesus Christ; that ye may become the sons of God; that when he shall appear we shall be like him, for we shall see him as he is; that we may have this hope; that we may be purified even as he is pure" (Moroni 7:48). Here he works backward, calling on his auditors to pray for love, which comes to those with faith in Jesus Christ, with the result that not just "ye" but "we" will have hope of being like him. Earlier in the sermon, Mormon showed how we can come unto Christ; at the end, he shows us how to become like him.

In all the sermons analyzed here, content is inextricably linked to form by such devices as parallelisms, rhetorical questions, and patterned arrangement of clauses or phrases.[31] As we have seen, King Benjamin's formal chiastic approach to covenant making focuses his auditors' attention on the central covenant implicit in the atonement of Christ. Alma's progressive cause-and-effect structure in the sermon to the poor Zoramites naturally grows out of the circumstances and lends itself perfectly to his organic analogy. And Mormon's interlocking of faith, hope, and charity shows relationships of these three elements and encourages the obtaining of all of them by the believer.

CHAPTER 6

"Their Fathers"
LETTERS AND AUTOBIOGRAPHY

The first purpose of the Book of Mormon, according to Moroni in the title page, is "to show unto the remnant of the House of Israel what great things the Lord hath done for their fathers." The "great things" are primarily the miracles of the Lord in bringing Lehi and his family out of Jerusalem and to the promised land (2 Nephi 1:1; Alma 9:9; 3 Nephi 5:20). To Nephi and Lehi, the "fathers" are their ancestors, especially Abraham, Isaac, and Jacob (1 Nephi 17:40). But Mormon and Moroni more likely intend "fathers" to refer primarily to Lehi and Nephi. Mormon speaks of "our fathers" whom the Lord brought "out of the land of Jerusalem" (3 Nephi 5:20). "Fathers" implicitly includes as well such other exemplars of faith as Ammon, Alma, and the twelve Nephite disciples. Moroni quotes Christ as saying "unto our fathers: If ye have faith ye can do all things which are expedient unto me" (Moroni 10:23; see also Moroni 7:33). Mormon speaking to Lamanites in the latter days says,

> Know ye that ye must come to the knowledge of your fathers, and repent of all your sins and iniquities, and believe in Jesus Christ. . . . and if ye believe [the Book of Mormon] ye will know concerning your fathers, and also the marvelous works which were wrought by the power of God among them. (Mormon 7:5, 9)

Conversely, the fathers of the Lamanites, Laman and Lemuel, began false traditions, saying Nephi was a liar and a robber (Alma 20:13). For the converted Lamanites, the Nephite fathers become their fathers as they accept the gospel through the Nephites. Thus Samuel the Lamanite says that those Lamanites who "know of the wicked and abominable traditions of *their fathers,* and are led to believe the holy scriptures, . . . have been made free" (Helaman 15:7–8). The time shall come, he continues, "which hath been spoken of by *our fathers* [meaning the Nephite prophets whom Samuel adopted as his fathers] . . . concerning the restoration of our brethren, the Lamanites, again to the knowledge of the truth" (Helaman 15:11).

Acceptance of Nephi and Lehi as fathers to the Lamanites is exemplified in King Lamoni's father. He has his people take upon themselves (and also gives to Lamoni's brother) the name of Anti-Nephi-Lehi, which could be interpreted to mean "in imitation of Nephi and Lehi." The prefix *anti-* means "against, facing, or opposite"—as is a reflection in a mirror. While it can have the negative meaning of a false imitation, *anti-* can also indicate a similarity or likeness. In this positive sense of being a reflection, *Anti* in *Anti-Nephi-Lehi* might well have signified the converted Lamanites' desire to be like the prophet-fathers Nephi and Lehi. In what must have been a similar intent, Helaman named his sons Nephi and Lehi so they would remember their "first parents who came out of the land of Jerusalem" (Helaman 5:6).

We come to know those "first parents" and their descendants in a book that reveals various personalities through styles of writing and that has many striking family relationships.[1] Personal voices appear in the literary genres of autobiography and letters. Such accounts provide direct access into the thinking and feeling of various "fathers" as well as of persons with whom they came into conflict.

AUTOBIOGRAPHY

Parts of the Book of Mormon could well be called autobiographies in giving us moving and searching confessionals or cries of the soul. They individualize the processes of redemption.

The first phrase of the book begins autobiographically, with "I, Nephi, having been born of goodly parents" (1 Nephi 1:1). Much of Nephi's record can be approached from that angle. The formula "I, Nephi" introduces most phases of Nephi's account of the Lehites' journey into the wilderness, the return for the plates, the voyage across the waters, and the arrival in the promised land. While these narratives are firmly told from Nephi's personal perspective, his confessions of the soul are the most moving parts of his autobiographical expressions. "As I sat pondering in mine heart I was caught away in the Spirit of the Lord," he says, "yea, into an exceedingly high mountain, which I never had before seen" (1 Nephi 11:1), and then he relates his visionary experience of seeing God's dealing with mankind to the end of time. Moving lyrically into what has been analyzed earlier as the psalm of Nephi, he reveals his deepest weaknesses and strengths:

> Nevertheless, notwithstanding the great goodness of the Lord,
> in showing me his great and marvelous works,
> my heart exclaimeth: O wretched man that I am!
> Yea, my heart sorroweth because of my flesh;
> my soul grieveth because of mine iniquities.
> I am encompassed about, because of the temptations and the
> sins which do so easily beset me.
> And when I desire to rejoice, my heart groaneth because of my
> sins;
> nevertheless, I know in whom I have trusted.
> My God hath been my support;
> he hath led me through mine afflictions in the wilderness;
> and he hath preserved me upon the waters of the great deep.
>   (2 Nephi 4:17–20)

Nephi's nephew, Enos, tells of the central event of his life, his "wrestle . . . before God," in which, like the eighteenth-century Puritan divine Jonathan Edwards, he supplicates God for his soul. Edwards in his private writings speaks of his "inward struggles and conflicts, and self-reflections. I made seeking my salvation the main business of my life." After describing his increased sense of divine things, he says: "It was my continual strife day and night, and constant inquiry, how I should *be* more holy, and *live* more holily, and more becoming a child of God, and a disciple of Christ."[2]

For his part, Enos confesses his experience in a forest:

> And my soul hungered; and I kneeled down before my Maker, and I cried unto him in mighty prayer and supplication for mine own soul; and all the day long did I cry unto him; yea, and when the night came I did still raise my voice high that it reached the heavens. And there came a voice unto me, saying: Enos, thy sins are forgiven thee, and thou shalt be blessed. (Enos 1:4–5)

The experience of Enos is reminiscent of Jacob's wrestle with an angel who blessed him and redeemed him from all evil (Genesis 32:24–29). As with the Old Testament account, Enos's experience is told simply. The word "and" is the main connective; modifiers are sparse ("*mighty* prayer"); and only the decisive points are emphasized.

The style here is similar to that of the biblical account of Abraham and Isaac as analyzed by Erich Auerbach in *Mimesis*. This style is first apparent in Auerbach's quotation of Genesis 22:1: "And it came to pass after these things, that God did tempt Abraham, and said to him, Abraham! and he said, Behold, here I am."[3] In both narratives, the syntactical connections are simple (*and* is the primary connective); there is "the externalization of only so much of the phenomena as is necessary for the purpose of the narrative";[4] modifiers are sparse ("*mighty* prayer" in Enos's account) or not to be found at all (in the passage from Genesis); and "the decisive points of the narrative alone are emphasized."[5]

The dialogue between Enos and the Lord continues in this sparse yet forceful way: "And I, Enos, knew that God could not lie; wherefore, my guilt was swept away. And I said: Lord, how is it done? And he said unto me: Because of thy faith in Christ, whom thou hast never before heard nor seen. And many years pass away before he shall manifest himself in the flesh; wherefore, go to, thy faith hath made thee whole" (Enos 1:6–8).

The transforming religious experience of Alma the Younger becomes more structured and more personal in his retelling of it to his sons. In the first instance, Mormon relates the story of Alma's being struck down, but he quotes the recovered Alma for the crucial recounting of his internal experience: After Alma receives his strength, he stands up and bids those around him to be of good comfort, "For, said he, I have repented of my sins, and have been redeemed of the Lord; behold I am born of the Spirit" (Mosiah 27:24). Alma continues to tell how his soul "was racked with eternal torment; but I am snatched, and my soul is pained no more" (Mosiah 27:29). To his son Helaman, Alma gives a more extensive and a remarkably chiastic version of his experience. In what John Welch calls a "conscious creation of an imaginative and mature artist," Alma succeeds in placing the turning point of his life at the turning point of his narrative.[6] This turning point is an intense movement from torment to mercy:

> And it came to pass that as I was thus racked with torment, while I was harrowed up by the memory of my many sins, behold, I remembered also to have heard my father prophesy unto the people concerning the coming of one Jesus Christ, a Son of God, to atone for the sins of the world. Now, as my mind caught hold upon this thought, I cried within my heart: O Jesus, thou Son of God, have mercy on me, who am in the gall of bitterness, and am encircled about by the everlasting chains of death. And now, behold, when I thought this, I could remember my pains no more; yea, I was harrowed up by the memory of my sins no more. And oh, what joy, and what marvelous light I did behold; yea, my soul was filled with joy as exceeding as was my pain! (Alma 36:17–20)

For his part, Mormon gives us a piecemeal autobiography and so does Moroni. In the first verse of Words of Mormon, before beginning his record, Mormon says: "And now I, Mormon, being about to deliver up the record which I have been making into the hands of my son Moroni, behold I have witnessed almost all the destruction of my people, the Nephites." Moroni, in turn, first tells us about himself and then gives an account of his people: "I even remain alone to write the sad tale of the destruction of my people" (Mormon 8:3).[7]

A distinguishing characteristic of each of these expressions is the necessity to confess deepest feelings as well as weaknesses or sins and religious experiences. Nephi, Enos, Alma, Mormon, and Moroni are impelled by the need to lay bare their souls and witness to future audiences.

LETTERS

Letters in the Book of Mormon have a claim to be examined as literature because they engage our interest both for what they say and for the way in which they are expressed. We take special interest in the personalities that are revealed in a genre the great letter writer Horace Walpole thought "ought to be nothing but extempore conversation upon paper."[8] Harold Binkley agrees that the familiar letter "is what we may call oral; it is read as we read drama, always with the sound of the words in our ears, and the image of personal manner and gesture before our eyes."[9] According to Ronald Corthell, "Demetrius, the most influential classical theoretician of the genre, distinguished the letter from other literary kinds by its style and corresponding ability to reveal the character or soul of the writer."[10]

The eight substantive, natural, and self-revelatory epistles or letters we find in the Book of Mormon are like conversations in revealing the souls of the writers.[11] These letters are from Captain Moroni to Ammoron (Alma 54:5–14), Ammoron to Moroni (Alma 54:16–24), Helaman to Moroni (Alma 56:2–58:41), Moroni to Pahoran (Alma 60:1–36), Pahoran to Moroni (Alma 61:2–21), Giddianhi to Lachoneus (3 Nephi 3:2–10), and Mormon to his son Moroni (Moroni 8:2–30; 9:1–26).[12] Those from Captain Moroni and Mormon notably reveal an intensity of feeling on the parts of these striking Book of Mormon personalities.

MORONI-AMMORON CORRESPONDENCE

The remarkable correspondence between Captain Moroni and the Lamanite warlord Ammoron comes after nine years of bloodshed in a war between the Lamanites and Nephites. This war was begun by Amalickiah, a cunningly brutal man of Nephite origin who installed himself as the king over the Lamanites by conspiring to kill the Lamanite ruler. Although he cursed God and swore to drink the blood of Moroni, Amalickiah was killed by Moroni's lieutenant, Teancum. Amalickiah was succeeded by his brother Ammoron, who continued the war.

In cosmic terms, these letters between Moroni and Ammoron have to do less with exchange of prisoners than with the irreconcilable conflict between the powers of God and Satan, with Moroni appearing as the Christian champion. As we read Moroni's letter, we remember Mormon's earlier encomium on Moroni as

> a strong and a mighty man; he was a man of a perfect under-standing; yea, a man that did not delight in bloodshed; a man whose soul did joy in the liberty and the freedom of his country, and his brethren from bondage and slavery; . . . and he was a man who was firm in the faith of Christ, and he had sworn with an oath to defend his people, his rights, and his country, and his religion, even to the loss of his blood. . . . If all men had been, and were, and ever would be, like unto Moroni, behold, the very powers of hell would have been shaken forever; yea, the devil would never have power over the hearts of the children of men. (Alma 48:11, 13, 17)

For his part, Ammoron, a Zoramite who has rejected his faith and turned into a Lamanite, epitomizes the apostate who repeatedly leads attacks on the Nephites.

Although at first Moroni rejoices at the request for an exchange, as he gets into his letter his pent-up anger flows forth. This is anger about years of conflict led by Ammoron's brother, the cunning and duplicitous Amalickiah; on a larger scale, it is a response to centuries of Lamanite-Nephite conflict. "Behold, I would tell you somewhat concerning the justice of God, and the sword of his almighty wrath, which doth hang over you except ye repent and withdraw your armies into your own lands," Moroni declares (Alma 54:6). In this cosmic context, God is on the side of the Nephites; the real battle is between God and Ammoron (both the man and the army).

The issues Moroni outlines are these: The purposes of Ammoron and of Amalickiah before him are blatantly murderous. In spiritual terms, the Lamanites have fought against the people of the Lord, and unless they abandon their plans, they will incur the wrath of God to their destruction (in Book of Mormon terms, the ultimate curse—one that eventually comes to the Nephites). For their part, the Nephites vow to stand firm in their religion and with their God. Because the Nephites are outnumbered, Moroni needs to arm his women and children—and would do so, in his extremity, to fight against the Lamanites.

The first half of Moroni's letter builds on a formula repeated four times: "except ye repent and withdraw" (Alma 54:6, 7) or "except ye withdraw" (Alma 54:9, 10) your armies and your murderous intentions, God's wrath and death will come upon you.[13] Moroni breaks off this theme with his angry declaration, "But behold, it supposeth me that I talk to you concerning these things in vain; or it supposeth me that thou art a child of hell" (Alma 54:11). Then continuing with the repeated declaration, "Behold," Moroni affirms not what God will do but what he, Moroni, will do:

> And behold, if ye do not this, I will come against you with my armies; yea, even I will arm my women and my children, and I will come against you, and I will follow you even into your own land, which is the land of our first inheritance; yea, and it shall be blood for blood, yea, life for life; and I will give you battle even until you are destroyed from off the face of the earth. (Alma 54:12)

Moroni ends his letter with three short, blunt affirmations that suggest the firmness of his character: "Now I close my epistle. I am Moroni; I am a leader of the people of the Nephites" (Alma 54:14).

In his letter, Moroni uses rhetorical devices to convey his "sincerity and force of utterance."[14] These devices, in classicist George Kennedy's words, are intended to persuade or motivate—to "affect the thought, actions, or emotions of an audience."[15] Moroni's letter can be analyzed in reference to rhetorical terms defined by linguist Edward Corbett in *Classical Rhetoric for the Modern Student* and by Northrop Frye, Sheridan Baker, and George Perkins in *The Harper Handbook to Literature*.[16] *Anaphora,* or initial repetition, is found in "Behold, Ammoron, I have written unto you . . . Behold, I would tell you . . . Yea, I would tell you . . . ; yea, I would tell you . . . " (Alma 54:5–7). This scheme, Corbett says, "is usually reserved for those passages where the author wants to produce a strong emotional effect."[17] Moroni uses *apophasis* (also called *paraleipsis,* a technique of irony in which one mentions a matter while appearing to pass over it) when he says to Ammoron he would tell him "somewhat concerning the justice of God" and would tell him "concerning that awful hell that awaits to receive such murderers as thou and thy brother have been" if Ammoron "were capable of hearkening" to these things (Alma 54:6–7). Moroni uses *isocolons* (repeated phrases of similar length and corresponding structure) when he writes: "for we will retain our cities and our lands; yea, and we will maintain our religion and the cause of our God" (Alma 54:10); "yea, and it shall be blood for blood, yea, life for life" (Alma 54:12). The latter in its equation of blood with life also illustrates *synecdoche* (substitution of a part for a whole). Close to *synecdoche* is *metonymy* (substitution of a name of one thing for that of another associated with it), as found in "the sword of [God's] almighty wrath" (Alma 54:6). A *parenthesis* (a verbal unit that interrupts the flow of the sentence) is found in the following: "I have written unto you somewhat concerning this war which ye have waged against my people, or rather which thy brother hath waged against them, and which ye are still determined to carry on after his death" (Alma 54:5). *Antithesis,* or the contrast of ideas in parallel phrases, is employed in "ye have sought to murder us, and we have only sought to defend ourselves" (Alma 54:13). There is an excellent example of *climax* (increasing weight or importance) in Alma 54:12 (quoted above), when Moroni enumerates the steps he will take toward his enemy's destruction. Moroni ends his letter with an *appositive* (a phrase that explains or modifies a previous phrase with the same grammatical construction): "I am Moroni; I am a leader of the people of the Nephites" (Alma 54:14).

For his part, Ammoron reveals his character and motives: bloodthirsty and brazen, he desires to avenge the death of Amalickiah. In the larger context, he asserts that the Nephite fathers wronged the Lamanites—"they did rob them of their right to the government when it rightly belonged unto them" (Alma 54:17). Ammoron desires to correct this wrong—a critical matter for him is who is rightfully in charge. The Nephites (when righteous) lead humbly and with a desire for liberty (exemplified by Mosiah, Alma, and Moroni); the Lamanites traditionally seek to subjugate others. That is shown in Ammoron's setting down exactly the condition he knows Moroni will not accept: an offer to end the war "if ye will lay down your arms, and *subject yourselves* to be governed by those to whom the government doth rightly belong" (Alma 54:18). Affirming a boldness equal to Moroni's, Ammoron vows to "wage a war which shall be eternal, either to the subjecting the Nephites to our authority or to their eternal extinction" (Alma 54:20). Protection against these alternatives has been Moroni's central concern for some time, especially as manifest when he rallied the people with the title of liberty. Ammoron will not consider the third alternative for the Lamanites, which, as we have seen earlier, is demonstrated by the people of Ammon—living in peace next to the Nephites and being neither conquerors nor slaves.

Ammoron's arrogant scorn is manifest in his declaration that though he does not know God, "neither do ye" (compare his statement to those of Korihor and Sherem). He continues with derision, "And if it so be that there is a devil and a hell, behold will he not send you there to dwell with my brother whom ye have murdered, whom ye have hinted that he hath gone to such a place?" (Alma 54:21, 22).

The aftermath of this exchange between Moroni and Ammoron has several ironies. Moroni is incensed at Ammoron's fraud and says, "Behold, I will not exchange prisoners with Ammoron save he will withdraw his purpose" (Alma 55:2). Knowing that this will not happen, however, Moroni plans a stratagem that has nothing to do with his apparent intent in the first letter. He responds to Ammoron's claim, "I am a bold Lamanite" (Alma 54:24), by getting a true Lamanite—fittingly named Laman and a descendant of Laman—to trick the Lamanites and free the prisoners in the city of Gid. (This Laman had been accused of murdering the king of the Lamanites, when the crime was actually Amalickiah's.) Rather than send a large army, Moroni sends only a small force with Laman. Arriving at the camp of the Lamanites, Laman claims that he has escaped from the Nephites. He then deceives the Lamanites by offering them wine as a symbol of conviviality—wine that has been strengthened in order to get them drunk. Moroni then makes good on his promise to Ammoron when, summoned by Laman, he and his men surround the sleeping Lamanites and arm the Nephite women and children who are prisoners in the city of Gid. They do not use their weapons, but their arms help persuade the Lamanites to surrender. In an ironic turnaround, once it is evident that the prisoners have power over the Lamanites, the captains of the Lamanites are the ones who take away their soldiers' weapons, throw them at the feet of the Nephites, and plead for mercy. Not one person is killed; no one is "destroyed." Thus, though in his letter Moroni unleashes his anger in words, afterwards he shows mercy in deeds.

HELAMAN TO MORONI

Helaman's letter to Moroni contrasts strikingly with the Moroni-Ammoron exchange. Written to "my dearly beloved brother, Moroni, as well in the Lord as in the tribulations of our warfare" (Alma 56:2), its tone is one of love, humility, gratitude, and faith. In it Helaman tells a remarkable story of 2,000 stripling Ammonites (later, 2,060) whose presence and valor change the course of the Lamanite-Nephite balance of power in the area by the west sea.

Helaman's love is evident in his salutation and in his repeated references to his 2,000 "sons"—"for they are worthy to be called sons," he says (Alma 56:10). Helaman's humility is revealed through his downplaying his own role in affairs. Though he was active in persuading the older Ammonites not to break their covenant regarding taking up weapons of war, he attributes his position as leader to the young men: they "would that I should be their leader" (Alma 56:5). Helaman's gratitude and faith are shown in his recounting the astounding preservation of all of the Ammonites after a fierce battle: "And we do justly ascribe it to the miraculous power of God, because of their exceeding faith in that which they had been taught to believe— that there was a just God, and whosoever did not doubt, that they should be preserved by his marvelous power" (Alma 57:26). His faith and gratitude are further shown in such statements as, "And blessed is the name of our God; for behold, it is he that has delivered us; yea, that has done this great thing for us" (Alma 57:35) and "The Lord our God did visit us with assurances that he would deliver us; yea, insomuch that he did speak peace to our souls, and did grant unto us great faith, and did cause us that we should hope for our deliverance in him" (Alma 58:11). Helaman closes his letter with an invocation of God's protection: "And now, my beloved brother, Moroni, may the Lord our God, who has redeemed us and made us free, keep you continually in his presence" (Alma 58:41).

Helaman's letter is particularly interesting in its gripping narrative of remarkable stratagems that recover one city after another for the Nephites. This narrative epitomizes the repeated Book of Mormon motif of a small force dealing successfully with an innumerable one—provided there is righteous commitment to a cause. Helaman's solution is to use ingenuity and plan creative stratagems, yet acknowledge the deliverance of the Lord: "It is by grace that we are saved, after all we can do," as Nephi said (2 Nephi 25:23).

In this respect, Mormon's edited retelling of Helaman's extended narrative points to a purpose of the "war chapters" in the Book of Mormon. If these chapters are to provide military history, it is strange military history indeed. By contrast with the 5,500 words of Helaman's account, the largest battle in the first 570 years is covered in 65 words. (In Alma 62:38 a great battle is dismissed in one sentence.)

> And in the fifty and seventh year [the Lamanites] did come down against the Nephites to battle, and they did commence the work of death; yea, insomuch that in the fifty and eighth year of the reign of the judges they succeeded in obtaining possession of the land of Zarahemla; yea, and also all the lands, even unto the land which was near the land Bountiful. (Helaman 4:5)

Rather, Helaman's narrative emphasizes the exercise of faith, direction by a great prophet-warrior, and help by the Lord in the face of superior numbers.[18]

MORONI TO PAHORAN

Contrasting sharply with Helaman's mild tone is Moroni's barely controlled anger in writing to the Nephite governor Pahoran. In expressing the need for reinforcements, Helaman had said in an earlier letter:

> Behold, we do not know but what ye are unsuccessful, and ye have drawn away the forces into that quarter of the land; if so, we do not desire to murmur. And if it is not so, behold, we fear that

there is some faction in the government, that they do not send more men to our assistance. . . . But, behold, it mattereth not—we trust God will deliver us, notwithstanding the weakness of our armies. (Alma 58:35–37)

When he received no response to his first letter requesting additional help for Helaman and having a serious setback in his own area, Moroni sends a second letter—or rather, an epistle—to Pahoran and other government officials with a powerful appeal that mounts into a condemnation, accusation, and threat.

The tone of Moroni's epistle is described by Hugh Nibley: "The letter seethes with the resentment of the man at the front for the easy-living ways of the 'VIP's' back at the capital—the old misunderstandings between the 'office' and the 'field.'"[19] In his thorough analysis of the letter, Nibley goes on to say:

> Moroni was bursting with pent-up emotions and the accumulated memories of reverses that could have been avoided and operations that could have ended the war had the necessary support been forthcoming from home. He knows, as Helaman suspects, that someone in high places is working against him, and for his noble and idealistic nature the thought that anyone should make capital of the miseries of others was simply maddening.[20]

Granted the bursting of pent-up emotions, the epistle nevertheless has a shape of development that makes it powerful and persuasive. (Moroni is incorrect in his surmise concerning Pahoran, yet he is right in his main suspicion, and the force of his challenge impels Pahoran to decisive action.) Though directing his epistle to Pahoran specifically, Moroni at first speaks generally "by the way of condemnation" to "those who have been chosen by this people to govern and manage the affairs of this war" (Alma 60:2, 1). He reminds them of their responsibility, tells how he and others have suffered afflictions, and then recounts the slaughter among the people—which, he asserts, might have been otherwise "if ye had rendered unto our armies sufficient strength and succor for them" (Alma 60:5).

The second phase of the epistle consists of Moroni's mounting accusations against the government leaders, prefaced by phrases such as "can you think" or "could ye suppose." "Can you think to sit upon your thrones in a state of thoughtless stupor," he asks disdainfully, "while your enemies are spreading the work of death around you? . . . Behold, could ye suppose that ye could sit upon your thrones, and because of the exceeding goodness of God ye could do nothing and he would deliver you?" (Alma 60:7, 11). Twice he declares, "if ye have supposed this ye have supposed in vain" (Alma 60:11, 12). (A comparison might be made here with George Washington's letters to the Second Continental Congress.)

In the third phase, Moroni develops a series of cause-and-consequence arguments in fearing that "the judgments of God will come upon this people": "Were it not for the wickedness which first commenced at our head, we could have withstood our enemies. . . . Yea, had it not been for the war which broke out among ourselves, . . . we should have dispersed our enemies" (Alma 60:14–16). Current military insufficiency, he says, is caused by recent civil strife instigated by those who sought to replace judges with a king.

Moroni then turns his criticism directly to the current rulers. With several rhetorical questions, Moroni ranges through possible reasons why the leaders have neglected him—and may even be traitors to their country. Have ye neglected us "because ye are in the heart of our country and ye are surrounded by security . . . ? Have ye forgotten the commandments of the Lord your God? Yea, have ye forgotten the captivity of our fathers?" His last question brings an obvious and sharp response: "Do ye suppose that God will look upon you as guiltless while ye sit still and behold these things? Behold I say unto you, Nay" (Alma 60:19–20, 23).

Moroni's forceful "Nay" is a bridge to the final phase of his epistle. "God has said that the inward vessel shall be cleansed first," he reminds them, "and then shall the outer vessel be cleansed also" (Alma 60:23). Moroni warns them that unless his leaders repent and send the armies relief and supplies, he will lead part of his army to the capital and stir up insurrections among them in the cause of freedom. Contrasting with the stasis of the supposedly *sitting* rulers, Moroni will act forcefully if his conditions are not met. If they do not act quickly, he will.

Moroni closes with an appeal to the authority of God and a calm affirmation of his unselfish purpose. The Lord has given him a directive to go to battle against the governmental leaders if they do not repent, and because "God will not suffer that we should perish with hunger, . . . see that ye fulfil the word of God. Behold, I am Moroni, your chief captain. I seek not for power, but to pull it down." In a balanced amplification of this statement he concludes, "I seek not for honor of the world, but for the glory of my God, and the freedom and welfare of my country" (Alma 60:35–36).

PAHORAN TO MORONI

If Moroni is bold, courageous, and strong-willed as the man of action, Pahoran is the hesitant, passive leader with an over-reliance on words. When he is chosen to be chief judge, he is on the right side of the cause of freedom but exhibits neither diplomacy nor forceful leadership. When a faction desiring to overthrow the free government and establish a king tries to change the law, Pahoran, we are told, does not "hearken to those who had sent in their voices with their petitions concerning the altering of the law" (Alma 51:3). When the king-men still try to get their way, it is others—not Pahoran—who resist them. Moroni, especially, rises to the fore with his petition to Pahoran representing "the voice of the people" in asking to be granted the "power to compel those dissenters to defend their country or to put them to death" (Alma 51:15).

In responding to Moroni's second epistle, Pahoran reveals both his good heart and his relative passivity:

I say unto you, Moroni, that I do not joy in your great afflictions, yea, it grieves my soul. But behold, there are those who do joy in your afflictions, yea, insomuch that they have risen up in rebellion against me, and also those of my people who are freemen. . . . And now, in your epistle you have censured me, but it mattereth not; I am not angry, but do rejoice in the greatness of your heart. I, Pahoran, do not seek for power, save only to retain my judgment-seat that I may preserve the rights and the liberty of my people. (Alma 61:2–3, 9)

Though he means well, Pahoran, in contrast to Moroni, does not do much. In the first part of his letter he emphasizes the actions of others: the king-men "have led away the hearts of many people. . . . They have driven me out before them. . . . They have got possession of the land" (Alma 61:4, 5, 8). After affirming that he does not seek for power, Pahoran gives passive responses that reverse Moroni's formula of "Except ye ___, I will ___." Pahoran says what he would not do: "We would not shed the blood of the Lamanites if they would stay in their own land. We would not shed the blood of our brethren if they would not rise up in rebellion and take the sword against us. We would subject ourselves to the yoke of bondage if it were requisite with the justice of God" (Alma 61:10–12). Rather than going forth to rally the people, as Moroni would have done, he sends forth a proclamation; his first resistance to evil is with words (Alma 61:14); and his advice to Moroni regarding the hardened and faithful warriors Lehi and Teancum is to "tell them to fear not, for God will deliver them" (Alma 61:21)—again, an overreliance on words. Pahoran's hesitancy to act is revealed especially in his saying to Moroni, "I do joy in receiving your epistle, for I was somewhat worried concerning what we should do, whether it should be just in us to go against our brethren. But ye have said, except they repent the Lord hath commanded you that ye should go against them" (Alma 61:19–20).

As revealed in their letters, the sharp outlines of the personalities of these two quite different leaders are striking.

Contrasting features of these two Nephite leaders subsequently appear in the differences between their sons. Moroni's son Moronihah is forceful, bold, and determined; Pahoran's sons are contentious, indecisive, and weak. His son Pacumeni, who becomes the ruler, ends up being killed against the wall of Zarahemla; Moronihah liberates the city.

GIDDIANHI TO LACHONEUS

The context for this letter from the robber chieftain Giddianhi to the Nephites' chief judge Lachoneus is a period of depredations by Gadianton robbers. These robbers, intent on gaining wealth and power by murder and by upsetting civil order, make forays out of their mountain hideouts to attack both Nephites and Lamanites and destroy their cities. Despite repeated efforts by the Nephites, "the Gadianton robbers did gain many advantages over them." Nephi adds that "the sword of destruction did hang over" his people, "insomuch that they were about to be smitten down by it, and this because of their iniquity" (3 Nephi 2:18–19).

Emboldened by successes of the robbers, Giddianhi threatens Lachoneus. Giddianhi's letter drips with gall, revealing an insolent, bold, and rapacious person. He begins with feigned flattery that moves into sarcasm:

> Lachoneus, *most noble* and chief governor of the land, behold, I . . . give unto you *exceedingly great praise* because of your firmness, and also the firmness of your people, in maintaining that which *ye suppose* to be your right and liberty; yea, ye do stand well, *as if* ye were supported by the hand of a god, in the defence of your liberty, and your property, and your country, *or that which ye do call so.*
>
> And it *seemeth a pity unto me, most noble* Lachoneus, that ye should be so foolish and vain as to suppose that ye can stand against so many brave men who are at my command, who do now at this time stand in their arms, and do await with great anxiety for the word—Go down upon the Nephites and destroy them.

161

And I, knowing of their unconquerable spirit, having proved them in the field of battle, and knowing of their everlasting hatred towards you because of the many wrongs which ye have done unto them, therefore if they should come down against you they would visit you with utter destruction.

Therefore I have written this epistle, sealing it with mine own hand, *feeling for your welfare,* because of your firmness in that which *ye believe* to be right, and your *noble spirit* in the field of battle. (3 Nephi 3:2–5)

Giddianhi impudently claims that the works of his secret society are good and that his robbers "dissented away from [the Nephites] because of [their] wickedness in retaining from them their rights of government" (3 Nephi 3:10). What he wants is nothing less than that the people of Lachoneus turn over their cities, lands, and possessions to the Gadianton band.

In his mail-fisted threats, Giddianhi reveals the claws that earlier were barely hidden: "If ye will not do this, I swear unto you with an oath, that on the morrow month I will command that my armies shall come down against you, and they shall not stay their hand and shall spare not, but shall slay you, and shall let fall the sword upon you even until ye shall become extinct" (3 Nephi 3:8).

Though there is no direct response by Lachoneus to Giddianhi that would reveal a contrast in personalities, we are given part of Lachoneus's proclamation to his people. He calls on them to gather into one central location with their families and enough substance for seven years, and he says they must repent or they will "in nowise be delivered out of the hands of those Gadianton robbers" (3 Nephi 3:15). His plan is successful. Giddianhi is slain, and the robbers are eventually defeated.

MORMON TO MORONI

Mormon's two pastoral letters to Moroni are just before the end of the Book of Mormon. In them we hear extensively the voice of the man who has given shape to the Book of Mormon

narrative from the book of Mosiah onward and whose commen-
taries have pointed the lessons he wanted his audience to
receive. The two letters are separated in time: the first coming
soon after Moroni is called to the ministry; and the second near
the end of Mormon's life, just before he delivers up the sacred
records to Moroni.

It is appropriate that these letters follow Mormon's sermon
on faith, hope, and charity because they put the essence of that
sermon to the test. They also prepare for the last chapter in the
Book of Mormon, Moroni's departing testimony and exhortation
regarding spiritual gifts, by showing the extremes of righteous
living and degraded wickedness. Mormon's closing prayer in
Moroni 7 is for the true followers of Jesus Christ to be purified
even as Christ is pure (Moroni 7:48). In his epistle in Moroni 8,
though, he fears that the Spirit has abandoned the Nephites as
they seek "to put down all power and authority which cometh
from God" (Moroni 8:28). In his second epistle he portrays a
"horrible scene" (Moroni 9:20) of a depraved people who are
"without order and without mercy. . . . And they have become
strong in their perversion; and they are alike brutal, sparing
none, neither old nor young; and they delight in everything save
that which is good" (Moroni 9:18–19).

Mormon's first letter is like a Pauline epistle in giving counsel to help regulate the Church. Like Paul in 1 Corinthians and
other epistles, Mormon begins with a salutation and thanksgiving: "My beloved son, Moroni, I rejoice exceedingly that your
Lord Jesus Christ hath been mindful of you, and hath called you
to his ministry, and to his holy work." He continues in a personal, affectionate manner of the sort Michael Goulder finds in
Paul.[21] "I am mindful of you always in my prayers," Mormon
says, paralleling his own caring to that of the Savior, "continually
praying unto God the Father in the name of his Holy Child,
Jesus, that he, through his infinite goodness and grace, will keep
you through the endurance of faith on his name to the end"
(Moroni 8:2–3).

The reference to Jesus the Child points to Mormon's main concern. In a systematic and well-structured argument, Mormon addresses the disputations that had come among the Nephites concerning the baptism of little children. He begins by quoting the words of Christ that came to him in a revelation: "Behold, I came into the world not to call the righteous but sinners to repentance; the whole need no physician, but they that are sick; wherefore, little children are whole, for they are not capable of committing sin; wherefore the curse of Adam is taken from them in me, that it hath no power over them" (Moroni 8:8). Mormon then develops the implications of this doctrine: Because little children need no repentance, they do not need baptism. Those who think children who have died without baptism are damned are themselves iniquitous and have "neither faith, hope, nor charity" (Moroni 8:14). Those who say little children need baptism deny the mercies of Christ. Indeed, "all little children are alive in Christ" (Moroni 8:22). Finally, repentance is for those who are condemned for breaking the law, which repentance is followed by baptism and remission of sins. In sum, according to Mark Thomas, "Mormon argues that to accept infant baptism is to deny one's own charity, the nature of God and the atonement."[22]

In harmony with his argument and his previously quoted sermon, Mormon's dominant characteristic revealed in this letter is love. He first affirms to his beloved Moroni that he always remembers him in his prayers. In the center of his argument he identifies with Christ as he testifies, "And I am filled with charity, which is everlasting love; wherefore, all children are alike unto me; wherefore, I love little children with a perfect love; and they are all alike and partakers of salvation" (Moroni 8:17).

The second letter reveals the full strength of Mormon's position. His people, he says, "have lost their love, one towards another; and they thirst after blood and revenge continually" (Moroni 9:5). Yet Mormon preserves his "perfect love" (Moroni 8:16) and remains uncontaminated by the evil around him.

Bracketed by Mormon's tender love and concern for Moroni, this letter gives a brief but pointed glimpse into the depths of the depravity of the collapsing and doomed Nephite civilization. The brutality of the Lamanites is evidenced by their feeding the Nephite women prisoners "upon the flesh of their husbands, and the children upon the flesh of their fathers" (Moroni 9:8). The depravity as well as brutality of the Nephites is shown by the men of Moriantum depriving many of the Lamanite young women of "that which was most dear and precious above all things, which is chastity and virtue," and then torturing the women to death and afterwards devouring their flesh "like unto wild beasts, because of the hardness of their hearts; and they do it for a token of bravery" (Moroni 9:9–10). Though he cannot recommend his people to God "lest he should smite me" (Moroni 9:21), Mormon can and does recommend his son Moroni to God, saying, "and I trust in Christ that thou wilt be saved; and I pray unto God that he will spare thy life, to witness the return of his people unto him, or their utter destruction" (Moroni 9:22). Then, in a tender close, Mormon invokes the grace of God upon Moroni and admonishes him to "be faithful in Christ; and may not the things which I have written grieve thee, to weigh thee down unto death; but may Christ lift thee up, and may his sufferings and death, and the showing his body unto our fathers, and his mercy and long-suffering, and the hope of his glory and of eternal life, rest in your mind forever" (Moroni 9:25). The storm is over; all that is left is for Moroni to conclude the record with this same exhortation to his unseen audience to "come unto Christ, and be perfected in him, and deny yourselves of all ungodliness; . . . and love God with all your might, mind and strength, . . . that by his grace ye may be perfect in Christ" (Moroni 10:32).

The eight letters we have examined show remarkable diversity in style and tone—from Captain Moroni's honest and angry forthrightness to Mormon's gentle charity toward children and his cry of the heart regarding the wickedness of his people. The letters likewise reveal clearly such various personality traits as Pahoran's vacillation and Giddianhi's arrogance. In total, they form part of the rich fabric of presentation of memorable individuals and families in the Book of Mormon.

CHAPTER 7

"Not Cast Off Forever"

IMAGERY

Moroni may be thinking imagistically when he says that through knowing the covenants the Lamanites can be assured "they are not cast off forever" (title page). The literal meaning of "cast off" is "being put away or separated from God." But used figuratively, it gains deeper meaning. In reflections that precede the prophecy of Samuel the Lamanite, Mormon says, "We read that in the great and last day there are some who shall be cast out, yea, who shall be cast off from the presence of the Lord" (Helaman 12:25). Samuel's words give force to that concept by comparing an unrepentant person to an unproductive tree: "Whosoever repenteth not is hewn down and cast into the fire; . . . for they are cut off again as to things pertaining to righteousness" (Helaman 14:18). In saying this, Samuel may be quoting from Zenos's allegory of the tame and wild olive trees: "the trees of my vineyard are good for nothing save it be to be hewn down and cast into the fire" (Jacob 5:42).

Imagery in a literary sense is "a picture made out of words."[1] It "refers to images produced in the mind by language, whose words and statements may refer to experiences which could produce physical perceptions were the reader actually to have those experiences, or to the sense-impressions themselves."[2] As Tremper Longman explains,

> In order to describe a person, object, or event, the [writer] will explicitly or implicitly compare the item with something or

someone else that is similar in some way but that is also different. The difference between the two causes the reader to recognize the presence of an image and stimulates him or her to search for the similarity within the difference that the image conceals.[3]

Though imprecise, Longman says, images are vivid and memorable, present old truths in new ways, and speak directly to the heart.[4]

The vividness and clarifying power of imagery are illustrated in Ammon's response to his and his brothers' missionary labors. He has been successful in helping the Lamanites know their true identity, acknowledge Nephite spiritual leadership, and accept covenants that keep them from being cast off from God forever. At the completion of this missionary service, Ammon tries to convey to his brothers his feelings. He is limited, though, in expression: "I cannot say the smallest part which I feel," he acknowledges (Alma 26:16). Nevertheless, the feelings he does communicate are presented indirectly and effectively through imagery. The Lamanites were "in darkness, yea, even in the darkest abyss, but behold, how many of them are brought to behold the marvelous light of God!" (Alma 26:3). Thousands have been brought "into the fold of God" (Alma 26:4) through missionary shepherds. Then comparing himself and his brothers to harvesters and their converts to sheaves, he says:

> The field was ripe, and blessed are ye, for ye did thrust in the sickle, and did reap with your might, yea, all the day long did ye labor; and behold the number of your sheaves! And they shall be gathered into the garners, that they are not wasted. Yea, they shall not be beaten down by the storm at the last day; yea, neither shall they be harrowed up by the whirlwinds; but when the storm cometh they shall be gathered together in their place, that the storm cannot penetrate to them; yea, neither shall they be driven with fierce winds whithersoever the enemy listeth to carry them. But behold, they are in the hands of the Lord of the harvest, and they are his; and he will raise them up at the last day. (Alma 26:5–7)

Continuing to convey his feelings with figurative language, Ammon compares his heart to a cup: "My heart is brim with joy" (Alma 26:11). The converts have been brought to "sing redeeming love" (Alma 26:13); they have been loosed "from the chains of hell" (Alma 26:14); and having been "encircled about with everlasting darkness," they now are brought into God's "everlasting light" (Alma 26:15). Reflecting on his and his brothers' own experience of conversion, Ammon wonders why God did not let the "the sword of his justice" fall on them (Alma 26:19). Instead, he brought them over "that everlasting gulf of death and misery" to the salvation of their souls (Alma 26:20). He has been mindful of them as part of "a branch of the tree of Israel . . . lost from its body in a strange land" (Alma 26:36). Thus, through use of imagery, Ammon calls on his auditors to enrich the meaning of his words by making associations from their experiences, just as Jesus did with his parables.

In a similar way, Mormon uses a series of metaphors to show the movement through peril to safety of those who covenant by baptism:

> Thus we see that the gate of heaven is open unto all . . . who will believe on the name of Jesus Christ. . . . Yea, we see that whosoever will may lay hold upon the word of God, which is quick and powerful, which shall divide asunder all the cunning and the snares and the wiles of the devil, and lead the man of Christ in a strait and narrow course across that everlasting gulf of misery which is prepared to engulf the wicked—and land their souls, yea, their immortal souls, at the right hand of God in the kingdom of heaven. (Helaman 3:28–30)

In this rapid shift of comparisons, Mormon uses pairs and triplets to intensify the effect of the images. The word (and *sword*) of God is "quick and powerful" in dividing "the cunning and the snares and the wiles" of the devil, and the course across the gulf of misery is "strait and narrow."

Had Abinadi declared, "The life of King Noah shall become of little value," his message would have lacked force and vitality. With imagery, his message is effective and stirring: the life of King Noah shall be "as a garment in a furnace of fire. . . . as a stalk, even as a dry stalk of the field, which is run over by the beasts and trodden under foot. . . . as the blossoms of a thistle, which, when it is fully ripe, if the wind bloweth, it is driven forth upon the face of the land" (Mosiah 12:10–12).[5]

Similarly, Helaman's instructions to his sons would have been weak and colorless had he said, "Remember to establish your lives on Christ, the Son of God, that when the devil causes trouble, he shall have no power over you because of the way you have lived." Instead, he expresses this idea memorably and with intensity by comparing his sons' faithful actions to building a weatherproof house:

> And now, my sons, remember, remember that it is upon the rock of our Redeemer, who is Christ, the Son of God, that ye must build your foundation; that when the devil shall send forth his mighty winds, yea, his shafts in the whirlwind, yea, when all his hail and his mighty storm shall beat upon you, it shall have no power over you to drag you down to the gulf of misery and endless wo, because of the rock upon which ye are built, which is a sure foundation, a foundation whereon if men build they cannot fall. (Helaman 5:12)

Moroni could have blandly said, "The Jaredites faced great difficulty in crossing the ocean." Instead, he makes the dangerous circumstances of the Jaredites immediate and real by reporting, "They were many times buried in the depths of the sea, because of the mountain waves which broke upon them, and also the great and terrible tempests which were caused by the fierceness of the wind" (Ether 6:6). Again speaking imagistically, Moroni says the Lamanites "are driven about as chaff before the wind . . . or as a vessel is tossed about upon the waves, without sail or anchor, or without anything wherewith to steer her" (Mormon 5:16, 18).

Imagery such as this helps make the Book of Mormon appeal to all our senses, including our spiritual sense. Indeed, some of our deepest responses to truth are through feelings. By stepping back and looking at imagery in the Book of Mormon as a whole, we can discover patterns hidden beneath the surface that increase the meaning and force of the book.

Imagery patterns in the Book of Mormon are important indexes to deep meanings. That is true especially in such repeated basic images as trees, rivers, and fire—things that to people like those in Lehi's group would be closely connected to survival. Images such as these are archetypes; that is, in the words of biblical scholar T. R. Henn, they

> are often linked to basic, recurrent and apparently universal symbols, which suggest conscious or subliminal meanings in many literatures. . . . For a people at first nomadic and then agricultural, cave, desert, river, well and fountain, storm and rain and drought, tower and wall, have a special immediacy. Images of the plough, the seed and the sower, the vineyard and the shepherd, are more germane to the settled life of the New Testament than the Old. The manifestations of God may commonly be perceived in thunder, lightning, in the pillar of fire, or even in the mulberry-trees. . . . Gold and silver, metals that are purified by smelting, serve to set forth the immortal character of the soul.[6]

Another well-known biblical scholar, Mircea Eliade, affirms that in primitive societies the importance of an object or an act is that it "imitates or repeats an archetype."[7]

To consider just one example of an archetype, crossing a river or an ocean is a widely accepted symbol for going from one life to another, for rescue, and for salvation. Literal, figurative, or prophetic crossings in the Book of Mormon develop salvation as a significant concern. Nephi sees the Gentiles going "forth out of captivity" "across the many waters" (1 Nephi 13:29). Once Lehi and his family have the Liahona, they begin the extensive part of their journey into the wilderness by first crossing the river Laman (1 Nephi 16:12). God tells Nephi to construct a ship so that "I may carry thy people across these waters" (1 Nephi 17:8). The Mulekites "were brought by the hand of the

Lord across the great waters" (Omni 1:16). The Lord miraculously provides light for the Jaredite barges and brings the people across the "raging deep" into the promised land (Ether 3:3). By contrast, some of those in Lehi's vision who do not hold fast to the iron rod are drowned in the river of filthy water; in the upheavals before Christ's coming, many notable cities are sunk into the sea, drowning their inhabitants. Commenting on the connection between water and death, literary critic Northrop Frye says water "traditionally belongs to a realm of existence below human life, the state of chaos or dissolution which follows ordinary death, or the reduction to the inorganic. Hence the soul frequently crosses water or sinks into it at death."[8]

PRINCIPAL ARCHETYPES IN THE BOOK OF MORMON

The most dominant images in the Book of Mormon are also the simplest and most basic. Either literally or figuratively they pertain to fire, light and darkness, captivity and deliverance, wilderness or wandering, trees and waters of life, and dust. We may think in this respect of the medieval division of life—both as microcosm and macrocosm—into earth, air, fire, and water. Overall, these images confirm the truth of Lehi's understanding that "it must needs be, that there is an opposition in all things" (2 Nephi 2:11) and that opposition ultimately can be beneficial to the righteous.[9]

With some of these images, the opposition is obvious, as in the contrast between light and darkness or between captivity and deliverance. But even the single images, like fire, are used to emphasize opposition. Fire accompanied Lehi's call to be a prophet just as it announced Moses' call at the burning bush. Whereas the righteous will be saved by fire, the wicked will be destroyed by it (1 Nephi 22:17). To approach the tree of life is to risk wandering into mists or death by drowning. For some of Lehi's family, salvation comes through departing into the wilderness with their tents, yet the rebellious sons see it in reverse:

from their perspective, Lehi has led them out to "perish in the wilderness" (1 Nephi 2:11). Thus, as with essentially all of the Book of Mormon images, though there is a risk of loss or death associated with an image such as fire or water, there are also great rewards that come from going through or over water, being enveloped in flames, coming out of dust, breaking the chains of bondage, wandering through the wilderness, and the like.

This two-sidedness will become clearer as we look closely at the six principal images.

Fire

Lehi's dream showed that the justice of God dividing the wicked from the righteous is like a flaming fire (1 Nephi 15:30). From that point on to the end of the Book of Mormon, fire operates in both helpful and destructive ways. At the extremes, the righteous will be "visited with fire and with the Holy Ghost" whereas their enemies will be destroyed by fire (3 Nephi 12:2; 1 Nephi 22:17).

Nephi's firelike strength in 1 Nephi 17 is a sign of his having the Lord's power but is a threat to his brothers, who would wither as dried reeds if they touched him. Quoting Isaiah, Nephi considers fire by night as blessing the righteous in being a sign of the Lord's presence, and he prophesies of terrors to the wicked through destructive fires at both the first appearance of Christ among the Nephites and before his second coming (2 Nephi 14:5; 26:6; 27:2). As for himself, Nephi says that God has "filled me with his love, even unto the consuming of my flesh" (2 Nephi 4:21).[10]

Fire dominates the martyrdom of Abinadi. Eventually King Noah and his wicked priests are also consumed by fire, but their destruction is that of the wicked and foretells their spiritual torment, which will be like a lake of fire and brimstone. On the other hand, the martyrdom of Abinadi serves as a testimony against the wicked. Further, as Alma perceives concerning the innocent Nephite martyrs at Ammonihah, "the Lord receiveth them up unto himself, in glory" (Alma 14:11).

Fire plays an unexpected role in the experience of the brothers Nephi and Lehi in prison. When they are about to be put to death, these prophets are encircled about by fire—which instead of destroying them leads to their release from prison. Likewise, their Lamanite captors, who had been imprisoned within the walls of their hatred and error, are set free when they repent and are encircled by a pillar of fire. Then all are "filled as if with fire" (Helaman 5:45) by the Holy Ghost. Although the Lamanites at first are immobilized by a cloud of darkness (typifying their spiritual condition), their eventual faith brings light out of darkness. Shaken by the tremors under the prison, the Lamanites are pierced to the soul by "a still voice of perfect mildness" and later hear "a pleasant voice" whisper peace unto them (Helaman 5:30, 46).

As part of the cataclysmic events in the New World associated with the crucifixion of Christ, the "refiner's fire" destroys the most wicked cities, such as Zarahemla and Jacobugath. Conversely, in the most holy scenes in 3 Nephi, fire comes out of heaven and encircles the little children and those who have been baptized (3 Nephi 9:3, 9; 17:24; 19:14). In like manner, Mormon says the righteous are to be baptized, "first with water, then with fire and with the Holy Ghost," while the holiness of Jesus Christ "will kindle a flame of unquenchable fire" upon the wicked (Mormon 7:10; 9:5). Thus, though the source of fire is ultimately the same, its effect of punishment or of glorification depends on the spiritual condition of the recipient.

Light and Darkness

As Christ is a fire, so is he a light in the wilderness (1 Nephi 17:13). In vision, Lehi saw the Son of God as glowing brighter than the sun (1 Nephi 1:9). He also saw Christ's apostles dressed in startlingly white garments (1 Nephi 1:10; 12:10; see also 3 Nephi 19:25). Both actually and figuratively, light and whiteness are associated with truth, purity, and divine guidance, just as darkness is associated with unbelief and error (see, for example, Alma 40:14).

Moving from darkness to light gives concrete meaning to the process of redemption. In his dream-journey, Lehi travels in darkness for many hours before being brought, through the mercy of the Lord, to the tree of life with its white fruit of the Savior's atonement and love (1 Nephi 8:8–11; 11:8–24). While unconscious, Lamoni enters into a dark condition but arises from it enlightened. Ammon

> knew that king Lamoni was under the power of God; he knew that the *dark* veil of unbelief was being cast away from his mind, and the *light* which did *light* up his mind, which was the *light* of the glory of God, which was a marvelous *light* of his goodness— yea, this *light* had infused such joy into his soul, the cloud of *darkness* having been dispelled, and that the *light* of everlasting life was *lit* up in his soul, yea, he knew that this had overcome his natural frame, and he was carried away in God. (Alma 19:6)

Alma's conversion is similarly framed in terms of his emerging from darkness into light. This experience prepares him to understand and prophesy about a stone or "interpreters" that the Lord will prepare for a future prophet. These interpreters (or Urim and Thummim) "shall shine forth in darkness unto light" in bringing "forth out of darkness unto light" the secret works and abominations of the Nephite people and make them known "unto every nation that shall hereafter possess the land" (Alma 37:23–25).

The most dramatic opposition of light and darkness is connected with the appearance of Jesus Christ. Samuel the Lamanite predicts that there will be great lights in heaven at the Savior's birth, but he prophesies also that darkness will attend the Savior's death (Helaman 14:3, 20). In the first part of Samuel's prophecy, light and order are associated with the Creator and creation (a new star). On the other hand, the chaos of things splitting apart as well as intense darkness—the opposites of

175

creation—are associated with the death of the Creator. Samuel the Lamanite says the earth shall shake and tremble and rocks shall be broken and torn in two, just as in Christ's death there is a division of body and spirit.

The Savior's coming to the Nephites out of darkness and great destruction is to them a great miracle of light. After the earth comes together again, a "Man" descends out of heaven clothed in a white robe and declares, "I am the light and the life of the world" (3 Nephi 10:10; 11:8, 11).[11] In a series of unforgettable instructions, the Savior teaches the gathered multitude to be "the light of this people" (3 Nephi 12:14), to realize that "the light of the body is the eye" (3 Nephi 13:22), and that "I am the law, and the light" (3 Nephi 15:9). They are also instructed to hold up their light "that it may shine unto the world" (3 Nephi 18:24). Then he causes the "light of his countenance" to shine upon his disciples, "and behold they were as white as the countenance and aiso the garments of Jesus" (3 Nephi 19:25).

The coming forth of the Book of Mormon is itself an experience of light. Calling on the power of light imagery, Moroni poetically declares:

> And blessed be he that shall bring this thing to light;
> for it shall be brought out of darkness unto light,
> according to the word of God;
> yea, it shall be brought out of the earth,
> and it shall shine forth out of darkness,
> and come unto the knowledge of the people;
> and it shall be done by the power of God.
> (Mormon 8:16)

Captivity and Deliverance

Joseph who saved his family in Egypt foretold that the Messiah would bring latter-day Lamanites "out of darkness unto light—yea, out of hidden darkness and out of captivity unto freedom" (2 Nephi 3:5). Here we see the contrast between darkness and light linked with captivity and deliverance. Both sets of images communicate to us a process, a movement, a rebirth, through which humans become whole by coming to a physical or spiritual promised land or condition.

Again and again, individuals or peoples in the Book of Mormon are delivered from captivity. Sometimes they are physically enslaved; other times the captivity is of the mind and spirit; or the two may be connected. In the wilderness, Nephi bursts the cords his brothers use to tie him up. Later, on board the ship, he is freed by a miracle from the ropes binding him. The first case of physical deliverance is followed by Lehi's vision of the tree of life, which promises spiritual deliverance; after the ship incident, the group is physically delivered and arrives at the land of promise.

Other individuals put into bondage, especially through being cast into prison, are Abinadi, Alma and Amulek, Ammon and his brethren, Nephi and Lehi, and the Three Nephites. What happens to them parallels the freeing of Moses and the Israelites by God's intervention, just as God takes direct action to save Lehi and his family (the two groups are often linked together, as in 1 Nephi 4:2 and Alma 36:28–29), Limhi and his people, and Alma and his followers. In each case, bondage is associated with the powers of Satan—with his prisons of death and hell—whereas deliverance comes through the power of God.

Bondage often seems to be necessary to prepare a person for conversion or salvation. After Aaron is freed (Alma 21:14–17), he and his brothers are tremendously successful. It is as though they somehow need to go through the experience of physical bondage in order to deliver others from spiritual bondage. Further, the captivity suffered by such peoples as Alma's group is beyond what humans can solve, requiring the power of God to be shown directly: "They were in bondage, and none could deliver them except it were the Lord their God" (Mosiah 24:21).

In like manner, oppressive spiritual bondage is miraculously overcome by the power of God. That is the core of the testimony of Alma the Younger, and it is also the experience of the

Lamanites taught by Ammon and his brethren. They are moved out of Satan's bonds of "everlasting darkness and destruction" into the refuge of God's "everlasting light" and "the matchless bounty of his love" (Alma 26:15).

As one who has experienced personal bondage, Alma bases his sermon to the people of Zarahemla on the captivity/deliverance theme while touching as well on the other images treated here. He appeals to the people to remember their fathers' captivity and says a merciful God has "delivered their souls from hell." The fathers were awakened "out of deep sleep, and they awoke unto God. Behold, they were in the midst of darkness; nevertheless, their souls were illuminated by the light of the everlasting word." Though they have been like sheep who have gone astray into the wilderness, they are encouraged to bring forth good fruit. Otherwise, the ax is poised at the root of the tree and the unrepentant shall be "hewn down and cast into the fire" (Alma 5:6, 7, 56).

Wilderness or Wandering

When God frees people from bondage, leading people out into and then through a wilderness often seems to be the way he does it. The pattern of escape into a wilderness is that of the Exodus under Moses. With many references to the children of Israel being led out of Egypt, miraculous escape is found in the stories of Lehi, Nephi, Mulek, Mosiah, Limhi, Alma, the Anti-Nephi-Lehies, Jared, and King Omer.

With the righteous, the wilderness can be a place of refuge and concealment; for the wicked or benighted, such as the people of Amulon or the Gadiantons or many of the Lamanites, the wilderness is a hideout or a permanent place of habitation. It can be a place of escape or a place of danger.

Responses to the wilderness are dramatically different. For righteous Nephi, the wilderness is a place of receiving revelation, but Laman and Lemuel fear perishing in it. Nephi's experience in the wilderness teaches faith, the rewards of obedience, and gratitude to God: "He hath led me through mine afflictions in the wilderness" (2 Nephi 4:20). For Laman and Lemuel and their posterity, it is a place where they become a "wild, and ferocious, and a blood-thirsty people, . . . dwelling in tents, and wandering about in the wilderness with a short skin girdle about their loins and their heads shaven" (Enos 1:20).

The essential difference is that the Lord intends his people to go through the wilderness (the command to Lehi) or else to civilize it (as in the case of Alma in the land of Helam), not simply to remain in it, as do the priests of Noah. Living in a tent is necessary for a time, but the permanence of building a temple is preferred. Even the most righteous Saints may wander through the land for a while (Jacob 7:26; Alma 26:36), but an aimless wandering is "losing one's way"—a root meaning of "wander." That is the spiritual condition of many of the descendants of Laman and Lemuel (Mormon 5:18). The way out is to have the word of Christ as guide, like a Liahona, to point "a straight course to eternal bliss" and to show that man's final destination is no spot in any earthly wilderness but the heavenly promised land (Alma 37:44, 45).

Trees and Waters of Life

In accordance with the Book of Mormon's system of opposition, it is fitting that in his dream Lehi must go through "a dark and dreary wilderness" to reach the tree "whose fruit was desirable to make one happy" (1 Nephi 8:4, 10). This tree of life is a rich, complex symbol. In different parts of the Book of Mormon it is linked with water, vineyards, and olive trees.[12] Its fruit stands for God's love, and faith in Christ is described as "a tree springing up unto everlasting life" (1 Nephi 11:22; Alma 32:41). Approaching the tree is a sacramental experience: "Come unto me," Alma quotes the Lord as saying, "and ye shall partake of the fruit of the tree of life; Yea, ye shall eat and drink of the bread and the waters of life freely; yea, come unto me and bring forth works of righteousness" (Alma 5:34–35).[13] On the other hand, those who refuse will be like dead trees that are "hewn down and cast into the fire" (Alma 5:34–35). Both alternatives depict Christ as the tree of life and the refiner's fire.

With Christ as its central focal point, the tree of life symbol in the Book of Mormon supports a number of the meanings attributed to this rich symbol over time. In Lehi's dream it is juxtaposed against a dark and dreary wilderness and mists of darkness, its fruit is of an exceeding whiteness, and only a few reach it (1 Nephi 8). Nephi considers it synonymous with "living waters" (1 Nephi 11:25) and sees it identified with the birth, life, mission, and death of Christ (1 Nephi 11:7–33).

In ancient Mesoamerica, according to Irene Briggs, the tree of life was depicted in the shape of a cross and also conventionalized as a maize plant—the staple food plant and therefore the "bread" of life.[14] Indeed, the Nahuatl word for cross, according to Constance Irwin, is *tonacaquahuitl,* meaning "tree of life."[15] As for the darkness and "living waters," Joseph Campbell says that in the monomyth, the tree of life (representing the "universe itself"), growing from the World Navel, "is rooted in the supporting darkness; the golden sun bird perches on its peak; a spring, the inexhaustible well, bubbles at its foot."[16] The whiteness of the fruit of the tree is related to E. A. S. Butterworth's finding that in the archetypal World Tree, "sometimes the sap is white and milk-like, but the liquid is found as often in the spring beneath as in the tree itself."[17] The journey to the tree is associated with legends; it is reported by Thomas Barns that the fruit of the sacred tree was to be taken only by the initiated.[18] The fruits of the tree, says Arnold Whittick, "especially bright fruits, are associated with the tree of wisdom and knowledge."[19] E. O. James finds that in St. John's Apocalypse, "the fruit of the Tree of Life was reserved for those who had overcome in the strife, and whose names were written in the Lamb's book of life."[20] And in many ancient cultures—as evidenced by the myths of Egypt, Mesopotamia, and Greece—the tree of life was associated with both birth and rebirth.[21]

Water and agricultural images work both ways. The fountain of living waters in Lehi's dream is opposed by the river of filthy waters. Compared to a ripe field, converted Lamanites have become sheaves gathered into garners, not to be beaten down by the storm at the last day; "they are in the hands of the Lord of the harvest" (Alma 26:5–7). On the other hand, the wicked condemned by Abinadi are as a "dry stalk of the field, which is run over by the beasts and trodden under foot"; they are as thistle blossoms blown across the land (Mosiah 12:11–12). The tree of life even has its opposite in the tree of death upon which the Gadianton leader Zemnarihah is hanged (3 Nephi 4:28–29).

Though the sea is a place where Lehi and his family come close to being swallowed up, the Lord also makes the sea their path (2 Nephi 1:2; 10:20). The Jaredites are "buried in the depths of the sea," yet eventually are brought through the "mountain waves" and "terrible tempests" to a chosen land set apart from the rest of the world by those very elements (Ether 6:6, 12).

The primary elements of water, fire, and earth are involved in the destruction of the Nephite and Lamanite cities recorded in 3 Nephi 8 and 9. Cities are sunk in the sea, burned, and covered with earth. Yet after the destruction, uplift and even salvation are said to come through those same three elements. For "the more righteous part of the people who were saved" from drowning, water becomes a medium for baptism (3 Nephi 10:12; 12:1–2). Spared from being burned in a city such as Zarahemla, the people gathered at the temple learn from the Savior that for them fire will bless, not curse, as they are baptized "with fire and with the Holy Ghost" (3 Nephi 12:1). Their little children are visited by angels and "encircled about with fire" (3 Nephi 17:24). And rather than being "buried up in the depths of the earth," these people are built upon Christ's rock (3 Nephi 9:8; 11:39).

Dust

The opposite of water and fruitfulness is dust. This image is associated in the Book of Mormon with mortality, humiliation, captivity, obscurity, destruction, and death.[22] The wicked, Nephi prophesies, will be "brought low in the dust," and the Jaredite prophets warn that the Jaredites, unless they repent, will be destroyed and their bones become "as heaps of earth upon the face of the land" (1 Nephi 22:23; Ether 11:6).

Yet out of the dust can come life and blessings. The Book of Mormon itself is prophesied to come "out of the dust" (2 Nephi 26:16). Echoing Isaiah, Moroni cries: "Arise from the dust, O Jerusalem; yea, and put on thy beautiful garments" (Moroni 10:31). Lehi exhorts Laman and Lemuel to "arise from the dust" (2 Nephi 1:14). After the Lamanites have been "brought down low in the dust, . . . yet the words of the righteous shall be written" and in the last days "shall whisper out of the dust" (2 Nephi 26:15–16).

At the very core, the six principal images in the Book of Mormon appeal to the senses in helping us *feel* the atoning power of Christ, which our minds cannot rationally grasp. The Lord is a refiner's *fire,* the *light* of Israel, *deliverer* of those who wander in the *wilderness,* the fountain of living *waters,* creator of humans from the *dust* of the earth, and the one who will retrieve us from dust again at the last day. Imaged forth is the purpose of the book itself, found in the title page, to "show unto the remnant of the House of Israel what great things the Lord hath done for their fathers" and to point the way for them to "be found spotless at the judgment-seat of Christ."

"AFFIXED OPPOSITE":
SIX OTHER IMPORTANT IMAGE CLUSTERS

Other image clusters as well develop an "opposition in all things" (2 Nephi 2:11) of the sort Lehi addressed. The Book of Mormon shows extremes in wickedness and holiness, life and death, happiness and misery, the sweet and the bitter (2 Nephi 2:11, 15). A cosmic truth it affirms time and again is that of God's children from the fall of Adam forward having choices between good and evil, between obedience and disobedience, with "a punishment . . . affixed opposite to the plan of happiness" (Alma 42:16). Linked loosely with darkness and light as well as with captivity and deliverance in sustaining these oppositions are the image pairs sleeping and waking, and heights and depths. Three significant structures—temples, tents, and palaces—compose a third set. Clothes imagery is next. A fifth set, connected with remnants of clothes and of rocks, has to do with wholeness or rending, quaking, or crumbling. Swords and other weapons are a sixth set.

The image clusters also use wordplay and multiple meanings to show transitions between the earthly or temporal and the spiritual. "The world is emblematic," Emerson said regarding relationships of this sort; "the whole of nature is a metaphor of the human mind."[23]

Sleeping and Waking

In several crucial encounters between the Nephites and the numerically superior Lamanites, the Lamanites simply fall asleep. Alma the Elder and his people are able to escape during the day because "the Lord caused a deep sleep to come upon the Lamanites" (Mosiah 24:19); Teancum is able to kill the dictator Amalickiah because sleep overpowers the fatigued Lamanites (Alma 51:33); Moroni captures the city Gid without loss of life "while the Lamanites [are] in a deep sleep and drunken" (Alma 55:16).

Physical sleep also symbolizes a type of spiritual darkness.[24] Anticipating his eldest sons' problems, Lehi challenges them (and their posterity) to "awake from a deep sleep, yea, even from the sleep of hell" (2 Nephi 1:13). Spiritually benighted Nephites also are awakened by the Lord "out of a deep sleep, and they [awake] unto God" (Alma 5:7). An example of this change is the story of the Lamanite king Lamoni. On believing the words of Ammon, Lamoni falls to the earth as though dead. After two days and two nights, Ammon tells Lamoni's queen that her husband "sleepeth in God, and on the morrow he shall rise again" (Alma 19:8). His rising is like a resurrection and redemption. Indeed, according to Moroni, the resurrection brings "a redemption from an endless sleep, from which sleep all men shall be awakened by the power of God when the trump shall sound" (Mormon 9:13).

Heights and Depths

As waking comes out of sleep, so heights are reached out of the depths. This again gives concrete meaning to the process of redemption.[25] When the Jaredites go through submersion in the depths of the ocean to reach the promised land, it is both a literal process and a symbol of salvation. The redeemed Alma declares, "I was in the darkest abyss; but now I behold the marvelous light of God" (Mosiah 27:29).

High places are usually holy but can at times be unholy. Nephi is caught up to "an exceedingly high mountain" (1 Nephi 11:1) to receive an expansive revelation; later, he is directed by the Liahona to go to the top of the mountain for game, for instructions on building a ship, and to pray. On the other hand, the total wars of the Jaredites and the Nephites-Lamanites culminate at a mountain (Ramah/Cumorah). While expressing deep humility, King Benjamin speaks to his people from the top of a tower. Yet the prideful Zoramites go one by one to the top of their Rameumptom, or "holy stand" (Alma 31:21), to express their vaunting prayer.[26]

Literally or figuratively, rising or falling in the Book of Mormon shows the relation of humans to God. Sherem, the antichrist who challenges Jacob, dramatizes the fall of man. He says his will, not God's, should be done. He boasts about himself and denies the atonement of Christ. Jacob is just the opposite. He calls for God's will, not his own, to be done, humbles himself, and affirms the atonement of Christ. When Sherem continues to deny the power of God, "the power of the Lord [comes] upon him, insomuch that he [falls] to the earth"

(Jacob 7:15). This is a damning fall of man, not one with potential salvation. After the people see Sherem die, confessing his sins, they in turn fall to the earth (Jacob 7:21). This fall, though, leads the way to their having "peace and the love of God" restored (Jacob 7:23).

The Nephite people, who had reached such heights in their civilization, fall to the lowest depths. Their fall brings Mormon's great cry of the heart: "O ye fair ones, how could ye have rejected . . . Jesus . . . ! Behold, if ye had not done this, ye would not have fallen. But behold, ye are fallen, and I mourn your loss" (Mormon 6:17–18). Mormon has hope for his son, though, and counsels him not to let "the things which I have written grieve thee, to *weigh thee down* unto death; but may Christ *lift thee up,* and may his sufferings and death . . . rest in your mind forever" (Moroni 9:25; see also 3 Nephi 27:4). This points to a central irony in the Book of Mormon concerning ascent and descent: It is only through the condescension of the Savior—his descending to the level of humanity and then suffering ignominy on the cross—(1 Nephi 11:16–33) that his people can be lifted up.

Temples, Tents, and Palaces

Wealth and poverty are a number of times connected in the Book of Mormon with three primary kinds of buildings: temples, tents, and palaces. In Lehi's vision, the palace is a "great and spacious building," symbolic of the wisdom and pride of the world, filled with people whose "manner of dress was exceeding fine" (1 Nephi 8:26–27). Later in the Book of Mormon this structure is made specific in the "spacious palace" wicked King Noah has built and ornamented "with gold and silver and with precious things" (Mosiah 11:9).

By contrast, father Lehi abandons his fine home with its treasures to depart into the wilderness. Nephi understates this sacrifice with the simple but meaningful declaration, "And my father dwelt in a tent" (1 Nephi 2:15). A temporary structure, a tent symbolizes Lehi's willingness to go wherever the Lord dictates;

further, there are scriptural parallels that identify tents with temples.[27] There is force in Nephi's repeated references to Lehi's tent—as though it stands for sacred space in contrast with the corrupted Jerusalem they have left behind. After he relates Lehi's vision of the mists of darkness, the great and spacious building, and the tree of life (another symbol of the temple), Nephi says, "And all these things did my father see, and hear, and speak, as he dwelt in a tent" (1 Nephi 9:1). Again, "All these things, of which I have spoken, were done as my father dwelt in a tent" (1 Nephi 10:16; see also 1 Nephi 16:6). As a location in which he receives and declares revelation, Lehi's tent is also a sanctified place.

After Lehi's family reaches the promised land, the Lamanites are noted for continuing to live in tents in the wilderness. The Nephites, though, build more permanent structures, particularly temples. The temple then becomes a positive gathering place, especially for the crowds who respond to King Benjamin's address and for those who behold Christ descend from heaven.[28]

Clothes

Wealth and poverty are also connected with clothes or the absence of clothes. Pride, the prevailing sin of Book of Mormon peoples, is presented imagistically in the silks and fine-twined linens prosperous Nephites find so attractive. By contrast, humility is suggested in the white robe worn by John the apostle and by Christ. And we are reminded several times of the paradox that the Saints' garments are made white in the blood of Christ (for example, 1 Nephi 12:10; Alma 5:21; 13:11).

Jacob opposes prideful sinfulness by taking off his garments and symbolically shaking them free of the iniquities of his auditors (2 Nephi 9:44). Alma enjoins his listeners at Zarahemla to be stripped of pride and envy just as they might remove pretentious clothing (Alma 5:22–29). Moroni says his audience loves money and fine apparel more than they love the poor and the needy. He then challenges them: "Why do ye adorn yourselves with that which hath no life, and yet suffer the hungry, and the needy, and the naked, and the sick and the afflicted to pass by you, and notice them not?" (Mormon 8:39).

The naked are frequently portrayed as spiritually humble as well as physically poor, and the Book of Mormon prophets constantly exhort their listeners—and readers—to clothe the naked and recognize their own symbolic nakedness before God. On the other hand, the Lamanites, who have stripped off their clothing intentionally (Enos 1:20; Alma 3:5; 43:20), are portrayed as reverting to savagery when they reject the Lord.

Wholeness and Rending

Portions of clothes also figure interestingly in the Book of Mormon. Captain Moroni rallies the people to the cause of liberty by tearing a piece from his coat and writing upon it, "In memory of our God, our religion, and freedom, and our peace, our wives, and our children" (Alma 46:12). He fastens it upon the end of a pole and then goes forth among the people,

> waving the rent part of his garment in the air, that all might see the writing which he had written upon the rent part, and crying with a loud voice, saying: Behold, whosoever will maintain this title upon the land, let them come forth in the strength of the Lord, and enter into a covenant that they will maintain their rights, and their religion, that the Lord God may bless them. (Alma 46:12, 19–20)

In response, the people cast their garments at the feet of Moroni and covenant that God "may cast us at the feet of our enemies, even as we have cast our garments at [Moroni's] feet to be trodden under foot, if we shall fall into transgression" (Alma 46:22). Using a remnant of his coat as a title of liberty, Moroni reminds the people that they are a remnant of Joseph and perhaps fulfill a prophecy of the biblical patriarch Jacob concerning a part of the remnant of the coat of Joseph that was preserved and had not decayed. "Even as this remnant of garment of my son hath been preserved," Moroni quotes Jacob as saying, "so shall a remnant of the seed of my son be preserved by the hand of God, and be taken unto himself, while the remainder of the seed of Joseph shall perish, even as the remnant of his garment" (Alma 46:24).[29]

Not only clothes are rent in the Book of Mormon. In prophetic vision, Nephi sees rocks rent and "mountains tumbling into pieces" (1 Nephi 12:4). Wicked people, we are told, will at the judgment wish for rocks to hide them from God's presence (Alma 12:14). It is prophesied that at the death of Christ the Rock, "the rocks which are upon the face of this earth, which are both above the earth and beneath, which ye know at this time are solid, or the more part of it is one solid mass, shall be broken up" (Helaman 14:21). In the fulfillment of this prophecy, at the time of the Crucifixion "the rocks were rent in twain; they were broken up upon the face of the whole earth" (3 Nephi 8:18). On the other hand, in its wholeness a rock is associated with Christ, the rock of salvation (1 Nephi 15:15). We may think of this when reading about Lehi's seeing a pillar of fire upon a rock or about the prophet Ether's hiding in the cavity of a rock. It is upon the rock of the Redeemer and his doctrine we may confidently build (Helaman 5:12; 3 Nephi 11:39–40).

Swords and Other Weapons

The book's paradoxes and wordplay are further illustrated by swords and other weapons. Jaredite swords found by the people of Limhi have blades cankered with rust (Mosiah 8:11). King Lamoni advises his followers to keep their swords bright by hiding them deep in the earth and refusing to stain them with the blood of their brethren. These swords then become "weapons of peace" as their burial keeps the repentant people of Anti-Nephi-Lehi from using them (Alma 24:12–16, 19). Another paradoxical turn on warfare is the method the Lamanites employ to destroy the Gadianton robbers—they preach to them, destroying them by saving them.

Pointing out a lesson from the prosperity of the church at the time of Helaman's sons, Mormon affirms that whosoever wants to can "lay hold upon the word of God, which is quick and powerful, which shall divide asunder all the cunning and the snares and the wiles of the devil" (Helaman 3:29).[30] Here the *word* of God becomes the *sword* of God, and the dividing asunder brings to mind cutting through a jungle with a sword or machete. In this respect we may think of other scriptural statements that "the sword of the Spirit . . . is the word of God" (Ephesians 6:17) and "the word of God is . . . sharper than any two-edged sword" (Hebrews 4:12).

Another play on *word* and *sword* is found in the confrontation between Nehor and Gideon. Because Gideon withstood Nehor "with the words of God," Nehor "drew his sword and began to smite him" (Alma 1:9). For this action, Nehor was condemned to death, and he acknowledged that what he taught was "contrary to the word of God" (Alma 1:15). After that, the people of Nehor did not dare to murder but still persecuted the people of the church of God "and did afflict them with all manner of words" (Alma 1:20).

Word and sword are connected in Alma's experience. Mormon observes that the preaching of the word "had had more powerful effect upon the minds of the people than the sword, or anything else, which had happened unto them—therefore Alma thought it was expedient that they should try the virtue of the word of God" (Alma 31:5).

Wordplay on weapons is developed pointedly by Jacob in Jacob 2. He laments that his words to the women and children will be not "the pleasing word of God" that "healeth the wounded soul" but sharp admonitions to offending men that for their wives and children will be like "daggers placed to *pierce* their souls and wound their delicate minds" (Jacob 2:8–9). Those offenders, Jacob says, are "under the glance of the *piercing* eye of the Almighty God. . . . O that he would show you that he can *pierce* you, and with one glance of his eye he can smite you to the dust!" (Jacob 2:10, 15). In an ironic turnaround, the adulterers who cause many hearts to die, "pierced with deep wounds," are under the piercing eye of God and can be thrust through to their own deaths (Jacob 2:35).

The sharp weapon featured most strikingly in the Book of Mormon is the sword of Laban. It is no ordinary sword. Nephi describes it in detail: "The hilt thereof was of pure gold, and the workmanship thereof was exceedingly fine, and I saw that the blade thereof was of the most precious steel" (1 Nephi 4:9). Nephi first uses it—at the Spirit's insistence—to keep the descendants of Lehi from perishing in unbelief (1 Nephi 4:13). Then he says that he modeled swords after the sword of Laban so his people would not be destroyed (2 Nephi 5:14). The people loved Nephi greatly, "he having been a great protector for them, having wielded the sword of Laban in their defence" (Jacob 1:10). Another great prophet-king, Benjamin, defensively stands at the head of his armies as their champion, "and he did fight with the strength of his own arm, with the sword of Laban." Afterwards, he leads other holy prophets in putting down contention and dissensions and in establishing peace by speaking "the word of God with power and with authority" and with "much sharpness" (Words of Mormon 1:13, 17).

This last subtle connection between the effectiveness of the sword of Laban and the sharpness of the word of God suggests the connections found elsewhere between the sword of Laban and the scriptures. Nephi tells of bringing with him to the land of Nephi the plates of brass, the compass (the Liahona), and the sword of Laban. In addition to the brass plates and the plates of Nephi, King Benjamin gives his son the sword of Laban and the Liahona, "which led [their] fathers through the wilderness" (Mosiah 1:16). Subsequent prophets continue to transmit these three items, as confirmed by the experience of the Three Witnesses: They are promised that the sacred items they shall see are the plates, the breastplate, the sword of Laban, the Urim and Thummim, and the Liahona (D&C 17:1). As for the Liahona,

Alma teaches his son Helaman (Alma 37) that it is a type of the word of Christ in that both help preserve the people and lead them to the promised land. Just as the sword of Laban is noted for its "exceedingly fine" workmanship (1 Nephi 4:9), so the Liahona is of "curious workmanship" (1 Nephi 16:10; see also Alma 37:39). Handled by an authorized servant of the Lord, each is a means of preserving the people. There will come a time, though, when neither is needed. During the Millennium, under Christ's reign of peace, swords will be beaten into plowshares (2 Nephi 12:4; Isaiah 2:4); the written word will be added to by direct revelation from the personally reigning Word.

Overview of Image Patterns as a Whole

After looking at single images and groups of images, it is appropriate that we look at imagery in the Book of Mormon as a whole. The work of the eminent literary critic Northrop Frye is helpful in this regard. We can readily apply to the Book of Mormon the kind of unified structure of significantly repeated images Frye finds in the Bible. In *The Great Code: The Bible and Literature,* Frye places biblical imagery into two main categories: the apocalyptic, which means the ideal world that the human creative imagination envisages; and the demonic. Apocalyptic paradisiacal imagery such as the Edenic tree of life has its demonic counterpart in a wasteland and sea of death; animal imagery such as the lamb in a flock has its demonic counterpart in beasts of prey; vegetable imagery of bread and wine is opposed by the harvest and vintage of wrath; and mineral imagery of a fortified city becomes demonic in the rubble of a destroyed city.

Seen from this angle, the apocalyptic image in the Book of Mormon of the tree rooted in the soil has a demonic counterpart in the unnatural building elevated above the ground. Further, against the living water near the tree is the stream of filthy water in which wanderers drown. Also in demonic counterpart to the tree of life, which is reminiscent of a mideastern oasis, is the "dark and dreary wilderness" persons must go through to reach the tree (1 Nephi 8:4).[31] The "great and spacious building" in its prideful elevation in the air (1 Nephi 8:26) is contrasted with Jesus' teachings on the importance of building on the rock.

After having settled in the promised land, the Nephites become associated primarily with pastoral apocalyptic imagery: they build cities and temples, tend their flocks and their fields, and are rewarded with harvests (except in times of war or drought brought on by wickedness). The Lamanites, on the other hand, are described by Enos as extremely degraded, being "led by their evil nature that they became wild, and ferocious, and a blood-thirsty people, full of idolatry and filthiness; feeding upon beasts of prey" (Enos 1:20).

The experience of Enos is a parable for the later conversion of many of these ferocious Lamanites. He goes "to hunt beasts in the forests," presumably for food, when he recollects the words of his father "concerning eternal life" (Enos 1:3). He thus discovers his need for spiritual food: "And my soul hungered," he says (Enos 1:4). Recognizing his soul's hunger, Enos fasts and prays all day and into the night. In answer to his prayer, he hears a voice forgiving him of his sins and instructing him concerning the future of the land. Then, in contrast with the idleness suggested in Enos's description of the Lamanites, he prays and labors "with all diligence" on behalf of the Lamanites, "that, perhaps, they might be brought unto salvation" (Enos 1:12–13). Enos and his compatriots are not successful in their efforts with the Lamanites, but from the time of his conversion he lives an exemplary life as a prophet among the Nephites who, by contrast with the Lamanites, "till the land, and raise all manner of grain, and of fruit, and flocks of herds, and flocks of all manner of cattle of every kind, and goats, and wild goats, and also many horses" (Enos 1:21). Then when the conversion of the Lamanites does come, under the missionary efforts of Ammon and the other sons of Mosiah, the converted people of Anti-Nephi-Lehi follow the pattern implicit in the story of Enos: They give up bloodshed of every kind, settle as farmers and herdsmen in Nephite territory, and are generous in their concern for others.

As for the mineral imagery of the city, the Book of Mormon sets up dramatic contrasts of the apocalyptic and the demonic. The destruction of Jerusalem is the original example of the later destruction of great cities. The wealthy but wicked city of Ammonihah, from which Alma was cast out, is destroyed in a day—and is then called Desolation of Nehors. The divine voice in 3 Nephi 9 declares a list of ruined cities. The first three the voice mentions have been destroyed by the elements of fire, water, and earth:

> Behold, that great city Zarahemla have I burned with fire, and the inhabitants thereof. And behold, that great city Moroni have I caused to be sunk in the depths of the sea, and the inhabitants thereof to be drowned. And behold, that great city Moronihah have I covered with earth, and the inhabitants thereof, to hide their iniquities and their abominations from before my face, that the blood of the prophets and the saints shall not come any more unto me against them. (3 Nephi 9:3–5)

Following the chaotic destruction of the demonic cities, the apocalyptic—that is, the divine—is asserted in a gathering of people "round about the temple which was in the land Bountiful" (3 Nephi 11:1).

IMAGERY FOR THE CHILDREN OF LEHI

The Book of Mormon is full of reversals: Good people rapidly become wicked, disbelievers are converted, those with hard hearts lose knowledge, and the ignorant are enlightened. To descendants of Lehi who might think of themselves as "cast off" from God (title page), there is comfort in Moroni's encouragement to his "brethren, the Lamanites" that they "come unto Christ, and be perfected in him" (Moroni 10:1, 32). That is a principal message of the Book of Mormon as a whole. It is not just stated, however, but shown. Literary devices such as image patterns can teach and motivate on a level that is apprehended by the senses. Especially the basic images of fire, light and darkness, captivity and deliverance, wilderness or wandering, water or fruitfulness, and dust might well appeal strongly to a living descendant of Lehi.

The Book of Mormon tells us that down through time the Lamanites would be scourged, including by fire. Under other circumstances, however, fire can purify and bless the Lamanites. This concept is demonstrated well in the imprisonment of the brothers Nephi and Lehi. The names of the brothers are particularly appropriate because they represent the "fathers" (title page) to the Lamanites. In their ignorance, the Lamanites at first want to put Nephi and Lehi to death. The Lamanites, however, are unlike the apostates described in Alma 14 who are crushed to death by a collapsing prison after they persist in trying to kill Alma and Amulek. Feeling imperiled by the shaking earth and frightened by the voice that speaks to them three times, the Lamanites ask the crucial question: "What shall we do, that this cloud of darkness may be removed from overshadowing us?" (Helaman 5:40). The answer is "Repent . . . until ye shall have faith in Christ" (Helaman 5:41). Doing so, they are brought into the light, and each is encircled about by a pillar of fire (signifying the Holy Ghost). Undoubtedly this was the incident the Savior meant when he said that the Lamanites at the time of their conversion "were baptized with fire and with the Holy Ghost, and they knew it not" (3 Nephi 9:20).

This event is a pattern of conversion. It points back to the spiritual darkness of the Lamanites during their first centuries in the promised land, anticipates the darkness and the thrice-repeated voice from heaven before the Savior's descent at Bountiful, and shows how Nephi's predictions are to be fulfilled. Nephi affirmed that latter-day Lamanites will hear the gospel of Jesus Christ and thus shall be restored unto the knowledge of their fathers, and also to the knowledge of Jesus Christ, which was had among their fathers. And then shall they rejoice; for they shall know that it is a blessing unto them from the hand of God; and their scales of darkness shall begin to fall from their eyes; and many generations shall not pass away among them, save they shall be a pure and a delightsome people. (2 Nephi 30:5–6)

With respect to the image cluster pertaining to captivity, the Book of Mormon shows that those who have hardened their hearts to the truth are in spiritual captivity. Lehi specifically refers to this kind of captivity in speaking to the latter-day posterity of Laman and Lemuel: "I have feared . . . that a cursing should come upon you for the space of many generations; and ye are visited by sword, and by famine, and are hated, and are led according to the will and *captivity* of the devil" (2 Nephi 1:17–18). People in that condition may gain heart by the pattern of deliverance imagery in the Book of Mormon.

In like manner, the Book of Mormon provides hope to a people who for many generations have inhabited the wilderness—both physically and spiritually. Through feeling as well as understanding the teachings and emotional emphases of the Book of Mormon, latter-day Lamanites may be brought to the condition of the Anti-Nephi-Lehies, an enlightened people who supported themselves by cultivating their lands. They may also be like the Lamanites who greeted the resurrected Christ at the temple.

Lehi challenged his Lamanite posterity in the latter days: "Awake, my sons; put on the armor of righteousness. Shake off the chains with which ye are bound, and come forth out of obscurity, and arise from the dust" (2 Nephi 1:23). Their renewal will come from feasting on the words of life that will come "out of the dust" (2 Nephi 26:16). In other words, latter-day Lamanites shall obtain renewal through repentance from a voice considered dead. Life will come out of death, and words of eternal life will be spoken by the voice out of the dust.

"That Jesus Is the Christ"
TYPOLOGY

Essentially every event or person in the Book of Mormon may well remind us of another event or person; the book is like a beautifully composed symphony with repeated themes and motifs. Reference to the deliverance of Lehi and his family from Jerusalem evokes the deliverance of Israel from Egypt. We are reminded of Noah by Lehi, of Joseph the Patriarch by Joseph the son of Lehi, and of Captain Moroni by Moroni the son of Mormon. Most significantly, all God-given events or God-directed persons in the Book of Mormon are reminders of Jesus Christ or his gospel. This is Nephi's point in saying, "Behold, my soul delighteth in proving unto my people the truth of the coming of Christ; for, for this end hath the law of Moses been given; and all things which have been given of God from the beginning of the world, unto man, are the typifying of him" (2 Nephi 11:4).[1] Abinadi says that all performances and ordinances of the law of Moses "were types of things to come" (Mosiah 13:31). Through their being types, the "things which have been given of God" in the Book of Mormon testify that Jesus is the Christ.

By "typifying" or "types," Nephi and Abinadi mean a likeness of Christ or something pertaining to him. That which is represented (for example, Christ) is the antitype. We might think of a type being the printed impression left on a sheet of paper and the antitype being the solid piece of metal or wood with a raised character on it used in making the impression. Similarly, a scriptural shadow could be compared to a tree's shadow, which in its shape is somewhat like the tree itself. A familiar type of the sacrifice of Jesus Christ is the intended sacrifice of Isaac by Abraham. Nephi's brother Jacob puts it this way: "And for this intent we keep the law of Moses, it pointing our souls to [Christ]; and for this cause it is sanctified unto us for righteousness, even as it was accounted unto Abraham in the wilderness to be obedient unto the commands of God in offering up his son Isaac, which is a similitude of God and his Only Begotten Son" (Jacob 4:5). Again, Moses' lifting up a brass serpent to heal the people was a type of Christ's being lifted up on the cross. "And behold a type was raised up in the wilderness," Alma taught the Zoramites, "that whosoever would look upon it might live. And many did look and live" (Alma 33:19).[2]

"Everything that happens in the Old Testament," says Northrop Frye,

> is a "type" or adumbration of something that happens in the New Testament, and the whole subject is therefore called typology. . . . Paul speaks in Romans 5:14 of Adam as a *typos* of Christ. . . . What happens in the New Testament constitutes an "antitype," a realized form, of something foreshadowed in the Old Testament. In I Peter 3:21, Christian baptism is called the *antitypos* of the saving of mankind from the flood of Noah.[3]

Frye goes on to say that typology

> is a figure of speech that moves in time: the type exists in the past and the antitype in the present, or the type exists in the present and the antitype in the future. What typology really is as a mode of thought, what it both assumes and leads to, is a theory of history, or more accurately of historical process: an assumption that there is some meaning and point to history, and that sooner or later some event or events will occur which will indicate what that meaning or point is, and so become an antitype of what has happened previously.[4]

Erich Auerbach in his essay "Figura" explains typology as a connection between two events or persons separate in time, "the

197

first of which signifies not only itself but also the second, while the second encompasses or fulfills the first." They exist in history, with promise and fulfillment being "real historical events." An understanding of the typological connection, Auerbach says, is "a spiritual act."[5]

Although typology in the Book of Mormon fits these definitions by Frye and Auerbach, there is also in the book a time structure in which a type exists in the past and the antitype in the future. The nature and purpose of this kind of type are clearly developed in Alma's reminder to the people of Ammonihah that

> the Lord God ordained priests, after his holy order, which was after the order of his Son, to teach these things unto the people. And those priests were ordained after the order of his Son, in a manner that thereby the people might know in what manner to look forward to his Son for redemption. And this is the manner after which they were ordained—being called and prepared from the foundation of the world according to the foreknowledge of God. . . . Now these ordinances were given after this manner, that thereby the people might look forward on the Son of God, it being a type of his order, or it being his order, and this that they might look forward to him for a remission of their sins, that they might enter into the rest of the Lord. (Alma 13:1–3, 16)

Typologically, those who received the Melchizedek Priesthood were "called and prepared from the foundation of the world," as was Jesus Christ (see also 1 Peter 1:20; Revelation 13:8). Detailed aspects of their ordination showed them the manner in which to look forward to Christ for redemption. And the priesthood they received was a type of Christ's order as well as his order itself.

The clearest explanation of typology in the Book of Mormon is Alma's enlightenment of his son Helaman regarding the Liahona, or compass, prepared by the Lord. First, Alma reviews how the "fathers" forgot to exercise their faith and therefore "tarried in the wilderness, or did not travel a direct course, and were

afflicted with hunger and thirst, because of their transgressions."
He continues,

> And now, my son, I would that ye should understand that these
> things are not without a shadow; for as our fathers were slothful to
> give heed to this compass (now these things were temporal) they
> did not prosper; even so it is with things which are spiritual. For
> behold, it is as easy to give heed to the word of Christ, which will
> point to you a straight course to eternal bliss, as it was for our
> fathers to give heed to this compass, which would point unto
> them a straight course to the promised land. And now I say, is
> there not a type in this thing? For just as surely as this director did
> bring our fathers, by following its course, to the promised land,
> shall the words of Christ, if we follow their course, carry us
> beyond this vale of sorrow into a far better land of promise. (Alma
> 37:42–45)

This is a textbook example of a type: according to the definitions of a type provided by various scholars, the type Alma
speaks of "exists in history and its meaning is factual"; it is "a
prophetic symbol . . . fixed at both of its poles of reference"; it
shows "evidence of the Divine *intention* in the correspondence
between it and the Antitype"; and it "was instituted to perform a
specific function in God's grand design." As with some types, it
also relates to "the progress of the individual soul through the
stages leading to redemption."[6]

Not only things that are alike may be paired as type and
antitype but opposite things may be as well: "We speak concerning the law," Nephi says, "that our children may know the
deadness of the law; and they, by knowing the *deadness* of the
law, may look forward unto that *life* which is in Christ, and
know for what end the law was given" (2 Nephi 25:27).

TYPOLOGICAL CONCEPTION OF HISTORY

In their conception of history, Book of Mormon prophets
consider types as significant, instructive, and persuasive in focusing on Christ's earthly advent, his visit to the Nephites, and his

second coming and heavenly kingdom. Nephi, for example, prophesies clearly of Christ and affirms that "as the Lord God liveth that brought Israel up out of the land of Egypt, . . . there is none other name given under heaven save it be this Jesus Christ . . . whereby man can be saved" (2 Nephi 25:20). In other words, the physical salvation of Israel from Egypt is a type of spiritual salvation by Christ. Faith sustained by the first develops faith in the second. King Benjamin preaches Christ directly but at the same time speaks of indirect likenesses of Christ: "And many signs, and wonders, and types, and shadows showed [Jehovah] unto [the Israelites under Moses], concerning his coming" (Mosiah 3:15). Abinadi before King Noah's court insists, "If ye teach the law of Moses, also teach that it is a shadow of those things which are to come" (Mosiah 16:14). Amulek teaches that "this is the whole meaning of the law, every whit pointing to that great and last sacrifice" (Alma 34:14). And Mormon says that the Anti-Nephi-Lehies "did look forward to the coming of Christ, considering that the law of Moses was a type of his coming. . . . Now they did not suppose that salvation came by the law of Moses; but the law of Moses did serve to strengthen their faith in Christ" (Alma 25:15–16).

Erich Auerbach in his *Mimesis: The Representation of Reality in Western Literature* sees a conception of history such as this as being structured vertically rather than horizontally. Two events are horizontal to each other if they are linked by time or causality. A vertical connection, however, "can be established only if both occurrences are vertically linked to divine Providence." God alone "is able to devise such a plan of history and supply the key to its understanding." Auerbach gives as an example of such a "figural interpretation" the sacrifice of Isaac as prefiguring the sacrifice of Christ. With Isaac the type and Christ the antitype, "in the former the latter is as it were announced and promised, and the latter 'fulfills' . . . the former." With typology, "the here and now is no longer a mere link in an earthly chain of events, it is simultaneously something which has always been, and which will be fulfilled in the future; and strictly, in the eyes of God, it is something eternal."[7]

This eternal perspective is illustrated especially well in Moroni's harking back to Nephite origins through the prophecies of Ether. In what Moroni initially thought would be his last word, he gives in a few verses a sweeping view of the role of his people in divine history. He quotes Ether as declaring that the promised land is "the place of the New Jerusalem, which should come down out of heaven, and the holy sanctuary of the Lord" (Ether 13:3). He then cites Ether's reference to the type, which is the Jerusalem from which Lehi should come and that would be built up again. Then he quotes Ether's declaration that

> a New Jerusalem should be built upon this land, unto the remnant of the seed of Joseph, for which things there has been a type. For as Joseph brought his father down into the land of Egypt, even so he died there; wherefore, the Lord brought a remnant of the seed of Joseph out of the land of Jerusalem, that he might be merciful unto the seed of Joseph that they should perish not, even as he was merciful unto the father of Joseph that he should perish not. Wherefore, the remnant of the house of Joseph shall be built upon this land . . . and they shall build up a holy city unto the Lord, like unto the Jerusalem of old. . . . And there shall be a new heaven and a new earth; and they shall be like unto the old save the old have passed away, and all things have become new. (Ether 13:6–9)

PURPOSE OF TYPES

From a religious-aesthetic perspective, types have a purpose similar to that of symbols, of which they may be considered a part—although symbols are open-ended, whereas types are fixed on both ends. Jonathan Edwards in "Types of the Messiah" says,

> The principles of human nature render TYPES a fit method of instruction. It tends to enlighten and illustrate, and to convey instruction with impression, conviction, and pleasure, and to help the memory. These things are confirmed by man's natural delight

in the imitative arts, in painting, poetry, fables, metaphorical language and dramatic performances.[8]

Hugh Nibley in "The Expanding Gospel" quotes the Gospel of Philip as saying, "Truth did not come into the world naked, but she came clothed in types and images. One cannot receive the truth in any other way."[9] Bruce R. McConkie affirms:

> To crystallize on our minds the eternal verities which we must accept and believe to be saved, to dramatize their true meaning and import with an impact never to be forgotten, to center our attention on these saving truths, again and again and again, the Lord uses similitudes. Abstract principles may easily be forgotten or their deep meaning overlooked, but visual performances and actual experiences are registered on the mind in such a way as never to be lost. It is one thing to talk of faith as an abstract principle, another to see the Red Sea parted by its power. It is one thing to talk of the word of God coming down from heaven, another to actually gather and taste the angelic manna. . . . [God] uses ordinances, rites, acts, and performances; he uses similarities, resemblances, and similitudes so that whatever is done will remind all who are aware of it of a greater and more important reality.[10]

It is this greater and more important reality that the Book of Mormon develops typologically, focusing on the affirmation that "JESUS is the CHRIST, the ETERNAL GOD, manifesting himself unto all nations" (title page). This is part of the consecrated life, seeing all divinely given things as a testimony of God and his purposes.

PERSONS AS TYPES

In both the Old Testament and the Book of Mormon, Joseph is a notable type of Christ.[11] The beloved son of his father, Joseph was stripped of his robe, thrown in a pit, betrayed and rejected by his brethren, and unjustly imprisoned. The name *Joseph* relates to Hebrew roots meaning "to add" and "to take away." In addition, Hugh Nibley quotes a Hebrew authority as saying that "*asaf* is 'sorrow' in that language, and that *asif* is 'servant,' and that the two are combined in the name of Joseph."[12]

Thus Joseph's name may also mean "sorrowing or suffering servant." In that capacity he came out of "burial" in prison to preserve for his brethren "a posterity in the earth, and to save [their] lives by a great deliverance" (Genesis 45:7). Both Joseph the man and Joseph the people are types repeated in the Book of Mormon. For instance, Lehi evokes the person and prophecies of Joseph the Patriarch in his blessing to his own son Joseph (2 Nephi 3). Captain Moroni rallies his people, "a remnant of the seed of Joseph," by reminding them how "a part of the remnant of the coat of Joseph was preserved and had not decayed." That led to Jacob's prophecy, "Even as this remnant of garment of my son hath been preserved, so shall a remnant of the seed of my son be preserved by the hand of God, and be taken unto himself, while the remainder of the seed of Joseph shall perish, even as the remnant of his garment" (Alma 46:23–24).[13]

Like Joseph, Nephi is a suffering servant, is resisted by older brothers who do not want him to be a ruler over them, is bound and threatened with death, fulfills his father's mission, and helps preserve the lives of those who earlier tried to take his life. Desiring to "be strong like unto Moses" (1 Nephi 4:2), he several times likens his situation to Moses'; his brothers dare not touch him because of the power of God within him; and like Moses he guides his people towards the promised land. Nephi's breaking the bonds put on him by his brothers is a type of the deliverance of the Nephites from the hands of their brethren, the Lamanites, in the promised land: "O Lord," Nephi prays, "according to my faith which is in thee, wilt thou deliver me from the hands of my brethren" (1 Nephi 7:17). Stilling the storm, as does Christ, Nephi is also directly like him in being an obedient son, a forgiving brother, a skillful carpenter, and a pilot.

Mosiah is like Moses and Lehi in leading his people into the wilderness (Omni 1:12). And in leading people out of a wicked or oppressive place, all three of these prophets are like Christ. Mosiah's son Benjamin also typifies Christ as an earthly king in the likeness of the heavenly King. Like the Christ to come,

Benjamin "was a holy man, and he did reign over his people in righteousness" (Words of Mormon 1:17). The typological connection is suggested by Benjamin himself. He reminds his people that if he "who has spent his days in [their] service, and yet has been in the service of God, [merits] any thanks from [them], O how [they] ought to thank [their] heavenly King" (Mosiah 2:19).

Abinadi is like Christ both indirectly and directly: "His face shone with exceeding luster, even as Moses' did while in the mount of Sinai" (compare this with the luster of Christ at the Transfiguration and in Lehi's first vision); he is cast into prison for three days; his persecutors shed his innocent blood; and at death, Abinadi cries, "O God, receive my soul" (Mosiah 13:5; 17:6, 10, 19).

Alma the Elder leads his flock into and then out of the wilderness, as do Moses, Lehi, and Mosiah. As a righteous judge, he prefigures Christ, the "Eternal Judge of both quick and dead" (Moroni 10:34). The conversion story of Alma the Younger echoes that of Jonah, of whom Christ said: "For as Jonas was three days and three nights in the whale's belly; so shall the Son of man be three days and three nights in the heart of the earth" (Matthew 12:40). Alma says: "I was three days and three nights in the most bitter pain and anguish of soul; and never, until I did cry out unto the Lord Jesus Christ for mercy, did I receive a remission of my sins"; "I was in the darkest abyss; but now I behold the marvelous light of God" (Alma 38:8; Mosiah 27:29; compare Jonah 1–2). Similarly, Lamoni "lay as if he were dead for the space of two days and two nights" and is followed in his trance by his queen who, upon recovery, declares she is "saved . . . from an awful hell" (Alma 18:43; 19:29).

Ammon is a type of Christ in saving many Lamanites, who were "in darkness, yea, even in the darkest abyss, but . . . are brought to behold the marvelous light of God" (Alma 26:3). And like Moses, Ammon leads his people through the wilderness to a promised land, giving the glory to Christ.[14] In turn, Captain Moroni, who with his standard of liberty demonstrates a type of the remnant of Joseph, is "a man like unto Ammon, the son of Mosiah, yea, and even the other sons of Mosiah, yea, and also Alma and his sons," who are "men of God" (Alma 46:24; 48:18).

The brothers Nephi and Lehi also have several experiences that prefigure Christ, or hark back to other types of Christ. When they are imprisoned and threatened with death by the Lamanites, they are preserved by a pillar of fire that encircles them (Helaman 5:23–24). That pillar of fire recalls the pillar of fire and cloud that accompanied the Israelites in the wilderness, which pillar the Israelites were told represented the presence of their God (Exodus 13:21). The fire also anticipates the pillar with which the Nephite children are encircled after the Savior blesses them (3 Nephi 17:24). The people within the prison walls hear a voice three times calling them to repentance and see Nephi's and Lehi's countenances shining as they converse with angels. When they call on Christ for forgiveness, the darkness around them disperses and they are themselves surrounded with the pillar of fire. Their experience anticipates the experience of the people spared destruction following the crucifixion of Christ. After three days of darkness, the remaining people gather at the temple, where a voice from heaven speaks to them. On the third time they hear the voice, they understand the words and remember the prophecies of the coming of Christ (3 Nephi 11). Nephi himself, like Moses, tries to prepare his people for this coming of Christ and, like Moses, sorrows that his prophecies have been denied (Helaman 8:11–13).

We also find categories of persons serving as types. Prophets speak by "the tongue of angels," and angels "speak the words of Christ" (2 Nephi 31:13; 32:3). Book of Mormon judges are in a likeness of Christ, the "Eternal Judge of both quick and dead" (Moroni 10:34), whose role is affirmed by both Nephi and Moroni in their parting testimonies. Such high priests as Alma and his posterity prefigure Christ, the great high priest, as clarified by Alma in his discourse on the Melchizedek Priesthood (Alma 13).

TYPOLOGICAL OBJECTS OR EVENTS

The sixteen stones gathered by the brother of Jared are typological objects like the Liahona. They "shine forth in darkness" (Ether 3:4), reminding us of the Lord's affirmation to Nephi, "I will also be your light in the wilderness," and of his later declaration, "I am the light of the world" (1 Nephi 17:13; John 8:12). With such a light, travelers are never in darkness.

Related to everlasting light is the pillar of fire seen by Lehi (1 Nephi 1:6). This memorable and dramatic type of Christ is like the pillars of fire in Helaman 5 and 3 Nephi 17. We may see them as representing or containing the God who "is a consuming fire" (Hebrews 12:29). As has been discussed, this fire can be either purifying or destroying. The righteous are baptized with fire and with the Holy Ghost, receive a remission of sins by fire, make their sacrifice—through purifying spiritual fire—of a broken heart and a contrite spirit instead of burnt offerings, are visited by a divine person "like a refiner's fire," and as part of that experience are "encircled about as if it were by fire" (3 Nephi 24:2; 19:14; see also 2 Nephi 31:17; 3 Nephi 9:19–20). But if the righteous shall be saved by fire, Mormon testifies that at the last judgment the unregenerate will be punished with unquenchable fire (Mormon 7:10; 9:5). Fire and brimstone are frequently presented as figurative torments; literal fire destroys Zarahemla, Jacobugath, and Kishkumen, which are described as extremely wicked (3 Nephi 9:9–10). These burned cities also represent the wicked places that will be destroyed at the end of time when "the world shall be burned with fire" (Jacob 6:3).

Directed or lighted by objects requiring faith for their operation, Nephi's ship and the Jaredite barges are connected with Noah's ark in being types of rebirth and baptism (1 Peter 3:20–21); further, the Jaredite vessels "were tight like unto the ark of Noah" (Ether 6:7). They all bring the occupants *through* the water into a new life, representing in the process the death, burial, and resurrection of Christ (Colossians 2:12). Or, reminiscent of Jonah, the Jaredites in their vessels, like "a whale in the midst of the sea," are "buried in the depths of the sea" (Ether 2:24; 6:6). This is part of a significant pattern woven throughout the Book of Mormon regarding outcasts of the world, who always consider themselves strangers and pilgrims (for example, Jacob 7:26; Alma 13:23). They wander through the wilderness or through darkness to escape destruction and to find a promised land—consider the Jaredites, Lehites, Zeniff, Limhi, Alma, and Ammon. They are miraculously brought through darkness and tribulation or are released from prison or servitude in a process that can also bring repentance. The darkness or death-in-life is several times described as lasting three days, the most notable example being the vapor of darkness following the great earthquake before Christ's coming (3 Nephi 8). There may be a voice out of heaven that calls for repentance and promises new life (Helaman 5:29; 3 Nephi 9). Then the "wanderers in a strange land" (Alma 13:23) whether they have been on an actual journey or not, are delivered into a promised land of light and fertility. (The Lehites plant seeds in the new land and bring forth the abundance of the earth [1 Nephi 18:24].) The ultimate journey, of which this is a type, is to the heavenly promised land. Mortals wander through life, often losing their way, and find direction to eternal life through the atonement of Christ, who is the way. (John 14:6: "I am the way, the truth, and the life.")

The process of being led out of bondage or away from destruction to a promised land could well be called an Exodus pattern. It is clear, as George Tate shows with much support, "that Nephi is conscious of replicating Exodus and that he reads texts and visions figurally."[15] In the remainder of the Book of Mormon, the pattern recurs with implications for individuals as well as communities. Redemption experiences in the Book of Mormon reenact the Exodus. The process is one of deliverance from worldliness (Egypt), rebirth, and trial to prove worthiness. As a summary of this pattern, Tate cites Alma's declaration that "God has delivered me from prison, and from bonds, . . . and he will still deliver me. . . . for he has brought our fathers out of Egypt, . . . and he has delivered them out of bondage and captivity from time to time. Yea, and he has also brought our fathers out of the land of Jerusalem; and he has also, by his everlasting power, delivered them out of bondage and captivity" (Alma 36:27–29). In sum, Tate asserts that

> in the Old Testament portion of the Book of Mormon, the Exodus pattern recurs in greater concentration than in the Bible, and its typology is more conscious because the narrators are understood to possess the Christological key to the fulfillment of the types from Nephi's vision forward, a fulfillment underscored by the patterning of 3 Nephi around the Exodus. The Exodus reverberates through the book, not only as theme but as pattern; and the overall design of the book generalizes the patterning of community in history while at the same time concentrating the Exodus in individual conversion.[16]

Just as deliverance from bondage is a type of Christ, so also is the tabernacle the people built in the wilderness under Moses' direction. Likewise, the temple in the Book of Mormon is a type of Christ. The "mountain of the Lord's house" built by Nephi (2 Nephi 12:2; 5:16) is the place where Jacob, by commandment, declares the word given him by the Lord and serves as the Lord's representative (Jacob 2:2). It is to the temple that King Benjamin's people gather to make holy covenants. In effect, they come unto the Savior. At the temple, King Benjamin gives thanks for deliverance. And the temple is the safe haven around which the multitude are gathered when Christ appears in glory to the Nephites. Here type and antitype converge: "Behold, I am Jesus Christ, whom the prophets testified shall come into the world" (3 Nephi 11:10). Christ emphasizes that he has "come to fulfill the law" (3 Nephi 15:5), as was promised throughout the ages. He says explicitly, "Behold, I am he of whom Moses spake, saying: A prophet shall the Lord your God raise up unto you of your brethren, like unto me" (3 Nephi 20:23).

The elements of wandering, deliverance, and coming unto Christ are all in the tree of life complex of symbolism. Lehi finds himself in a dark and dreary wilderness; through prayer and faith, however, and leadership by a man in a white robe (a Moses-Christ figure), he is led to the tree of life (akin to the heavenly destination). Many are drowned in the depths of the fountain or lost in the mist of darkness, connected for Nephi with the "mist of darkness on the face of the land of promise" that he prophesied would be part of the great destruction preceding the appearance of the Lamb of God (1 Nephi 12:4). The vision foretells the antitype of Christ's appearance, being in himself a fruit white and pure, upon which, Alma says in his version of the tree of life story, "ye shall feast . . . even until ye are filled, that ye hunger not, neither shall ye thirst" (Alma 32:42; see also John 6:35). The vision also projects figuratively the destruction of the Nephite people as a result of pride and temptations, but the full sweep of history on the promised land leads to the restoration of other scripture and to Christ's manifesting himself to all nations (1 Nephi 12:17–19; 13:38–42).

Typology, as we have seen, involves a person or event having some point in common with another. In a book full of events or relationships that are doubled and redoubled, the two prison scenes have special typological significance. Alma and Amulek are faced by murderous Nephites who do not repent and consequently are themselves destroyed; the lives of Nephi and Lehi are threatened by Lamanites who become converted and turn from their murderous intentions. The first experience is a figure of the ultimate destruction of a wicked Nephite nation; the second, a pattern of the conversion of the Lamanites. Nephi and Lehi are cast into the same prison into which the explorer Ammon was cast by the servants of Limhi. This action reminds us that Limhi came close to putting to death the principal instrument of the Lord in leading his people to freedom. Likewise, the Lamanites are incarcerating the prophets who can lead them to spiritual freedom.

Nephi and Lehi stand for the "fathers," for whom, according to the title page of the Book of Mormon, the Lord has done great things, and the heavenly voice penetrating the darkness conveys a message for Lamanites down through time: "Repent ye, repent ye, and seek no more to destroy my servants whom I have sent unto you to declare good tidings" (Helaman 5:29). Feeling imperiled by the shaking earth and frightened by the voice that speaks to them three times, the Lamanites ask the crucial question: "What shall we do, that this cloud of darkness may be removed from overshadowing us?" (Helaman 5:40). The answer is "Repent . . . until ye shall have faith in Christ" (Helaman 5:41). Doing so, they are brought into the light, and each is encircled about by a pillar of fire (signifying the Holy Ghost). This powerfully presented event echoes the Lamanites' previous spiritual darkness and anticipates the darkness and the thrice-repeated voice from heaven before the Savior's descent at Bountiful. As a pattern of conversion of latter-day Lamanites, this event images forth the prediction of Nephi that

> the gospel of Jesus Christ shall be declared among [the remnant of Lehi's seed]; wherefore, they shall be restored unto the knowledge of their fathers, and also to the knowledge of Jesus Christ, which was had among their fathers. And then shall they rejoice; for they shall know that it is a blessing unto them from the hand of God; and their scales of darkness shall begin to fall from their eyes. (2 Nephi 30:5–6)

THE BOOK OF MORMON AS PROPHECY

As we study the book intently, it becomes clear that not only does it contain prophecy and fulfill prophecy but it *is* prophecy. As we have seen, when Moses was instrumental in healing the Israelites through lifting up a brazen serpent, that event was both history and prophecy. The Savior himself attested that the healing power of the raised serpent was a type of his being lifted up on a cross. Likewise, the story of Jonah being swallowed by a whale and then delivered up has significance in itself but perhaps has even more importance as a type of Christ's death, burial, and resurrection.

In a similar manner, events in the Book of Mormon have significance in a later time as well as in the time they occurred. For example, in his farewell to his sons (2 Nephi 1–4:11), Lehi is like Jacob in Genesis 48 in speaking to a people even more than to the individuals standing before him. Thus Lehi's concern in 2 Nephi 1:17 that Laman and Lemuel would be cut off and destroyed forever applies to their family lines. He fears a cursing will come upon them "for the space of many generations" (2 Nephi 1:18); and he challenges them to "come forth out of obscurity" (2 Nephi 1:23), caused by disobedience and by repressions of latter-day Gentiles. Likewise, the Savior in 3 Nephi 20 is addressing a multiple audience: both the Nephites and Lamanites before him and also their descendants living in the end-time. "Then shall ye, who are a remnant of the house of Jacob, go forth" among the Gentiles (3 Nephi 20:16), he says, at a time just before the coming of the New Jerusalem.

According to Moroni's title page, the Book of Mormon is written primarily to the Lamanites, to show them, the "remnant of the House of Israel," what great things the Lord has done for their fathers. As becomes apparent by subsequent references, the "great things" are the events associated with the deliverance of Lehi's family from Jerusalem. The book is also to teach the latter-day Lamanites the covenants of the Lord and to convince them they are not cast off forever. The secondary audiences of the Book of Mormon are the Jews and the Gentiles. To the first of these, the book testifies that "Jesus is the very Christ"; to the second, that "Jesus is the Christ, the Eternal God" (2 Nephi 26:12). As the Savior said to the Nephites regarding the Jews, "The time cometh, when the fulness of my gospel shall be preached unto them; and they shall believe in me, that I am Jesus Christ, the Son of God, and shall pray unto the Father in my name" (3 Nephi 20:30–31). For Gentiles who profess a belief in Jesus but deny his power (Mormon 8:28), the Book of Mormon testifies of a "God of miracles" (Mormon 9:11).

THE PROPHETIC TYPE AND TITHING

The instructions of the resurrected Jesus concerning tithing are given for the benefit of "future generations" (3 Nephi 26:2), especially people who would live before the time of his second coming. Seen in the context of the Book of Mormon as a whole, these instructions have typological significance and explain why those who tithe will not be burned.

Tithing prepares God's people "against the day of vengeance and burning"; "he that is tithed shall not be burned at [the Son of Man's] coming" (D&C 85:3; 64:23). According to the scripture from Malachi that the Savior quotes, burning is the consequence for those who do not tithe. After the Lord challenges his people to bring "tithes into the storehouse" (3 Nephi 24:10), he affirms that "the day cometh that shall burn as an oven; and all the proud, yea, and all that do wickedly, shall be stubble; and the day that cometh shall burn them up" (3 Nephi 25:1). That is the same consequence the Lord speaks of in the Doctrine and Covenants following his promise to tithe payers: "Tomorrow all the proud and they that do wickedly shall be as stubble; and I will burn them up, for I am the Lord of Hosts; and I will not spare any that remain in Babylon" (D&C 64:24).

The reason those who do not tithe could be burned is suggested in the phrase "remain in Babylon." The capital of Babylonia was itself a type of a wicked city, which in the book of Revelation probably denotes Rome or apostate Jerusalem.[17] Modern scripture also designates Babylon as the world (D&C 1:16). At the beginning of the Book of Mormon, Lehi and his family do not remain in Babylon (apostate Jerusalem); also, Lehi, Sariah, Sam, and Nephi choose the way to the tree of life. By contrast, Laman and Lemuel, by implication, choose to enter the great and spacious building—defined as "the pride of the world"

(1 Nephi 11:36). The essential difference is that the first group were tithe payers, and Laman and Lemuel were not. That is, Lehi and some of his family had consecrated all that they had to the Lord and thus were willing to leave behind "gold and silver, and all manner of riches" to follow God's commandment to flee out of Jerusalem, which "must be destroyed," presumably by fire (1 Nephi 3:16–17). Laman and Lemuel, on the other hand, were tied to what they considered to be *their own* "precious things" and sided with murderous Jews in Jerusalem (1 Nephi 2:11, 12).

As Nephi understands, there will come a time when "all the proud and they who do wickedly shall be as stubble; and the day cometh that they must be burned." The righteous, though, will "be preserved." How? They will be saved by a prophet like unto Moses: the Holy One of Israel (1 Nephi 22:15–21). This rescue is repeatedly described as a deliverance of the covenant people (for example, see 2 Nephi 6:17). The Exodus pattern also applies here; that is, a covenant people are in danger and the Lord leads them out. For example, Jacob prophesies to the Nephites that the Lamanites "shall scourge you even unto destruction," and except the Nephites repent, the Lamanites will "possess the land of your inheritance, and *the Lord God will lead away the righteous out from among you*" (Jacob 3:3–4).

The most graphic portrayal of this type is the deliverance of the righteous from Zarahemla followed by the destruction of the city by fire. After the cataclysmic destructions attending Christ's crucifixion, people are heard to cry, "O that we had repented before this great and terrible day, and then would our brethren have been spared, and they would not have been burned in that great city Zarahemla" (3 Nephi 8:24). Zarahemla, along with other cities, was burned with fire because "there were none righteous among them" (3 Nephi 9:11). On the other hand, "it was the more righteous part of the people who were saved, and . . . they were spared . . . and they were not burned by fire" (3 Nephi 10:12–13).

The principle involved here is essentially this: those who were bound to their material goods and ignored or disobeyed God's commandments remained in Jerusalem, Jacobugath, or Zarahemla and were burned. Those who understood tithing and considered themselves simply stewards over what God had given them were ready to leave their homes and material goods and follow their prophets to safety. The primary gathering place for such people was the temple.

Thus the Book of Mormon sets up the type of a people willing to abandon most of their worldly possessions and be gathered to a place of refuge. They are the ones of whom Nephi prophesies, "For the time speedily cometh that the Lord God shall cause a great division among the people, and the wicked will he destroy; and he will spare his people, yea, even if it so be that he must destroy the wicked by fire" (2 Nephi 30:10). This division is similar to the one—accomplished by free choice—of which President Benson spoke in his 1988 prophetic testimony: "As the issues become clearer and more obvious, all mankind will eventually be required to align themselves either for the kingdom of God or for the kingdom of the devil."[18] According to Malachi, as quoted by Jesus, the Lord will spare those who tithe and align themselves with him "as a man spareth his own son that serveth him" (3 Nephi 24:17). "Zion shall escape" if she keeps God's commandments; otherwise, the Lord will "visit her according to all her works, . . . with devouring fire" (D&C 97:25–26). The righteous that "hearken unto the words of the prophets, and . . . look forward unto Christ with steadfastness . . . , they are they which shall not perish" (2 Nephi 26:8).

WARFARE IN THE BOOK OF MORMON
AS A PROPHETIC TYPE

Warfare is part of the history of the Book of Mormon peoples; it is included in the Book of Mormon for purposes that pertain to the people who would receive the book. As a type, it speaks to all those who are "enlisted till the conflict is o'er."[19]

Warfare is a scriptural metaphor for Christian action. The metaphor is found in the standard of liberty (Alma 51:20), in the prophet's mouth being like a sharp sword (Isaiah 49:2; 1 Nephi 21:2), in the sword of justice (Alma 26:19; 60:29), and in the sword of the Lord's Spirit (D&C 27:18). Lehi challenges his sons to "put on the armor of righteousness" (2 Nephi 1:23), just as the Lord's people are to "take unto [them] the whole armour of God"—including the "shield of faith" and the "helmet of salvation" (Ephesians 6:13–17; D&C 27:15–18). An exemplary Christian leader, King Mosiah "warred a good warfare, walking uprightly before God" (Alma 1:1).

Besides being metaphorical, warfare is also typological. Typology is suggested by the implications of Nephi's revelation concerning the last days in which he "beheld that the great mother of abominations did gather together multitudes upon the face of all the earth . . . to fight against the Lamb of God" (1 Nephi 14:13). This conflict pertains to "things both temporal and spiritual" (1 Nephi 22:3). In both respects, the numbers of "the church of the Lamb of God . . . [will be] few" and they will be "scattered upon all the face of the earth," yet they will prevail because they are "armed with righteousness and with the power of God in great glory" (1 Nephi 14:12, 14). The instances in the Book of Mormon when a righteous few in number prevail against, outwit, or elude superior forces determined to destroy them serve as types of warfare involving saints in the last days.

"We are as the army of Helaman," begins the chorus of a song in which Latter-day Saint children identify themselves with the 2,000 stripling warriors serving under the direction of Helaman. Having been taught faith by their mothers, these youthful soldiers are spared death at the hands of superior forces. Their experiences are related at length in great detail, even though their accomplishments are only a portion of a much larger war going on. Conversely, great battles are dismissed with a few words (for example, the account in Helaman 4:5 of the Lamanites' obtaining possession of all the Nephite lands up to the land Bountiful). The Book of Mormon does give in considerable detail accounts of the exercise of faith, inspired stratagems, the Lord's protection, and the direction by great prophet-warriors. Time and again, it demonstrates how the Lord protects or helps the few in the face of the enemy's much greater numbers. For example, when the Amlicites join the Lamanites, the foes are "as numerous almost, as it were, as the sands of the sea" (Alma 2:27). Yet the Nephites, "being strengthened by the hand of the Lord, having prayed mightily to him that he would deliver them out of the hands of their enemies, therefore the Lord did hear their cries, and did strengthen them, and the Lamanites and the Amlicites did fall before them" (Alma 2:28).

On the other hand, iniquity brings on the destruction of the people (Alma 4:11). There is a definite relationship between the degree of spiritual righteousness and the vulnerability of the people to warfare. Indeed, in several places success or failure in battle is directly attributed to righteousness or wickedness. In this choice land, says Moroni to a latter-day audience, "he that doth possess it shall serve God or shall be swept off; for it is the everlasting decree of God. And it is not until the fulness of iniquity among the children of the land, that they are swept off" (Ether 2:10).

The Book of Mormon is a witness to conflicts before the Second Coming. At that day, Satan will "rage in the hearts of the children of men, and stir them up to anger against that which is good" (2 Nephi 28:20). The Lord will "cause a great division among the people" (2 Nephi 30:10) comparable to that between the Nephites and the Lamanites in which "the true worshipers of Christ . . . were called Nephites . . . [and] they who rejected the gospel were called Lamanites" (4 Nephi 1:37–38). In conflicts in the Book of Mormon, those who are "faithful in keeping the commandments of the Lord [are] delivered at all times" (Alma 50:22). That is not to say that the lives of all believers are spared; the death by fire of the converted women and children of the people of Ammonihah shows that. But the Book of Mormon contains many accounts and promises of deliverance of the righteous.[20] Those accounts foreshadow the division into opposing groups and deliverance of God's people in the latter days as prophesied by President Benson:

> I testify that as the forces of evil increase under Lucifer's leadership and as the forces of good increase under the leadership of Jesus Christ, there will be growing battles between the two until the final confrontation. . . . As these conflicts rage, either secretly or openly, the righteous will be tested. God's wrath will soon shake the nations of the earth and will be poured out on the wicked without measure. . . . But God will provide strength for the righteous and the means of escape; and eventually and finally truth will triumph.[21]

"All the nations that fight against Zion, and that distress her," Isaiah says, quoted by Nephi, "shall be as a dream of a night vision" (2 Nephi 27:3). In this spirit, the Book of Mormon shows the fundamental nature of latter-day warfare and gives hope to the Lord's people. With accounts of the victories of small minorities against overwhelming odds (often with no lives of the righteous being lost) or of escapes from their enemies (as with the people of Lehi, Nephi, Mosiah, Alma the Elder, and Limhi), it confirms the truth of President Benson's words: "God will provide strength for the righteous and the means of escape." It illustrates that ultimately God fights the battles for the "true worshipers of Christ" (4 Nephi 1:37). As the Lord says through Nephi, "I will show unto them that fight against my word *and against my people,* who are of the house of Israel, that I am God, and that I covenanted with Abraham that I would remember his seed forever" (2 Nephi 29:14).

THE BOOK OF MORMON AS A TYPE

As with the fruit of the tree of life, the Book of Mormon itself is considered of great worth. Indeed, as the word of God, it is a figure of Christ the Word. It is also a treasure, typifying Christ "in whom are hid all the treasures of wisdom and knowledge" (Colossians 2:3). In the beginning of the book, Laman and Lemuel represent the unbelievers who lament leaving "their gold, and their silver, and their precious things, to perish in the wilderness," or so they suppose (1 Nephi 2:11). On the other hand, Nephi is willing to give up the family's material treasures to try to obtain the heavenly treasure represented by the contents of the brass plates. When he is finally successful in obtaining the plates, he finds them in the treasury. Later, Nephi's younger brother Jacob admonishes the rich whose hearts are set upon their treasures that "their treasure shall perish with them" (2 Nephi 9:30). The same lesson is preached by Samuel the Lamanite. Treasures hidden up not unto the Lord are lost; the riches are cursed, says Samuel, "because ye have set your hearts upon them, and have not hearkened unto the *words* of him who gave them unto you" (Helaman 13:21). The capstone instruction is given by Christ himself to "lay up for yourselves treasures in heaven" rather than earthly treasures (3 Nephi 13:20). The book ends with Moroni hiding up—unto the Word—the words of life, an echo of the Lord's instruction to the brother of Jared to "treasure up the things which ye have seen and heard" (Ether 3:21). With an awareness that Christ is the ultimate treasure, Moroni admonishes his future readers to "come unto Christ, and lay hold upon every good gift, and touch not the evil gift" (Moroni 10:30). Seen as a type, then, the Book of Mormon itself is a precious treasure of the earth and as such is a figure of the treasures of heaven.[22]

CHAPTER 9

"At the Judgment-Seat of Christ"
LARGER PERSPECTIVES

Though Mark Twain defined a classic as "a book which people praise and don't read,"[1] the Book of Mormon more properly fits another definition of a classic: "A book that wears you out before you wear it out."[2] On each rereading, the book becomes more significant, deep, and powerful—and its overall patterns and purposes become more apparent. It is especially instructive to read the beginning from the end. That is, Moroni's parting words are helpful in orienting the reader to the meanings and purposes of the Book of Mormon on the largest scale. In part, Moroni is responding to his father's perspective—one of both looking backward at the histories of the Nephites and Jaredites and looking down through time "until the end shall come, when all the saints shall dwell with God," when Mormon and Moroni can "rest [their] souls in the kingdom of God" and have confirmed the hope of Christ's "glory and of eternal life" (Moroni 8:26; 9:6, 25). In a similar manner, Moroni in his closing exhortation wants his readers to consider the Lord's mercies "from the creation of Adam even down unto the time that ye shall receive these things" (Moroni 10:3). Affirming that God is "the same yesterday, today, and forever," Moroni speaks "unto all the ends of the earth" in declaring that the time comes speedily when they shall see him, Moroni, "at the bar of God" and hear again his testimony (Moroni 10:19, 24, 27).

In the title page—the preface to the book—Moroni hopes his latter-day audience will accept the things of God so as to "be found spotless at the judgment-seat of Christ." He closes his record with similar words: he promises to meet us "before the pleasing bar of the great Jehovah, the Eternal Judge of both quick and dead" (Moroni 10:34). In presenting the Book of Mormon in such a framework, Moroni establishes the largest possible context for the book. It deals with time and eternity, earth and heaven. It looks at such questions as what is God's way and how does it differ from the way of the "natural man" (Mosiah 3:19) and what is necessary to inherit eternal life. This earthly life, as Moroni understood and as Alma taught, is "a probationary state; a time to prepare to meet God; a time to prepare for that endless state which has been spoken of by us, which is after the resurrection of the dead" (Alma 12:24). Thus, judgment day is the meeting point between time and eternity. It is when we will be "raised from this mortality to a state of immortality" and "brought before the bar of God, to be judged according to our works" (Alma 12:12). It is when the righteous will "see as they are seen, and know as they are known" (D&C 76:94; see 1 Corinthians 13:12). It is when faith and obedience are rewarded and when the unfaithful find it is everlastingly too late for them.

The testimonies or teachings of Nephi, Jacob, King Benjamin, Alma the Younger, Nephi the son of Helaman, Jesus, Mormon, and Moroni all culminate in reference to the last judgment.[3] For example, in his parting words, Nephi confirms the truthfulness of his writings by saying, "Christ will show unto you, with power and great glory, that [my writings] are [Christ's] words, at the last day; and you and I shall stand face to face before his bar" (2 Nephi 33:11). By directing our thoughts to the last judgment, these prophets give the Book of Mormon the largest possible sweep of concern pertaining to both time and timelessness, mortality and immortality. That concern is set forth in several overall artistic structures. Examining those structures helps us understand better how the book truly is designed for our day in testifying to a disbelieving world that miracles are real—that earth can and does meet heaven.

HEAVEN MEETS EARTH:
THRESHOLDS IN THE BOOK OF MORMON

Many of the characteristics of God's ways pertain to thresholds—or, to use a word derived from *limen,* the Latin word for *threshold,* they are *liminal.* The judgment day itself could be called *liminal,* being on the edge, or threshold, between different places and conditions.

A perfect artistic rendition of liminality is Michelangelo's painting in the Sistine Chapel of the creation of Adam. The recumbent Adam is partially lying on earth at a slightly lower level than God, who is in a cloud of heaven. The Father is reaching out toward Adam, His forefinger almost touching Adam's. Though this creation, or birth, of man is liminal in itself, the slight space between the finger of God and the finger of Adam is electrically charged as a threshold between the powers of heaven and the potentials of earth.

In a similar way, the Book of Mormon portrays the connections between heaven and earth. The book begins with Nephi, on earth, recounting his father's being carried away in a vision in which he sees Christ descend "out of the midst of heaven" and with twelve others going "forth upon the face of the earth" (1 Nephi 1:9, 11). At the end of the book, Moroni on earth is soon to go to rest in paradise "until my spirit and body shall again reunite, and I am brought forth triumphant through the air" (Moroni 10:34). The Book of Mormon's story of the fall and return of man portrays limitations, such as materialism and pride, of earthbound people and, on the other hand, aspirations toward heaven. Awe-inspiring experiences show heaven coming down to earth in the form of the angels that minister to the repentant Lamanites who had imprisoned the brothers Nephi and Lehi

(Helaman 5) or in the descent of the resurrected Jesus Christ himself (3 Nephi 11).

The term *liminal* was introduced by Arnold van Gennep in *The Rites of Passage*. There he applies it to people who undergo a "rite of transition," literally or figuratively going through such "neutral zones" as deserts or forests.[4] Liminal persons, according to anthropologist Victor Turner, are "betwixt and between the positions assigned and arrayed by law, custom, convention, and ceremonial."[5] Liminal actions or events are transitions into or across boundaries. "To cross the threshold," van Gennep says, "is to unite oneself with a new world." In the case of entering a temple, it is to move "between the profane and sacred worlds."[6] Purifications, such as Christian baptism, "constitute rites of separation from previous surroundings; there follow rites of incorporation [such as] . . . a shared meal" or naming.[7]

In the Book of Mormon, these liminal actions include going across water (the Lehites and the Jaredites); going into or out of prison (Alma and Amulek, the brothers Nephi and Lehi); falling into and coming out of trances (Alma, Lamoni, Ammon); escapes (Lehi's family, the people of Limhi); conversion from a world of wickedness to one of righteousness (Alma); initiations (covenant making by King Benjamin's people); and transformations (Zeezrom's change from cunning lawyer to humble missionary).

In the Book of Mormon, liminal persons are those without class or status or those who minimize their status. Although it seems paradoxical, even kings can be liminal. As a good example of this, King Benjamin minimizes his status, reminding the people he has labored with his own hands for his support and identifying himself as a beggar before God. Although holding titles and authority, such kings as Nephi and Mosiah and such high priests as Jacob and Alma the Elder are meek and unpretentious. Mosiah exemplifies humility and warns his people not to let "pride nor haughtiness disturb their peace," but rather, "every man should esteem his neighbor as himself" (Mosiah 27:4). For his part, Alma the Younger readily gives up his status as a judge to preach as a missionary. Captain Moroni and those who rally behind him are liminal persons in desiring freedom and equality.

Liminal persons are also in transition. For them, this world is not their final home. Jacob, for instance, laments that "our lives passed away like as it were unto us a dream, we being a lonesome and a solemn people, wanderers, cast out from Jerusalem, born in tribulation, in a wilderness, and hated of our brethren" (Jacob 7:26). Mormon's son Moroni is a totally isolated wanderer who remains "alone to write the sad tale of the destruction of [his] people" (Mormon 8:3).

A group of liminal persons, according to Victor Turner, form a community marked by spontaneity, freedom, and equality.[8] Turner uses the term *communitas* to define this group who bond together in an unstructured or only rudimentarily structured community. In the Book of Mormon, an ideal *communitas* is found in the disciples of Jesus, who have "all things common among them, every man dealing justly, one with another" (3 Nephi 26:19). Likewise, when the Nephites and Lamanites following Christ's visit are converted,

> there were no contentions and disputations among them, and every man did deal justly one with another. And they had all things common among them; therefore there were not rich and poor, bond and free, but they were all made free, and partakers of the heavenly gift. . . . There were no robbers, nor murderers, neither were there Lamanites, nor any manner of -ites; but they were in one, the children of Christ, and heirs to the kingdom of God. (4 Nephi 1:2–3, 17)

Conversely, nonliminal persons and places assert structure and classes. In the Book of Mormon, the "natural man," who is an enemy to God (Mosiah 3:19), inevitably wants to establish classes, whereas the Saint, who is meek and humble, is without status, like a child. King Noah is a perfect example of a nonliminal person. Taxing his people heavily, he builds a large palace and equips it with a throne that is "of fine wood and . . .

ornamented with gold and silver and with precious things." For his high priests, he provides seats "above all the other seats" and which "he did ornament with pure gold." His tower is built high so he can proudly "look over all the land round about" (Mosiah 11:9, 11, 12).

Those who occupy the great and spacious building in Lehi's dream are nonliminal. The building itself is defined as the "vain imaginations and the pride of the children of men" (1 Nephi 12:18). The people in it wear "exceedingly fine" clothes denoting their status, and they mock those who partake of the fruit of the tree of life (1 Nephi 8:27). Subsequently, severe structuring of society, with its accompanying abuse of the poor and humble, is evidenced by the wearing of "fine-twined linen" and the like (Alma 4:6). The Zoramites exemplify a classed society: they cast out their poor as pariahs, a group to whom Alma is able to preach successfully his message of faith and love. Other structured persons distinguish themselves "by ranks, according to their riches and their chances for learning" (3 Nephi 6:12). Two centuries after the coming of Christ, the breakdown of Nephite society begins with some prosperous people being

> lifted up in pride, such as the wearing of costly apparel, and all manner of fine pearls, and of the fine things of the world. And from that time forth they did have their goods and their substance no more common among them. And they began to be divided into classes; and they began to build up churches unto themselves to get gain, and began to deny the true church of Christ. (4 Nephi 1:24–26)

On the other hand, the great covenant making that King Benjamin sets up for his assembled people is a thoroughly liminal experience. The people stay in tents, linking up with their ancestors in observing what John Tvedtnes has described as a Nephite Feast of Tabernacles.[9] They have come to a liminal place—the temple—and there they undergo a transformation. They humble themselves and "become as little children" (Mosiah 3:18), without class or status. When the people awaken to a sense of their nothingness and their worthless and fallen state, they understand the atonement of Christ, enter into a covenant with God to do his will and keep his commandments, and receive a rebirth and a new name—"the children of Christ" (Mosiah 5:7).

We can understand better the nature and significance of liminality in this experience by considering it as a great Year Rite. Hugh Nibley says that in the ancient East,

> all things center in a single supreme rite, performed in its completeness only at a particular place, the shrine that stands at the center of the earth, and a particular time, the New Year's day, when all things are born and the earth is created anew. Since everyone was required by law to be present at this great event, to do homage to the king and receive his blessing for the new age, the result was a tremendous assembly. . . . "The New Year was the birthday of the human race and its rites dramatized the creation of the world; all who would be found in 'the Book of Life opened at the creation of the World' must necessarily attend."[10]

Nibley finds thirty-six ways in which King Benjamin's gathering is a Year Rite. Besides the time (New Year) and place (the temple), these include such liminal elements as giving the people a name, providing a vivid form of instruction unfolding to view the mysteries of God, and renunciation—even reversal—of the conventional claims of kingship.[11]

To be on the threshold or to cross boundaries is not necessarily a positive experience. Liminality—"that which is neither this nor that and yet is both"[12]—is by its nature ambiguous. Fire, a liminal element, can purify or destroy; a visitation by heavenly powers can terrify rather than bless. That duality is especially true with respect to the cataclysmic events that occur at the time of the crucifixion.

The events in Third Nephi are the culmination of liminal imagery and events. The very structures of the earth are shaken and changed as violent earthquakes and accompanying fires and whirlwinds create destruction. After hearing a voice from heaven, the multitude gathered at the temple see "a Man descending out of heaven" who declares himself to be Jesus Christ, "the light and the life of the world" (3 Nephi 11:8, 11). This mediator between heaven and earth parts the veil and allows the people to touch him and hear him. He calls on the people to undergo a transformational process: "Ye must repent, and become as a little child, and be baptized in my name" (3 Nephi 11:37), he says; he teaches them to be one, a *communitas;* then he administers the sacrament to them—a sacred shared meal that van Gennep would call a rite of incorporation.

Earlier, the voice of Jesus was heard telling about the deaths of the unrighteous; later, Jesus in person stands before the people as an affirmation of the resurrection—which is the great transition from death to eternal life. The Holy One of Israel, whose coming the prophets had foretold, now personally covenants with his people. He affirms his power to effect transitions by healing all their sick, opening the eyes of their blind, unstopping the ears of their deaf, and raising a man from the dead. His parting words include an admonition to "repent, all ye ends of the earth, and come unto me and be baptized in my name, that ye may be sanctified by the reception of the Holy Ghost, that ye may stand spotless before me at the last day" (3 Nephi 27:20).

In the book of Ether, which follows soon after Third Nephi and which serves as a microcosm of the whole Book of Mormon, the threshold between heaven and earth is again made transparent. Here Moroni speaks of those like the brother of Jared "whose faith was so exceedingly strong, even before Christ came, who could not be kept from within the veil, but truly saw with their eyes the things which they had beheld with an eye of faith, and they were glad" (Ether 12:19).

Though the book of Ether contains an account of an ancient people, it speaks to a future one in richly liminal language. "Come unto me, O ye Gentiles," Moroni quotes Jesus as saying, and I will show unto you the greater things, the knowledge which is *hid* up because of unbelief. . . . Behold, when ye shall rend that *veil* of unbelief which doth cause you to remain in your awful state of wickedness, and hardness of heart, and *blindness* of mind, then shall the great and marvelous things which have been *hid* up from the foundation of the world from you— . . . then shall my revelations which I have caused to be written by my servant John be *unfolded* in the eyes of all the people. (Ether 4:13, 15–16)

One of the chief "marvelous things," Moroni is told, is the record Moroni is involved in writing. It shall come forth "out of the earth," Moroni says, "in a day when it shall be said that miracles are done away; and it shall come even as if one should speak from the dead" (Mormon 8:26). The book thus is "betwixt" and between the dead and the living (Alma 40:6); of earthly origins, it asserts that it contains the revelations of God; a liminal "voice . . . from the dust" (2 Nephi 33:13), it speaks today with power and beauty.

In Moroni's title page the Book of Mormon shows God's dealings with the fathers (heaven contacting earth), presents transformational covenants (such as baptism), and convinces that Jesus Christ is the Son of God—the mediator between heaven and earth. The last assertion of the book resolves liminal tensions: the earthly person can be made heavenly through being "sanctified in Christ by the grace of God"; in the resurrection, Jehovah is "the Eternal Judge of both quick and dead" (Moroni 10:33–34).

In Michelangelo's painting of the creation of Adam, birth comes from God's reaching to man. Rebirth, as the Book of Mormon develops it, is initiated by a person's reaching to God and is answered by an outstretched arm of mercy. It completes and perfects the meeting at the threshold between heaven and earth. This process is described by the voice of the Lord to the Nephite people who are spared the destruction of their cities: "If ye will come unto me ye shall have eternal life," he says, regarding their obligation. For his part, he says, "Behold, mine arm of mercy is extended towards you, and whosoever will come, him will I receive; and blessed are those who come unto me" (3 Nephi 9:14). Thus, the most liminal person of all is Jesus Christ. He is "the keeper of the gate" (2 Nephi 9:41), "the way" (John 14:6), the divine mediator "standing betwixt [the children of men] and justice" (Mosiah 15:9), the One who descended below all things and whose mercy can satisfy justice and thus allow fallen humankind to be redeemed. The saving power defined in the Book of Mormon hinges on Jesus Christ. "Come unto me," he says, and be "even as I am"; the true disciple "putteth off the natural man and becometh a saint through the atonement of Christ the Lord" (3 Nephi 12:20; 27:27; Mosiah 3:19). This, ultimately, is the sacred liminal connection and transformation.

BEING CENTERED IN CHRIST AND LIFTED UP BY HIM

The experience of coming to Christ is the emotional and spiritual focal point of the Book of Mormon. The visit of the resurrected Jesus Christ to the surviving descendants of Lehi is the main event all the prophets anticipate or look back upon. This event brings all else in the book to surround it.[13] Christ the temple (John 2:19) comes to the Nephite temple where the people are gathered "round about the temple" (3 Nephi 11:1). In effect, they surround the temple as a center and then Christ appears "in the midst of them" (3 Nephi 11:8).

Every temple, Mircea Eliade argues, is a "Sacred Mountain—where heaven and earth meet—[and] is situated at the center of the world. . . . Being an *axis mundi,* the sacred city or temple is regarded as the meeting point of heaven, earth, and hell."[14] Thus it is appropriate that the temple be the site where Christ teaches the people and establishes ordinances related to that meeting point.[15] The resurrected Christ, himself the center, provides a memorable scene in which heaven touches earth and others become centers as well. The people see "angels descending out of heaven as it were in the midst of fire." It is reported that the angels "came down and encircled [the] little ones about, and they were encircled about with fire; and the angels did minister unto them" (3 Nephi 17:24).

Heaven and hell both encircle. Lehi declares to his family, "I am encircled about eternally in the arms of [the Lord's] love" (2 Nephi 1:15); Nephi pleads for the Lord to "encircle me around in the robe of thy righteousness" (2 Nephi 4:33); and Amulek teaches that mercy "encircles [the penitent] in the arms of safety" (Alma 34:16). Conversely, before being spiritually delivered, the fathers "were encircled about by the bands of death, and the chains of hell" (Alma 5:7); Zeezrom is "encircled about by the pains of hell" (Alma 14:6); and Ammon testifies that his Lamanite brethren were formerly "encircled about with everlasting darkness and destruction" (Alma 26:15). These are part of the larger Book of Mormon circles that either save or damn.

Put another way, humanity, the Book of Mormon says, is either encircled and lifted up through mercy or encircled by chains and brought down to hell. This movement, rising and falling, or ascent and descent, develops a way to see the book as a whole as the story of mankind's journey through life, fall, and redemption. Catherine Thomas made this point in her presentation at the 1991 Sidney B. Sperry Symposium on "Types and Shadows of Deliverance in the Book of Mormon." She notes:

> All major journeys in the Book of Mormon are allegorical as well as actual and reflect not only the different kinds of the Lord's deliverances but also the principles on which the deliverances depend. All these journeys typify every person's sojourn on earth and the tasks that each is given to accomplish. . . . The destination of each divinely guided journey is a promised land where spiritual enlargement will be possible.[16]

The book begins with Lehi's vision of the descent of Christ and others in white clothing and ends with Moroni's anticipation of being lifted up and "brought forth triumphant through the air" at the last judgment (1 Nephi 1:9–10; Moroni 10:34). In this account of many journeys (which can be seen as figures of the journey of life), materialistic and proud earthbound people move downward to destruction; by heeding angels and other messengers of God, other people, through the grace of Christ, are lifted up. At the end of the book, Moroni and his father are witnesses of the fall of the Nephite people. In his great cry of the heart, Mormon laments: "O ye fair ones, how could ye have rejected that Jesus . . . ! Behold, if ye had not done this, ye would not have fallen. But behold, ye are fallen, and I mourn your loss" (Mormon 6:17–18). Countering that downward movement of the Nephites generally is Mormon's hope for his son Moroni. "Be faithful in Christ," Mormon says to him, "and may not the things which I have written grieve thee, to *weigh thee down* unto death; but may Christ *lift thee up*" (Moroni 9:25).

The Savior defines to his disciples how he lifts up others. It necessitates that he first had to be forcibly lifted up and put to death:

> And my Father sent me that I might be lifted up upon the cross; and after that I had been lifted up upon the cross, that I might draw all men unto me, that as I have been lifted up by men even so should men be lifted up by the Father, to stand before me, to be judged of their works, whether they be good or whether they be evil—And for this cause have I been lifted up; therefore, according to the power of the Father I will draw all men unto me, that they may be judged according to their works. (3 Nephi 27:14–15)

In other words, Christ came down to earth and suffered pain and death that he might lift up others. It was he "that ascended up on high, as also he descended below all things" (D&C 88:6; see also Psalm 68:18; Ephesians 4:8–10). The fallen Adam is allowed to stand again through the resurrection of the Second Adam.

"ALPHA AND OMEGA, THE BEGINNING AND THE END"

Christ is both the center and the circumference of the Book of Mormon. "I am Alpha and Omega," he tells the righteous people spared destruction, "the beginning and the end" (3 Nephi 9:18). The destruction and redemption associated with his coming to the Nephites make this a time of judgment—and connect it with the last judgment: Christ will yet be "the Eternal Judge of both quick and dead" (Moroni 10:34). His chosen servants also have a perspective of the beginning and the end. Such prophets as Lehi, Nephi, Alma, Ether, the brother of Jared, Mormon, and Moroni have visions of God's dealings with man from the beginning until the last judgment and see how events in their own time will be repeated in the future. As a prominent example, remembering his father's view that secret combinations were the cause of Nephite destruction, Moroni looks down through time to when the record he hides will be brought forth, and says to the people of that time:

> Whatsoever nation shall uphold such secret combinations, to get power and gain, until they shall spread over the nation, behold, they shall be destroyed. . . . Wherefore, O ye Gentiles, it is wisdom in God that these things should be shown unto you, that thereby ye may repent of your sins, and suffer not that these murderous combinations shall get above you. (Ether 8:22–23)

The historical perspective of Book of Mormon prophets is sweeping. The brother of Jared is shown "all the inhabitants of the earth which had been, and also all that would be; and [the Lord] withheld them not from his sight, even unto the ends of the earth" (Ether 3:25). "The Lord knoweth all things from the beginning," Nephi says, and then he is shown things reserved to be written by John the Revelator (1 Nephi 9:6; 14:24–26). He foretells a sealed book containing a revelation of "all things from the foundation of the world unto the end thereof" and prophesies that eventually the words which were sealed "shall be read upon the house tops" (2 Nephi 27:10–11).[17] After King

Benjamin's speech, his people declare that through the manifestations of God's Spirit they "have great views of that which is to come; and were it expedient, we could prophesy of all things" (Mosiah 5:3). In a culminating revelation, the resurrected Christ expounds "all things, even from the beginning until the time that he should come in his glory—yea, even all things which should come upon the face of the earth, even until the elements should melt with fervent heat, and the earth should be wrapt together as a scroll, and the heavens and the earth should pass away" (3 Nephi 26:3).

Because Christ is both the beginning and the end, his course, Nephi says, "is one eternal round" (1 Nephi 10:19). In a divine perspective, the passing away of one condition can usher in the beginning of another—as happens in the New World after the Crucifixion. There is physical and spiritual chaos (for example, rocks are broken up, and people are left desolate); yet out of this destruction comes renewal and hope. The intent of these "signs and these wonders," Samuel prophesies, is that "whosoever will believe might be saved, and that whosoever will not believe, a righteous judgment might come upon them" (Helaman 14:28–29).

One way to look at "the course of the Lord" (1 Nephi 10:19) through time is to apply some of Northrop Frye's ideas about phases in the Bible to the Book of Mormon. Frye argues that the Bible progresses through seven phases: creation, revolution or exodus, law, wisdom, prophecy, gospel, and apocalypse.[18] It could be argued that the Book of Mormon also roughly follows this pattern, but Frye's ideas about creation and apocalypse are especially helpful in seeing how the Book of Mormon treats beginnings and endings of life or civilization. The "beginning," Frye says, is "the moment of waking from sleep, when one world disappears and another comes into being."[19] The Book of Mormon begins with this transition from one world to another: Anticipating the imminent destruction of Jerusalem, it gives us

Lehi as an Adam starting a new life in the promised land. Lehi is also like Noah in taking seeds of every kind with him. In the new world, creation is reenacted by the actions of Lehi and his family in cultivating the land and taking possession of it. As Mircea Eliade notes, when "possession is taken of a territory . . . rites are performed that symbolically repeat the act of Creation."[20]

Frye defines *apocalypse,* the Greek word for *revelation,* as "the vision of staggering marvels placed in a near future and just before the end of time." It "ends with the restoration of the tree and water of life."[21] The last three books of the Book of Mormon—those of Mormon, Ether, and Moroni—contain both of these aspects of the apocalyptic vision. The marvels are the destructions of two great civilizations presented first by Mormon and ended by his son. These destructions are types of the end-time "wars, rumors of wars, and earthquakes in divers places" before "that great day when the earth shall be rolled together as a scroll, and the elements shall melt with fervent heat" (Mormon 8:30; 9:2). Current readers are actively brought into the picture by Moroni, who looks centuries into the future and speaks to them "as if ye were present" (Mormon 8:35). Readers are challenged to contemplate the apocalyptic vision Moroni presents in the context of imagining themselves "in that great day when [they] shall be brought to stand before the Lamb of God" (Mormon 9:2). Moroni ends with a powerful future-time joining of writer and reader by testifying that as a resurrected person he would "meet you" before the bar of Jehovah (Moroni 10:34).

With God all things are an eternal round: There is an implied creation at the end of the book as the dust of death gives way to Moroni's call for Israel to "arise from the dust" (Moroni 10:31). Moroni's voice is not stilled when he writes his last words on the plates of Nephi. Rather, it comes to life again in the translated record we read.

TO MORONI'S "BRETHREN, THE LAMANITES"

To the Gentiles who would profess a belief in Christ but deny miracles, the Book of Mormon affirms the continuing power of God (Mormon 8; Ether 4; Moroni 7). To the Jews who have not yet recognized Jesus Christ as the Messiah, the Book of Mormon affirms that "Jesus is the very Christ" (2 Nephi 26:12). To the Lamanites, the primary audience, the Book of Mormon shows them who they really are and points the way to their redemption.[22]

With respect to modern-day Lamanites, the overall structure of the Book of Mormon is like a triangle. The book begins and ends with concern for the Lamanites' receiving the gospel. The title page is balanced with Moroni's final exhortation to his "brethren, the Lamanites" (Moroni 10:1). Nephi's account reiterates the main points of the title page in emphasizing that through the Book of Mormon the Lamanites shall know they are of Israel and through it "they shall be restored unto the knowledge of their fathers, and also to the knowledge of Jesus Christ" (2 Nephi 30:1–5). Toward the end of the record, Mormon says much the same thing: "Know ye that ye are of the house of Israel. . . . Know ye that ye must come to the knowledge of your fathers, and repent of all your sins and iniquities, and believe in Jesus Christ" (Mormon 7:2, 5). At the apex of the triangle is an account of a great spiritual change among the Lamanites. That is the turning point because it is the climax of centuries of efforts to bring the gospel to the Lamanites and because of the opposing forces it brings on.

This apex occurs in the physical center of the Book of Mormon. The section of Alma that includes chapters 23 through 26 (which is just one chapter, Alma 14, in the first edition) treats a wholesale conversion of the Lamanites. This central part begins with the decree of the king of the Lamanites that Ammon and his brethren should be free to preach the word of God throughout all the land and ends with gratitude expressed by these great missionaries for the thousands of Lamanite souls "brought to behold the marvelous light of God" (Alma 26:3). The earlier war-like and reprobate nature of the Lamanites has given way to their wholehearted acceptance of the gospel once converted. In their larger context, these chapters provide uplifting lessons of faith and redemption for latter-day Lamanites—which is the persistent prayer of the book's authors, the main purpose of the Book of Mormon as stated on the title page, and the anticipation of Mormon and Moroni at the end of the book. Then memorably repeated at emotionally charged places are definitions of the gospel, prophetic forewarnings, and examples of a righteous people. Thus this missionary book *about* the conversion of the Lamanites is primarily *for* the conversion of the Lamanites, coming forth as a voice "out of the dust" (2 Nephi 26:16) expressly for that purpose.

As pertaining to the Lamanites, but also to the Jews and Gentiles, the sections of the Book of Mormon progress in this manner: The title page says the abridgment of the record of the people of Nephi was "hid up unto the Lord, that they might not be destroyed"—with the plural *they* referring most appropriately back to the Lamanites. If so, the destruction prevented here would surely be a spiritual destruction, the loss forever of the gospel in their lives. Lehi has the same concern, fearing that his oldest sons and their families will be "cut off and destroyed forever" (2 Nephi 1:17). He calls on them to follow Nephi's leadership and obey God's commandments.

The First Book of Nephi defines what it means to keep the commandments. Further, it presents the story of God's dealings with the "fathers" and tells "the marvelous works which were wrought by the power of God among them" so that latter-day Lamanites will know they are a "remnant of the seed of Jacob" and are "numbered among the people of the first covenant" (Mormon 7:9–10). One part of the message of 1 Nephi is that "the tender mercies of the Lord are over all those whom he hath chosen, because of their faith, to make them mighty even unto the power of deliverance"; the other part, with which Nephi ends 1 Nephi, is that "if ye shall be obedient to the commandments, and endure to the end, ye shall be saved at the last day" (1 Nephi 1:20; 22:31). To both of these truths, Nephi says, "I and my father . . . have testified" (1 Nephi 22:31). The latter-day Lamanites need to know not only of their fathers' deliverance but also of their fathers' disobedience, and they need to desire to turn away from the sins of the fathers.

If the main purpose of 1 Nephi is to affirm a testimony of Christ and to assure the Lamanites they are a covenant people with the promises and responsibilities of the same, the main purpose of 2 Nephi is to convince primarily the Jew and also the Gentile that Jesus is the Christ and that he will fulfill his covenants with Israel. A key to the method in 2 Nephi is suggested by 1 Nephi 15:17–20, in which Nephi's prophecies concerning the "covenant which should be fulfilled in the latter days" are supported and fleshed out by Lehi's and Isaiah's prophecies concerning the same matter. In like manner, in 2 Nephi the testimonies of Lehi, Nephi, Jacob, Joseph, and Isaiah are brought together to testify that Jesus Christ is the promised Messiah, the God of Abraham, Isaac, and Jacob. In this respect, Nephi both clarifies and is a second witness of the truth of Isaiah, whereas Isaiah is a second witness of the truth of Nephi's prophecies.

The selections from Isaiah also have direct relevance for our time. They are verified by Christ and provide an independent witness that the Savior is the promised Messiah. Further, the chosen passages from Isaiah deal with the primary motifs of the Book of Mormon: the truth of the first coming of Christ and the basic prophecies connected with the Restoration and the gathering of Israel in the last days, culminating in the second coming of Christ and followed by the Millennium. A voice out of Israel's past, Isaiah establishes the grand connection with the house of Israel in the Old World (particularly the Jews), the remnant of

Israel in the New World (the Lamanites), and modern-day Israel (especially the blood of Israel intermixed with the Gentiles).

In the accounts of the people of King Benjamin and of Alma we have examples of those who keep the commandments and become the kind of pure and holy people God desires. Set against them are examples of those who, like King Noah, are headed for destruction. Abinadi is an important prophet-messenger who teaches about Christ and declares the possibilities of faith and repentance or destruction. Abinadi's teachings and testimony set in motion the subsequent events of the books of Mosiah and Alma—leading up to the central conversion of the Lamanites.

The war chapters in the book of Alma show the incursions of apostate-led Lamanites as a consequence of the conversion of the Anti-Nephi-Lehies. These chapters give selective accounts of the inspired activities of the threatened Nephites. At stake is the lust for power over man, best exemplified by Zerahemnah, Amalickiah, and Ammaron, in opposition to reliance on God's power, demonstrated by Moroni and Helaman. Moroni's courageous assertion, "Ye cannot destroy this our faith" (Alma 44:3), shows his confidence in the Book of Mormon promise regarding the rewards of keeping God's commandments.

The kind of wickedness found in King Noah and his court is intensified in the account of the beginnings of Gadiantonism. Remembering that the promise of blessings for the obedient is balanced by the curse of destruction, we can well see the nature of the secret combinations that destroyed both the Nephites and the Jaredites and that will be the chief threat to Gentiles in the last days (Ether 8:20–25).

A prophetic spokesman like Abinadi, Samuel the Lamanite has a similar message about blessings through Christ and his atonement and about calamities to the unrepentant. He, too, prepares the way for the kind of pure and holy people God desires. In this case, they are those converted by Christ's coming.

Most of 3 Nephi then describes the teachings and covenants adhered to by the elect. It describes them in clear and simple language, with the emphasis being on baptism—as it was in the account of Alma's righteous people who joined him at the waters of Mormon (Mosiah 18). Indeed, after the Savior has the multitude come forth to recognize him as the God of Israel, the very first instruction he gives pertains to baptism. Likewise, baptism is at the core of Nephi's counsel at the end of his prophesying unto his "beloved brethren" (2 Nephi 31), as it is in Mormon's parting challenge to the Gentiles (3 Nephi 30) and in his last words to the Lamanites (Mormon 7:10). Baptism is the individual covenant; the group covenant is to receive the Book of Mormon, leading to acceptance of the Savior and baptism.

The gospel message to all three audiences is given prominence in the Book of Mormon. After his teachings about baptism and the Holy Ghost, Nephi declares in his parting testimony: "I have charity for my people. . . . I have charity for the Jew. . . . I also have charity for the Gentiles. But behold, for none of these can I hope except they shall be reconciled unto Christ, and enter into the narrow gate, and walk in the straight path which leads to life, and continue in the path until the end of the day of probation" (2 Nephi 33:7–9). This testimony is echoed again by King Benjamin, by the Savior, and finally by Mormon in his great sermon on faith, hope, and charity (Moroni 7). The essential message, then, is to have faith, repent, be baptized, receive the Holy Ghost, and endure to the end, having faith, hope, and charity.

THE BOOK OF ETHER AS A PARABLE FOR OUR TIME

In its testimony to its three-part audience, the Book of Mormon has many warnings directed to the Gentiles. These are specified particularly in Mormon 8 and 9 and in the book of Ether. Indeed, by stepping back and looking at its structure, we can see how the book of Ether is a parable for our time. It is the presentation of key ideas with support by elements from a true story rather than a story interrupted by comments. It sets the conditions for prolonged physical and spiritual survival in America, and it warns against secret combinations and resulting destruction.

We get closer to the essence of the book of Ether by looking at its structure in the 1830 edition of the Book of Mormon. Originally it was made up of six chapters: 1 (chapters 1–4 in our current Book of Mormon), 2 (our chapter 5), 3 (chapters 6–8), 4 (chapters 9–11), 5 (chapter 12), and 6 (chapters 13–15). All but one of these chapters begin with "And now I, Moroni," and the fourth sentence of the remaining chapter (5) begins with "And now I, Moroni"—emphasizing the central position of Moroni in the presentation and structure of the book of Ether.

The preface of the book of Ether is the last chapter in the previous book, Mormon (chapter 4 in the 1830 edition; chapters 8 and 9 in the current one), from which we learn that Moroni is the sole survivor "to write the sad tale of the destruction of my people" (Mormon 8:3). He writes specifically for people whom he has seen living when the Book of Mormon will come forth, cataloging their sins as similar to those that led to the capsizing of the Nephite civilization: pride, materialism, vanity, lack of charity, and sustaining of secret combinations. As does Mormon, Moroni frequently uses a phrase like "thus we see" to signal that he is speaking to his latter-day audience and drawing a moral especially for them.

Having detailed the destruction of the Nephite people, Moroni begins the book of Ether by saying it deals with "those ancient inhabitants who were destroyed by the hand of the Lord" (Ether 1:1). The first chapter (our chapters 1–4) implicitly compares the experience of the Jaredites with that of the Nephites, shows in the account of the brother of Jared the kind of faith that brings the Jaredites to the land of promise where its inhabitants are promised freedom if they "will but serve the God of the land, who is Jesus Christ," and warns modern-day Gentiles to repent "that ye may not bring down the fulness of the wrath of

God upon you as the inhabitants of the land have hitherto done" (Ether 2:12, 11).

The second chapter (our chapter 5), Moroni's words to the future translator of the book, attests that the Book of Mormon will come forth and that Moroni has authority from God to bear the testimony he does.

The third chapter (6–8) shows patterns of righteousness and unrighteousness by the Jaredites in the promised land, with prophetic warnings that the people will be destroyed if they do not repent and with details of the introduction of a secret combination into the Jaredite society. The specific audience for which the book of Ether was intended, modern-day Gentiles, are warned that secret combinations have caused the destruction of the Jaredites and also of the Nephites—and that "whatsoever nation shall uphold such secret combinations . . . shall be destroyed." On the other hand, Moroni pleads that his audience will "come unto the fountain of all righteousness and be saved" (Ether 8:21–22, 26).

The fourth chapter (9–11) shows the disastrous effect of secret combinations among the Jaredites, the rise and decline of generations of Jaredites who are warned to possess the land unto the Lord or be destroyed when ripened in iniquity, and Ether's coming on the scene as the last of a series of prophets warning of utter destruction.

The fifth chapter (12) introduces Ether with his appeal for faith and then almost immediately presents Moroni's teachings on faith, hope, and charity as the antidote his modern-day audience will need. Implicitly, Moroni identifies with Ether. Each is a prophet who hides to witness the end of his people and then testifies of it to future inhabitants of the land.

The final section (13–15) is Moroni's completion of his record "concerning the destruction" (Ether 13:1) of the Jaredites. Rejecting the kind of faith and charity outlined in the previous chapter, the people are corrupted by secret combinations (Ether

13:18). Then we see in powerful detail the final destruction of the Jaredites.

Thus the essential elements of the book of Ether are instructions on faith, beautifully illustrated by the brother of Jared; details of the nature and danger of secret combinations; and an account of the destruction of a people who turned away from Jesus Christ, the God of the land. All of this is pointed at the Gentiles among whom the Book of Mormon would come: it is a pattern of what will happen if they do not repent, and it shows how those who heed can turn to the Savior—in whom all who believe on his name shall have "life, and that eternally" (Ether 3:14).

The simplest and most emphasized theme of the Book of Mormon, that of covenant making, is given special point in the book of Ether. "Have faith, repent, and be baptized" is the message each prophet puts in an emphatic place; it is the principal instruction of the resurrected Christ; and it is the culmination of the quoted directions of Jesus Christ to Moroni in the book of Ether. "Come unto me, O ye Gentiles, . . . Come unto me, O ye house of Israel," Moroni quotes Jesus as saying; "then shall ye know that the Father hath remembered the covenant which he made unto your fathers, O house of Israel. . . . Therefore, repent all ye ends of the earth, and come unto me, and believe in my gospel, and be baptized in my name" (Ether 4:13–15, 18). As is epitomized in these simple words, ultimately all of the Book of Mormon is centered in Jesus Christ and his gospel.

In the larger context, the book of Ether is a key to its latter-day audience on how to read the Book of Mormon. As with the book of Ether, the Book of Mormon is a highly selected work that is prophetically focused for our time. It has as its main injunction, "Inasmuch as ye shall keep [God's] commandments ye shall prosper in the land; and inasmuch as ye will not keep [God's] commandments ye shall be cut off from [his] presence" (2 Nephi 4:4; compare Ether 2:9). It illustrates the conditions of salvation as well as the conditions of physical and spiritual destruction, and it affirms throughout and at the very end the need for faith, hope, and charity. Truly, the Nephite record in the Book of Mormon—and the book of Ether, which is a second witness of it—is designed for our time.

THE BOOK OF ETHER:
A MINIATURE OF THE BOOK OF MORMON

In the book of Ether we get answers to questions we have been led to anticipate throughout the Book of Mormon. In the title page we are informed that the book tells about the people of Jared dating back to the Tower of Babel. Our interest is piqued by the bits and pieces of the Jaredite story subsequently presented: A large stone found in the days of Mosiah gives an account of Coriantumr, whose "first parents came out from the tower" but whose people were destroyed "and their bones lay scattered in the land northward" (Omni 1:20, 22). The people of Limhi are fascinated with twenty-four engraved gold plates that they presume will tell them about the people who have been destroyed; consequently, they anticipate the translation of the records by Mosiah, a seer through whom shall "secret things be made manifest, and hidden things shall come to light" (Mosiah 8:17). After the people of Zeniff arrive in Zarahemla, King Mosiah translates the plates of gold because his people are "desirous beyond measure to know concerning those people who had been destroyed." This account, we are told, "shall be written hereafter; for behold, it is expedient that all people should know the things which are written in this account" (Mosiah 28:12, 19). We are next tantalized with the twenty-four plates in Alma's instructions to his son Helaman. The plates, he says, contain the Lord's warning that if the people did not repent "they should be destroyed from off the face of the earth." Through his servant Gazelem, the Lord says the secrets and abominations of the destroyed Jaredites will be brought to light

242

"unto every nation that shall hereafter possess the land" (Alma 37:22, 25).

From the preface forward, then, our curiosity has been building about the Jaredites with one tantalizing piece of information after another. The key elements are these: a record is hidden up unto God, to come forth by the power of God; it will tell about a people who were destroyed; it will answer the question of who were the fathers; it will be translated by a seer; it contains both a warning (bringing sorrow) and knowledge (causing rejoicing).

In effect, the end of the Nephites is recounted just before the full story of the Jaredites is finally given us. In Mormon 8, Moroni is writing after the "great and tremendous battle at Cumorah" and tells us that "I even remain alone to write the sad tale of the destruction of my people" (Mormon 8:2–3). He will write and hide the records in the earth. "Behold," he says, in a starkly simple statement that echoes the prophecies regarding the time of the Nephite demise, "four hundred years have passed away since the coming of our Lord and Savior" (Mormon 8:6). Moroni then turns from the past to the future: "And whoso receiveth this record . . . , were it possible, I would make all things known unto you. . . . And whoso shall bring [the record] to light, him will the Lord bless. . . . And it shall shine forth out of darkness, and come unto the knowledge of the people; and it shall be done by the power of God" (Mormon 8:12, 14, 16).

The same elements are here that were part of the Jaredite mystery: a hidden record to come forth by the power of God, to be translated by a seer, and to tell about a people destroyed through secret combinations and through turning away from their covenants with the Lord. At this culminating juncture of the Nephite and Jaredite stories, we see nearly simultaneously the causes of the destruction of both civilizations and our questions are answered.

The questions set forth about the Jaredites are essentially the same ones implied about the Nephites and their record: Who were these people? Where did the Lamanites come from? What do we have in this strange book, a book written in "reformed Egyptian" (Mormon 9:32)? Where did it come from? What does it mean? What happened to the people it describes? In what ways—and why—were they preserved for a season, and why were they destroyed? This last question is the one with which Mormon mourns his fallen people: "O ye fair ones, how could ye have rejected that Jesus, who stood with open arms to receive you!" (Mormon 6:17).

A counterpart to Mosiah, Joseph Smith was Gazelem, who used interpreters to translate the hidden record.[23] The record he translated has a relationship to its audience today similar to the relationship the twenty-four gold plates had to the people of Limhi and others assembled before King Mosiah to hear his translation. The implied expected response is both sorrow and rejoicing. From a historical perspective, the book ends in the tragic annihilation of a civilization. From an eternal perspective, in God's time, the book ends hopefully. Moroni expects the bar of God to be pleasing to him and to others who have accepted his parting challenge to "come unto Christ" (Moroni 10:32).

FEASTING ON THE WORD

A person is led to Christ, Nephi explains in figurative language, by feasting on the word:

> If ye shall follow the Son, with full purpose of heart, . . . then cometh the baptism of fire and of the Holy Ghost; and then can ye speak with the tongue of angels. . . .
>
> Angels speak by the power of the Holy Ghost; wherefore, they speak the words of Christ. Wherefore, I said unto you, feast upon the words of Christ; for behold, the words of Christ will tell you all things what ye should do. (2 Nephi 31:13; 32:3)

The Book of Mormon is rich in its direct quotation of Christ—indeed, there are nearly 26,000 of the Lord's words.[24] Feasting on them brings an identification with Christ, an ability through the power of the Holy Ghost to speak his words. It is also implicitly a sacramental experience, a feasting on the Word. "I am the bread of life," Jesus said to his disciples in the Old World. "He that cometh to me shall never hunger; and he that believeth on me shall never thirst. . . . I am the living bread which came down from heaven: if any man eat of this bread, he shall live for ever: and the bread that I will give is my flesh, which I will give for the life of the world" (John 6:35, 51).

Both Nephi and Christ poetically use metaphors to communicate most effectively.[25] Feasting has connotations of partaking of a rich and elaborate meal and also of being at a religious festival. "In ancient biblical times," according to Alvin R. Dyer, "the 'feast' was a time of gathering, a time of harvest, a time of rejoicing, and what is more particularly significant, 'the feast' was designated by the Lord as a time of remembrance."[26] Feasting on the sacramental bread is both communal sharing and individual covenant making. And as the most common and universal food, bread, together with water or wine, is life sustaining; the Word, or Bread of Life, brings everlasting life.

The Book of Mormon is itself the word of God, meant to be feasted on. Just as the Nephite disciples ate the bread Jesus broke and blessed and "were filled" (3 Nephi 18:4), so all who "hunger and thirst after righteousness" shall "be filled with the Holy Ghost" (3 Nephi 12:6). Through the Book of Mormon, including through its literary elements that engage the senses, Jesus bids his disciples to "come unto me, that ye might feel and see" (3 Nephi 18:25). The book that is a testament of him and by him calls to those who approach it, "Taste and feast."

A WITNESS AND TESTIMONY

From an eternal perspective, the Book of Mormon is designed by Jesus Christ for our day, just as he is responsible for continuing revelation. I believe that though individual authors wrote with distinctive styles and concerns, the final shape of the book is what God intended. Thus he foreknew and provided for Martin Harris's loss of the 116 pages of the Book of Mormon just as he foreknew Martin Harris would visit Charles Anthon (2 Nephi 27). And though Moroni several times thought his end was near, I believe he was allowed to continue writing so he could include the book of Ether where it is and give his latter-day audience all it was supposed to receive from him. Despite his and Mormon's efforts over years of time in "abridging" the Book of Mormon, he did not expect the book to be read until centuries in the future.

The intended audience, structure, and selected materials of the Book of Mormon, then, all prophetically emphasize the latter-day significance of the book. Just as the Savior gave scriptures to the assembled multitude because it was wisdom in the Father "that they should be given unto future generations," so the Book of Mormon as we have it was written "to the intent that they [a 'lesser part' of Christ's teachings and, by extension, all of Mormon's writings] may be brought again unto this people [the modern-day Lamanites], from the Gentiles, according to the words which Jesus hath spoken" (3 Nephi 26:2, 8).

These writings in all their richness of style, complexity of poetry, vividness of imagery, and memorability of narrative, reach both the mind and the heart. The content of the Book of Mormon is inseparable from the way it is presented.[27] It is a literary testimony of Christ. Why literature? An answer is found in Nephi's purpose in appealing to the writings of Isaiah, considered some of the most beautiful literature of all time. This purpose applies in turn to the persuasive beauty of Nephi's own writings: "that I might more fully persuade them to believe in the Lord their Redeemer I did read unto them that which was written by the prophet Isaiah; for I did liken all scriptures unto us, that it might be for our profit and learning" (1 Nephi 19:23). Similarly, the literary character of the Book of Mormon helps "more fully persuade" (1 Nephi 19:23) us. Nephi follows this statement and prefaces his quotation of Isaiah with words that are reminiscent of Isaiah's poetry:

> Hear ye the words of the prophet,
> ye who are a remnant of the house of Israel,
> a branch who have been broken off;
> hear ye the words of the prophet,
> which were written unto all the house of Israel,
> and liken them unto yourselves,
> that ye may have hope as well as your brethren
> from whom ye have been broken off.
>
> (1 Nephi 19:24)

These parallel ideas preface Nephi's quotation of Isaiah that continues Nephi's concern with "hearing":

> Hearken and hear this, O house of Jacob,
> who are called by the name of Israel . . . .
>
> (1 Nephi 20:1)

For those who will hearken to it, the book's message is clear: If the Gentiles in America keep the commandments, they shall prosper; if they do not, they shall be cut off from the Lord. To Lamanites long in a condition of spiritual captivity, the Book of Mormon provides deliverance through their coming to know the promises of the Lord in "the latter times" (Helaman 15:12–13). They are challenged to "arise from the dust," aided by the record that will cry unto them "out of the dust" (2 Nephi 1:14; Moroni 10:27). To the Jews, the Book of Mormon testifies that the Holy One of Israel, Jesus Christ, is the Messiah.

Once we have received the Book of Mormon, we are exhorted to ponder it in our hearts and to ask God, the Eternal Father, about it with a sincere heart and with real intent (Moroni 10:3–4). Further application of the various literary approaches introduced here can help in that pondering. There is much in the book that is plainly in view and yet still to be seen. Its words can and will be more meaningful as the Book of Mormon is studied with "heed and diligence," as Alma puts it; the book increasingly will disclose a greater "portion of his [God's] word" (Alma 12:9). To the person who "will not harden his heart," Alma says, "to him is given the greater portion of the word, until it is given unto him to know the mysteries of God until he know them in full" (Alma 12:10).

Considered from this perspective, the Book of Mormon is a Liahona. It provides heaven-sent direction "according to the faith and diligence and heed" given to it (1 Nephi 16:28). Apparently some in Lehi's party accepted the ball too casually and overlooked it because of its simplicity. For the Liahona to work properly, Alma taught, it was necessary to take it seriously and diligently observe it with faith (Alma 37). So too with the Book of Mormon. And in its literary dimension as well, the Book of Mormon is like a Liahona. Alma uses the example of the Liahona to make concrete to his son Helaman the abstract experience of following Christ. He says,

> For just as surely as this director did bring our fathers, by following its course, to the promised land, shall the words of Christ, if we follow their course, carry us beyond this vale of sorrow into a far better land of promise. (Alma 37:45)

The Book of Mormon, too, gains effectiveness and memorability by presenting doctrines and covenants through figurative language, narratives, typology, and the like.

To shift to another of Alma's metaphors, the tree of life (Alma 32), it is not enough to read the Book of Mormon once and say, "I believe." That would be like considering the first blossoming of a fruit tree to be the complete horticultural success. The tree needs to be fertilized, watered, pruned, and otherwise nourished until it reaches its full purpose in bearing fruit. Growth (and inspired learning) cannot come without help from God, but much effort is required on our part. As the apostle Paul put it, "I have planted, Apollos watered; but God gave the increase" (1 Corinthians 3:6). Or in Nephi's words, "It is by grace that we are saved, after all we can do" (2 Nephi 25:23). We are like Oliver Cowdery: to read God's word and translate it fully into our lives, we need to give it our best effort and God will then do his part (D&C 8, 9).

The words of the Book of Mormon weigh into God's judgments. As Nephi says, "The nations who shall possess [the things he writes] shall be judged of them according to the words which are written" (2 Nephi 25:22). Our further searching of the Book of Mormon "by study and also by faith" (D&C 88:118) prepares us to be favorably judged by its words. We will have to account to those inspired prophets who prepared the Book of Mormon for us—to Nephi, whose testimony sealed on earth "shall be brought against [us] at the judgment bar" (2 Nephi 33:15); to Jacob, who will meet his brethren "before the pleasing bar of God" (Jacob 6:13); to Mormon, who has promised that if we follow the example of our Savior, "it shall be well with [us] in the day of judgment" (Mormon 7:10); and to Moroni, who will bear his testimony again "at the judgment-seat of Christ" (title page).

NOTES

CHAPTER 1

"To Come Forth in Due Time"
INTRODUCTION

1. Ralph Waldo Emerson, "Address at the Opening of the Concord Free Public Library," in *Miscellanies*, vol. 11 of *The Complete Works of Ralph Waldo Emerson* (Boston: Houghton, Mifflin, 1911), 501.

2. William Wordsworth, "Preface to the *Lyrical Ballads*," in *English Romantic Poetry and Prose*, ed. Russell Noyes (New York: Oxford University Press, 1956), 363.

3. Robert Frost, "Education by Poetry: A Meditative Monologue" and "The Constant Symbol," in *Robert Frost: An Introduction*, ed. Robert A. Greenberg and James G. Hepburn (New York: Holt, Rinehart and Winston, 1961), 84, 87.

4. Orson F. Whitney, "Oratory, Poesy and Prophecy," *Improvement Era* 29 (April and May 1926): 530, 628.

5. Here, as with all Book of Mormon phrases and verses quoted and set as poetry in this book, lineation has been added.

6. Although this is the first book-length examination of the literary qualities of the Book of Mormon, several people have written on many aspects of the topic. One of the first to consider this approach was Roy A. West, who looked at literary forms and values in the Book of Mormon in his *An Introduction to the Book of Mormon* (Salt Lake City: LDS Department of Education, 1940). Another early treatment is Evan Shute's article, "The Book of Mormon as Literature," which appeared in *The Saints Herald*, 27 February 1943. "As it is primarily a theological work," Shute notes, "a 'Golden Bible,' one naturally turns to the Hebrew Bible for comparisons." To him, the Book of Mormon "has much of the Mosaic thunder, much of the noble melodrama of Daniel, and great stretches reminiscent of Isaiah (who is extensively quoted) and of Jeremiah and their lesser brethren. It contains much of the personal, simple, quotable teaching of the Gospels and a great deal of theological

exposition, suggesting Paul and the great apostles" (7, 8). "The Book of Mormon as Literature" was also the title of a highly detailed radio address given in 1946 by Franklin S. Harris Jr. It was published in *The Book of Mormon Message and Evidences* (Salt Lake City: Corporation of the President of The Church of Jesus Christ of Latter-day Saints, 1953). In another pioneering work on the topic that was developed at the same time, Sidney B. Sperry defined various literary types found in the Book of Mormon and wrote out the Psalm of Nephi in poetic form (see note 22, below, for a more detailed discussion of Sperry's work). In 1947, Robert K. Thomas completed a B.A. thesis at Reed College entitled, "A Literary Analysis of the Book of Mormon." In it he defined these various literary types found in the Book of Mormon: narrative prose, poetry, parable, oratory, prophetic discourse, symbolic prophecy, prophecy of vision, prophetic dialogue, pastorals, and war letters. He subsequently published his main findings in a summary article, "A Literary Critic Looks at the Book of Mormon," in *To the Glory of God*, ed. Charles D. Tate Jr. and Truman G. Madsen (Salt Lake City: Deseret Book, 1972), 149–61. Thomas's discussion on diversity of style is anticipated in a brief reference to the topic by James E. Talmage in chapter 15 of *The Articles of Faith* (Salt Lake City: The Church of Jesus Christ of Latter-day Saints, 1913).

7. William Shakespeare, *The Tragedy of King Lear*, IV. vi. 152. Nathaniel Hawthorne, *The Scarlet Letter*, vol. 1 of *The Centenary Edition of the Works of Nathaniel Hawthorne*, ed. William Charvat et al. (Columbus: Ohio State University Press, 1962), 260.

8. Arthur Henry King, in "Language Themes in Jacob 5: 'The vineyard of the Lord of hosts is the house of Israel (Isaiah 5:7),'" in *The Allegory of the Olive Tree: The Olive, the Bible, and Jacob 5*, ed. Stephen D. Ricks and John W. Welch (Salt Lake City: Deseret Book and FARMS, 1994), 171, says the richness of the Book of Mormon "cannot be properly appreciated unless the book is read aloud and listened to."

9. The text of the Book of Mormon cited throughout by book, chapter, and verse is the one published in 1981 by The Church of Jesus Christ of Latter-day Saints. Other texts consulted are the 1830 edition (in a 1980 facsimile) and the three-volume *Book of Mormon Critical Text: A Tool for Scholarly Reference* (Provo, Utah: FARMS, 1984–87).

10. Gary Lee Walker elaborates the lessons for our time found in 3 Nephi in his essay "The Downfall of the Nephite Nation: Lessons for Our Time (3 Nephi 6–10)," in Kent P. Jackson, ed., *Alma 30 to Moroni*, Studies in Scripture Series, vol. 8 (Salt Lake City: Deseret Book, 1988).

11. In *Ensign* 16 (November 1986): 6. In his October 1986 general conference address, President Benson reaffirmed what he had said in the April 1975 general conference ("The Book of Mormon Is the Word of God," *Ensign* 5 [May 1975]: 63): "The Book of Mormon was written for us today. God is the author of the book. . . . Mormon, the ancient prophet after whom the book is named, abridged centuries of records. God, who knows the end from the

beginning, told him what to include in his abridgment that we would need for our day." Daniel H. Ludlow expressed much the same view in his article "The Book of Mormon Was Written for Our Day," *Instructor* (July 1966): 265: "Through the power of vision and prophecy, these writers were shown the people of our day, for whom they were writing their records. Thus, from the voluminous records at their disposal, they were able to select those principles and experiences which would be most useful in helping us to meet our challenges and solve our problems."

12. Hugh Nibley, *The Prophetic Book of Mormon* (Salt Lake City: Deseret Book and FARMS, 1989), 365.

13. Ibid., 500.

14. Gordon B. Hinckley, in October 1979 general conference, published in "'An Angel from on High, the Long, Long Silence Broke,'" *Ensign* 9 (November 1979): 8.

15. Boyd K. Packer, *Teach Ye Diligently* (Salt Lake City: Deseret Book, 1975), 227–28.

16. Samuel Taylor Coleridge, *Biographia Literaria,* in *English Romantic Poetry and Prose,* 427.

17. Leland Ryken finds these characteristics in biblical literature in *How to Read the Bible as Literature* (Grand Rapids, Mich.: Academie Books, 1984), 23.

18. Here, as with all italicized Book of Mormon words and phrases quoted in this book, the italics have been added.

19. Nibley, *Prophetic Book of Mormon,* 68.

20. Joseph Smith attributed the writing of the title page to Moroni: "I wish to mention here that the title-page of the Book of Mormon is a literal translation, taken from the very last leaf, on the left hand side of the collection or book of plates, which contained the record which has been translated, the language of the whole running the same as all Hebrew writing in general" (Joseph Smith, *History of The Church of Jesus Christ of Latter-day Saints,* ed. B. H. Roberts, 2d ed. rev. [Salt Lake City: The Church of Jesus Christ of Latter-day Saints, 1932–51], 1:71).

21. Robert K. Thomas examines varying styles in his 1947 Reed College thesis. Glade L. Burgon provides an extensive treatment of style in his 1958 Brigham Young University M.A. thesis, "An Analysis of Style Variations in the Book of Mormon." Regarding the writings of Moroni, he concludes that they are "made beautiful and impressive by the abundance of well formed synthetical and antithetical parallelisms" (43).

22. The types, or genres, dealt with in this book are ones more narrowly considered under belletristic literature. A broader list of genres in the Book of Mormon is provided by Sidney B. Sperry in his pioneering work, *Book of Mormon Compendium* (Salt Lake City: Bookcraft, 1970), which was an expansion of his earlier work *Our Book of Mormon* (Salt Lake City: Bookcraft, 1947). Much of *Our Book of Mormon* has been reprinted in a special issue of *Journal of Book of Mormon Studies* 4, no. 1 (1995). Sperry gives the following literary

types: allegory, didactic exposition, editorial reflection or commentary, epistle, exhortation, genealogy, gospel, historical narrative, hortatory discourse, lamentation, memoir, oratory, patriarchal admonition, patriarchal blessing, prayer, prophecy of doom, prophetic dialogue, prophetic discourse, prophetic narrative, prophetic prediction, psalm, religious teaching, revelation, sermon, song of praise, symbolic prophecy, and war epistle. Additional types are aphorism, apocalyptic writing, judgment, and farewell speech.

23. Leland Ryken, *Words of Delight: A Literary Introduction to the Bible* (Grand Rapids, Mich.: Baker, 1987), 16.

24. Hugh Nibley, *The World and the Prophets* (Salt Lake City: Deseret Book and FARMS, 1987), 214.

25. David Noel Freedman, "Pottery, Poetry, and Prophecy: An Essay on Biblical Poetry," in *The Bible in Its Literary Milieu,* ed. John R. Maier and Vincent L. Tollers (Grand Rapids, Mich.: Eerdmans, 1979), 95.

26. George A. Kennedy, *New Testament Interpretation through Rhetorical Criticism* (Chapel Hill: University of North Carolina Press, 1984).

CHAPTER 2
"To Show unto the Remnant of the House of Israel"
NARRATORS AND NARRATIVES

1. For a fruitful lead for further exploration of Book of Mormon narratives, see Edgar C. Snow Jr., "Narrative Criticism and the Book of Mormon," *Journal of Book of Mormon Studies* 4, no. 2 (1995): 93–106.

2. Grant R. Hardy, "Mormon as Editor," in *Rediscovering the Book of Mormon,* ed. John L. Sorenson and Melvin J. Thorne (Salt Lake City: Deseret Book and FARMS, 1991), 22.

3. Repetition is also an important characteristic of certain biblical narratives. For example, James S. Ackerman comments on "the unusual amount of doubling in the Joseph story: three sets of dreams occur in pairs—by Joseph, by his fellow prisoners, and by Pharaoh. Joseph is twice confined—in the pit and in prison. The brothers make two trips to Egypt for grain, have two audiences with Joseph on each occasion, twice find money in their grain bags, make two attempts to gain Jacob's permission to send Benjamin to Egypt, and finally receive two invitations to settle in Egypt." And so on. "Joseph, Judah, and Jacob," in *Literary Interpretations of Biblical Narratives,* ed. Kenneth R. R. Gros Louis (Nashville: Abingdon Press, 1982), 2:85.

4. The apostle John taught this law in the Old World when he said: "For there are three that bear record in heaven, the Father, the Word, and the Holy Ghost: and these three are one. And there are three that bear witness in earth, the Spirit, and the water, and the blood: and these three agree in one" (1 John 5:7–8).

5. Robert Alter, *The Art of Biblical Narrative* (New York: Basic Books, 1981), 181.

6. Ibid., 180–81.

7. Ibid., 181.

8. Ibid., 47–62, 181.

9. Susan Taber analyzes this comparison in her essay, "Mormon's Literary Technique," finding that the "structure of the book of Mosiah, and to some extent the first half of Alma, is parallelism, contrasting and reinforcing" (*Mormon Letters Annual* [Salt Lake City: Association for Mormon Letters, 1983], 118). In "Mosiah: The Complex Symbolism and the Symbolic Complex of Kingship in the Book of Mormon" (*Journal of Book of Mormon Studies* 2, no. 1 [1993]), Gordon C. Thomasson also makes the point that the Book of Mosiah is a study in contrasts between good and bad kings.

10. Leland Ryken, *How to Read the Bible as Literature* (Grand Rapids, Mich.: Academie Books, 1984), 14.

11. Hugh Nibley, *Since Cumorah* (Salt Lake City: Deseret Book and FARMS, 1988), 380.

12. Chauncey C. Riddle, "Korihor," in *The Book of Mormon: It Begins with a Family* (Salt Lake City: Deseret Book, 1983), 135–37.

13. These connections are noted in *Book of Mormon Critical Text: A Tool for Scholarly Reference*, vol. 2 (Provo, Utah: FARMS, 1986).

14. For perceptive and thorough treatments of the Exodus pattern in the Book of Mormon, see George S. Tate, "The Typology of the Exodus Pattern in the Book of Mormon," in *Literature of Belief: Sacred Scripture and Religious Experience,* ed. Neal E. Lambert (Provo, Utah: BYU Religious Studies Center, 1981), 245–62, and S. Kent Brown, "The Exodus Pattern in the Book of Mormon," *Brigham Young University Studies* 30, no. 3 (1990): 111–42.

15. See also 1 Nephi 2:20–21; 2 Nephi 1:9; 4:4; Enos 1:10; Jarom 1:9–10; Omni 1:6; Alma 9:13; 36:1; 37:13; 48:25; 50:20; 3 Nephi 5:22; 4 Nephi 1:18; and Ether 2:7–10.

CHAPTER 3

"Great Things the Lord Hath Done"
EPIC ELEMENTS

1. E. M. W. Tillyard, *The English Epic and Its Background* (New York: Barnes and Noble, 1966).

2. Leland Ryken, *Words of Delight: A Literary Introduction to the Bible* (Grand Rapids, Mich.: Baker, 1987), 127–29.

3. M. H. Abrams, *A Glossary of Literary Terms* (Fort Worth: Harcourt Brace Jovanovich, 1993), 54–55.

4. John P. McWilliams Jr., *The American Epic: Transforming a Genre, 1770–1860* (New York: Cambridge University Press, 1989), 217, 6.

5. Abrams, *Glossary,* 52.

6. McWilliams, *American Epic,* 28.

7. Gabriel Josipovici, *The Book of God: A Response to the Bible* (New Haven: Yale University Press, 1988), 61.

8. Abrams, *Glossary,* 55.

9. Hugh Nibley, *An Approach to the Book of Mormon* (Salt Lake City: Deseret Book and FARMS, 1988), 33–55. In "Tenting, Toll, and Taxing," *Western Political Quarterly* 19, no. 4 (1966): 599, Nibley says regarding an epic milieu: "It was not until early in the present century that H. M. Chadwick [in *The Heroic Age*] pointed out what should have been obvious to everyone, namely that epic literature, a large and important segment of the human record, is the product not of unrestrained poetic fancy but of real years of terror and gloom through which the entire race has been forced to pass from time to time. We now have good reason to believe . . . that the violence of the elements that forms the somber backdrop of the 'Epic Milieu' was more than a literary convention." (This article was reprinted in Hugh Nibley, *The Ancient State: The Rulers and the Ruled* [Salt Lake City: Deseret Book and FARMS, 1991].)

10. Nibley, *Approach,* 39–40.

11. This relationship of Nephi to his people is central to an epic. According to Cleanth Brooks, R. W. B. Lewis, and Robert Penn Warren in *American Literature: The Makers and the Making* (New York: St. Martin's Press, 1973), 2:2190, an epic gives us "the story of a hero who typifies a people and whose career provides us with a sense of the history of a people enacted and of a civilization realized or transformed."

12. E. Douglas Clark and Robert S. Clark in *Fathers and Sons in the Book of Mormon* (Salt Lake City: Deseret Book, 1991), 229–32, show a number of parallels between Mormon and Nephi, including preparation in the "learning of my people" or "learning of my father" (Mormon 1:2; 1 Nephi 1:1), being visited by the Lord, and being military leaders of their people.

13. See also Jarom 1:9; Omni 1:6; Mosiah 1:7; Alma 9:13; 36:30; 37:13; 3 Nephi 5:22.

14. Northrop Frye, *Anatomy of Criticism: Four Essays* (Princeton: Princeton University Press, 1957), 317.

CHAPTER 4
"By the Spirit of Prophecy"
POETRY

1. Susan Easton Black, *Finding Christ through the Book of Mormon* (Salt Lake City: Deseret Book, 1987), 11.

2. Indeed, Kent P. Jackson in his essay on Nephi and Isaiah, in Kent P. Jackson, ed., *1 Nephi to Alma 29,* Studies in Scripture Series, vol. 7 (Salt Lake City: Deseret Book, 1987), 138, says, regarding the Book of Mormon, "Nowhere in it (except when Old Testament prophets are quoted) do we have

revelation presented in poetic style." I trust that in this chapter we shall see otherwise.

3. See Richard Dilworth Rust, "Book of Mormon Poetry," *New Era* (March 1983): 46–50; Paul Cracroft, "A Clear Poetic Voice," *Ensign* 14 (January 1984): 28–31; Angela M. Crowell, "Hebrew Poetry in the Book of Mormon," *Zarahemla Record* 32 and 33 (1986): 2–9, and 34 (1986): 7–12; Angela M. Crowell, "The Hebrew Literary Structure of the Book of Mormon," *Restoration Studies V,* ed. Darlene Caswell (Independence, Mo.: Herald Publishing House, 1993), 156–69; Donald W. Parry, "Climactic Forms in the Book of Mormon," in *Reexploring the Book of Mormon,* ed. John W. Welch (Salt Lake City: Deseret Book and FARMS, 1992), 290–92; and Donald W. Parry, *The Book of Mormon Text Reformatted According to Parallelistic Patterns* (Provo, Utah: FARMS, 1992). With respect to the last work, though not every unit containing parallelism is poetry (nor is every passage of poetry reformatted here), Parry's reformatted text reveals visually much of the poetry in the Book of Mormon. I should add that most of the Book of Mormon text still remains prose, and I think Wade Brown takes a good thing too far in formatting the entire text into poetic and parallelistic structures in *The God-Inspired Language of the Book of Mormon: Structure and Commentary* (Clackamas, Oreg.: Rainbow Press, 1988).

4. Hugh Nibley says that "in Lehi's day an inspired leader had to be a poet" (*An Approach to the Book of Mormon* [Salt Lake City: Deseret Book and FARMS, 1988], 268).

5. David Noel Freedman, "Pottery, Poetry, and Prophecy: An Essay on Biblical Poetry," in *The Bible in Its Literary Milieu,* ed. John Maier and Vincent Toller (Grand Rapids, Mich.: Eerdmans, 1979), 92. In my essay "Book of Mormon Poetry," I comment that "Book of Mormon prose may be likened to a highway: it moves sequentially from one place to the next. Book of Mormon poetry, on the other hand, is cumulative: one idea builds upon another. It is like a beautiful structure such as the Salt Lake Temple" (50).

6. Robert Alter, *The Art of Biblical Poetry* (New York: Basic Books, 1985), 141. He also makes this telling point about the connection of poetry and prophecy: "As a rule the formal resources of poetry—its pronounced reliance on figurative language; its strong tendency in parallelism to underscore and complicate connections between related sounds, words, images, and motifs; its gravitation toward symbolic structures; its impulse to realize the extreme possibilities of the themes it takes up—all these lead the prophets to a different order of statement when they cast their vision in verse" (160–61).

7. Orson F. Whitney, "Joseph Smith in Literature," *Improvement Era* 9 (December 1905): 136.

8. T. R. Henn, "The Bible as Literature," in *Peake's Commentary on the Bible,* ed. Matthew Black and H. H. Rowley (Surrey, England: Thomas Nelson & Sons, 1962), 12–13.

9. Edgar Allan Poe, "*Twice-told Tales,* by Nathaniel Hawthorne: A Review," *Graham's Magazine* 20 (May 1842): 298.

10. Ralph Waldo Emerson, "The Poet," in *Essays: First and Second Series* (New York: Vintage Books and the Library of America, 1990), 225.

11. As stated before, with these passages and all the poetry that follows, the line arrangements are mine; likewise, all italicization of Book of Mormon words or phrases is mine. Because the poetry in the Book of Mormon is Hebraic in character, my model for lineation by parallelistic ideas is lined-out Old Testament poetry as found in books like *The Bible and the Common Reader*, by Mary Ellen Chase (New York: Macmillan, 1956) and *The Dartmouth Bible: An Abridgment of the King James Version, with Aids to Its Understanding as History and Literature, and as a Source of Religious Experience* (Boston: Houghton Mifflin, 1950).

12. Victor L. Ludlow, in *Isaiah: Prophet, Seer, and Poet* (Salt Lake City: Deseret Book, 1982), 31–39, illustrates seven types of semantic parallelism in Hebraic poetry: (1) "Synonymous parallelism: a theme of the first line *repeats* itself in the second line, but in slightly different words." (2) "Antithetic parallelism: a thought of the second part of a couplet *contrasts* with an opposite theme in the first." (3) "Emblematic parallelism: the ideas of two lines are *compared* by means of a simile or metaphor." (4) "Synthetic parallelism: the second line *completes* or *complements* the thought of the first." (5) "Composite parallelism: three or more phrases *develop* a theme by amplifying a concept or defining a term." (6) "Climactic parallelism: part of one line (a word or phrase) is repeated in the second and other lines until a theme is developed which then *culminates* in a main idea or statement." (7) "Introverted parallelism: a pattern of words or ideas is stated and then repeated, but in a *reverse* order. This parallelism is also called chiasmus."

13. As might be expected, a much more technical analysis can be made. Some of the principal indicators of Hebraic poetry set forth by Wilfred G. E. Watson in *Classical Hebrew Poetry: A Guide to Its Techniques* (Sheffield, England: JSOT Press, 1984), 46–47, are evident line-forms, ellipsis, unusual vocabulary, conciseness, unusual word-order, regularity and symmetry, parallelism in various forms, word-pairs (e.g., day/night), chiastic patterns, envelope figures, and repetition in various forms. In his *Hebrew Poetry: Traditional Techniques in Classical Hebrew Verse* (Sheffield, England: Sheffield Academic Press, 1994), Watson expands on his earlier indicators and includes chapters specifically devoted to word-pairs, chiasmus, and rhetorical devices. See also Parry, *Book of Mormon Text Reformatted;* Crowell, "Hebrew Poetry in the Book of Mormon"; and Alter, *Poetry.*

14. Ruth apRoberts, "Old Testament Poetry: The Translatable Structure," *PMLA* 92 (1977): 999; Alter, *Poetry,* 18–19. In her book *The Biblical Web* (Ann Arbor: University of Michigan Press, 1994), 20–23, apRoberts shows that biblical poetry with its rhyme of parallel ideas is readily translatable.

15. According to Freedman, a purpose of chiasmus, or inverted parallelism, is to "concentrate the reader's or hearer's interest on the central expression" (in John W. Welch, ed., *Chiasmus in Antiquity: Structures, Analyses, Exegesis*

[Hildesheim, West Germany: Gerstenberg, 1981], 7). Other purposes, according to John Welch, are to strengthen each element individually upon its chiastic repetition, help in memorization, make the work suitable for use in ritual settings, and help in oral transmission (11–14).

A good example of chiasmus is the quotation from Isaiah in 2 Nephi 16:10 (cf. Isaiah 6:10):

a Make the *heart* of this people fat,
  b and make their *ears* heavy,
    c and shut their *eyes*—
    c' lest they see with their *eyes*,
  b' and hear with their *ears*,
a' And understand with their *heart*,
and be converted and be healed.

16. Alter, *Poetry*, 76.

17. Moshe Greenberg, "Job," in *The Literary Guide to the Bible*, ed. Robert Alter and Frank Kermode (Cambridge: Harvard University Press, 1987), 303.

18. Isaiah 55:1–2 reads:

Ho, every one that thirsteth, come ye to the waters,
and he that hath no money; come ye, buy, and eat;
yea, come, buy wine and milk without money and without price.
Wherefore do ye spend money for that which is not bread?
and your labour for that which satisfieth not?
hearken diligently unto me, and eat ye that which is good,
and let your soul delight itself in fatness.

19. James L. Kugel in *The Idea of Biblical Poetry: Parallelism and its History* (New Haven: Yale University Press, 1981), 59–95, discusses the difficulty of positively identifying the presence of poetry in the Bible and notes instances of parallelism within prose. Tremper Longman III in *Literary Approaches to Biblical Interpretation* (Grand Rapids, Mich.: Academie Books, 1987) says, "Poetry may be defined over against prose by reference to ordinary speech. Prose represents a certain departure from normal speech patterns and poetry a further departure. Poetry is a more self-consciously structured language. It is self-referring in the sense that increased attention is given to how something is said as well as to what is said. In this manner, poetry is characterized by a higher level of literary artifice than prose. . . . Instead of characterizing prose and poetry as discrete literary forms, we may better represent them as poles on a continuum" (120–21).

20. Sidney B. Sperry, *Our Book of Mormon* (Salt Lake City: Bookcraft, 1947), 110–11. A carefully detailed analysis of this poem is provided by Stephen P. Sondrup, "The Psalm of Nephi: A Lyric Reading," *Brigham Young University Studies* 21, no. 3 (1981): 357–72.

21. Alter, "Psalms," in *Literary Guide to the Bible*, 248.

22. "That which is of God inviteth and enticeth to do good continually;

wherefore, every thing which inviteth and enticeth to do good, and to love God, and to serve him, is inspired of God" (Moroni 7:13).

23. William Everson, Note (n.p.) to Walt Whitman, *American Bard;* the original preface to *Leaves of Grass* arranged in verse by William Everson (New York: Viking Press, 1982). Unlike Whitman's preface, though, most of the Book of Mormon is in prose, not poetry.

24. "A Conversation with Clinton F. Larson," *Dialogue* 4 (1969): 75. Similarly, Larson calls Nephi "a fine symbolist poet" with "the same vision that his father Lehi had, a vision which involved profound metaphors and the affective interpretation of metaphors" (74).

25. For a lined-out presentation of this poem similar to mine, see J. N. Washburn, *The Miracle of the Book of Mormon* (Orem, Utah: Book Production Services, 1984), 153–54.

26. S. Kent Brown argues persuasively in his essay "The Prophetic Laments of Samuel the Lamanite" (*Journal of Book of Mormon Studies* 1 [Fall 1992]: 163–80) that Mormon responded to prophetic and poetic laments by Samuel the Lamanite, especially the lament that people would say, "O that we had remembered the Lord our God in the day that he gave us our riches, and then they would not have become slippery that we should lose them" (Helaman 13:33; cf. Mormon 2:10–11).

27. Hugh Nibley, *Since Cumorah* (Salt Lake City: Deseret Book and FARMS, 1988), 152.

28. Welch, *Chiasmus in Antiquity,* 201.

29. Ludlow, *Isaiah,* 3.

CHAPTER 5
"Know the Covenants of the Lord"
SERMONS

1. Although it is not examined in detail here, the resurrected Jesus' initial sermon to the Nephites—which corresponds considerably to the Sermon on the Mount—has remarkable literary qualities. The rhetorical effectiveness of the Sermon on the Mount has been discussed by George A. Kennedy, *New Testament Interpretation through Rhetorical Criticism* (Chapel Hill: University of North Carolina Press, 1984), 39–63. The paradoxical nature of the Beatitudes is treated by Frank Kermode, "Matthew," in *The Literary Guide to the Bible,* ed. Robert Alter and Frank Kermode (Cambridge: Harvard University Press, 1987), 391. Striking differences between the Sermon on the Mount and its equivalent in 3 Nephi, especially the pervasively Christ-centered pattern of the latter, have been pointed out by Krister Stendahl, "The Sermon on the Mount and Third Nephi," in *Reflections on Mormonism: Judaeo-Christian Parallels,* ed. Truman G. Madsen (Provo, Utah: BYU Religious Studies Center, 1978), 139–54. Arthur R. Bassett shows the organic unity of this sermon in "Jesus' Sermon to the

Nephites," in *The Book of Mormon: It Begins with a Family* (Salt Lake City: Deseret Book, 1983), 204–13.

2. Additional important sermons in the Book of Mormon, or what Sidney B. Sperry more exactly calls "prophetic discourse," are Nephi's expounding the prophecies of Isaiah to his brethren (1 Nephi 22); Nephi's prophetic declarations to his people (2 Nephi 25–33); Lehi's exhortation found in 2 Nephi 1:1–4:11; Jacob's sermon in Jacob 2–3; Jacob's introducing and expounding the allegory of the olive tree (Jacob 5–6); Limhi's oration (Mosiah 7:18–33); Abinadi's exhortation and testimony (Mosiah 12–16); Alma's sermon in Alma 12–13; Amulek's story and testimony (Alma 10:17–23, Alma 34); religious dialogue between Ammon and King Lamoni (Alma 18); religious dialogue between Aaron and the king over all the land (Alma 22); dialogue of Ammon with his brethren (Alma 26); Alma's blessings and instructions to his sons (Alma 36–42); the impromptu sermon by Nephi the son of Helaman (Helaman 7:13–29); Nephi's speech renewed (Helaman 8:11–28); Samuel the Lamanite's testimony (Helaman 13–15); sermons and teachings of the resurrected Christ (much of 3 Nephi 11–28); and Moroni's final admonition to his future readers (Moroni 10).

Having in mind prophetic discourses such as those found in 2 Nephi 29 and Jacob 6, Sperry says in *Our Book of Mormon* (Salt Lake City: Bookcraft, 1947), 117, "This type of literature is relatively simple and may be thought of as the equivalent of our modern sermon in which description, reflection, and warning are intermingled in a fervor of appeal." As good examples of prophetic discourse in the Old Testament, he cites Isaiah 1–4, Jeremiah 23–32, and Ezekiel 34.

3. The Nephites would have seen a close connection between an earthly king and a heavenly king—they considered their kings to be appointed by God. Stephen D. Ricks points out this fact in "The Ideology of Kingship in Mosiah 1–6," in *Reexploring the Book of Mormon*, ed. John W. Welch (Salt Lake City: Deseret Book and FARMS), 114–16.

4. In his essay "King, Coronation, and Covenant in Mosiah 1–6" (in *Rediscovering the Book of Mormon*, ed. John L. Sorenson and Melvin J. Thorne [Salt Lake City: Deseret Book and FARMS, 1991], 209–19), Stephen Ricks shows how the elements of covenant renewal found in Exodus, Deuteronomy, and Joshua are found in Mosiah 1–6: "(1) the king/prophet gives a preamble that introduces God as the one making the covenant or that introduces his prophet as spokesman for God; (2) the king/prophet gives a brief review of God's relations with Israel in the past; (3) the king/prophet notes the terms of the covenant, listing specific commandments and obligations that God expected Israel to keep; (4) the people bear witness in formal statements that they accept the covenant; (5) the king/prophet lists the blessings and curses for obedience or disobedience to the covenant; and (6) the king/prophet makes provisions for depositing a written copy of the covenant in a safe and sacred place and for reading its contents to the people in the future" (215–16). See

also Ricks's earlier essay, "The Treaty/Covenant Pattern in King Benjamin's Address (Mosiah 1–6)," *Brigham Young University Studies* 24, no. 2 (1984): 151–62.

5. Hugh Nibley in *An Approach to the Book of Mormon* (Salt Lake City: Deseret Book and FARMS, 1988), 243–56 shows how this gathering was the Great Assembly at the New Year. Also, John A. Tvedtnes, Gordon C. Thomasson, and John W. Welch have noted how the setting of this speech is proximate to a celebration of the Feast of Tabernacles. (Tvedtnes, "King Benjamin and the Feast of Tabernacles," in *By Study and Also by Faith: Essays in Honor of Hugh W. Nibley*, ed. John M. Lundquist and Stephen D. Ricks [Salt Lake City: Deseret Book and FARMS, 1990], 2:197–237; Thomasson, "Expanding Approaches to the Book of Mormon: Pre-exilic Israelite Religious Patterns" [unpublished]; Welch, "Chiasmus in the Book of Mormon," in *Chiasmus in Antiquity: Structures, Analyses, Exegesis,* ed. John W. Welch [Hildesheim, West Germany: Gerstenberg, 1981], 202.)

6. George Kennedy, *Classical Rhetoric and Its Christian and Secular Tradition from Ancient to Modern Times* (Chapel Hill: University of North Carolina Press, 1980), 123–24.

7. Ibid., 127.

8. Kennedy, *New Testament Interpretation,* 36.

9. Ibid., 10.

10. Ibid., 23–24.

11. Ibid., 15.

12. Kennedy, *Classical Rhetoric,* 123.

13. This is one of many elements that make, as Welch shows, Benjamin's speech a classic ancient farewell address (*Reexploring the Book of Mormon,* 120–23).

14. Radical Christian rhetoric, Kennedy says, is "a form of 'sacred language' characterized by assertion and absolute claims of authoritative truth without evidence or logical argument" (*New Testament Interpretation,* 104).

15. Many of these elements are also found in other Book of Mormon sermons. For example, *Authority:* Alma commands the people of Zarahemla "in the language of him who hath commanded me" (Alma 5:61). *Clear one's conscience:* Jacob desires to rid his garments of blood (Jacob 1:19; 2:2). *Speak plainly:* Alma says, "I have spoken unto you plainly that ye cannot err, or have spoken according to the commandments of God" (Alma 5:43). *Purpose of discourse given:* Alma asks the people of Zarahemla challenging questions that will stir them to repentance (Alma 5:8–59). *People enjoined to repent:* Abinadi's exhortation (Mosiah 12–16). *Choice between following God and following Satan:* Jacob says, "Reconcile yourselves to the will of God, and not to the will of the devil and the flesh" (2 Nephi 10:24). *A prophecy given of the future:* Samuel the Lamanite's prophecies (Helaman 13–15). *Prophet's testimony to be confirmed:* Nephi says, "I speak unto you as the voice of one crying from the dust: Farewell until that great day shall come. . . . For what I seal on earth,

shall be brought against you at the judgment bar" (2 Nephi 33:13, 15). *Audience response:* The poor of the Zoramites interact with Alma (Alma 32–33).

16. Welch, *Chiasmus in Antiquity,* 203.

17. Ibid.

18. Ibid. Also very instructive on chiasmus is Welch's earlier essay on the topic: "Chiasmus in the Book of Mormon," *Brigham Young University Studies* 10, no. 1 (1969): 69–84.

19. Welch, *Chiasmus in Antiquity,* 205.

20. John S. Tanner characterizes Jacob's style and themes well in "Jacob and His Descendants as Authors" (*Rediscovering the Book of Mormon,* 52–66). Jacob is "intimate, vivid, vulnerable" (59).

21. Marilyn Arnold, in *Sweet Is the Word: Reflections on the Book of Mormon, Its Narrative, Teachings, and People* (American Fork, Utah: Covenant, 1996), 51, responds to "how effectively Jacob melds content and form, how what he says is enhanced by his use of language." A brief but effective analysis of the sermon is provided by C. Terry Warner in his essay "Jacob," in *The Book of Mormon: It Begins with a Family,* 47–48.

22. Kennedy, *New Testament Interpretation,* 19. Kennedy refers to the three species of rhetoric formulated by Aristotle—judicial, deliberative, and epideictic—and says, "The species is judicial when the author is seeking to persuade the audience to make a judgment about events occurring in the past; it is deliberative when he seeks to persuade them to take some action in the future; it is epideictic when he seeks to persuade them to hold or reaffirm some point of view in the present." More specifically, *epideictic* means "the praise or blame of a man" as defined by Kennedy in *Classical Rhetoric,* 73.

23. Welch, *Reexploring,* 66–68; see also Welch, "The Temple in the Book of Mormon," in *Temples of the Ancient World,* ed. Donald W. Parry (Salt Lake City: Deseret Book and FARMS, 1994), 334–36.

24. This Book of Mormon sermon is exceptional in containing elements akin to the pattern of Puritan sermons: explication of biblical text, a derivation of doctrine from it, reasons for that doctrine, and uses of it. For the form of Puritan sermons, see Phyllis M. Jones and Nicholas R. Jones, eds., *Salvation in New England: Selections from the Sermons of the First Preachers* (Austin: University of Texas Press, 1977), 6; Perry Miller, *The New England Mind: The Seventeenth Century* (Cambridge: Harvard University Press, 1954), 332–33; or Kenneth R. Murdock, "The Colonial and Revolutionary Period," in *The Literature of the American People,* ed. Arthur Hobson Quinn (New York: Appleton-Century-Crofts, 1951), 43.

25. Welch aptly calls these "Jacob's Ten Commandments," in *Reexploring the Book of Mormon,* 69–72. Welch says Jacob's "statement is an admirable summary of the basic religious values of the Nephites, cast in a form fully at home in ancient Israel and in the Near East" (72).

26. This concept of ridding garments of the blood (sins) of others is

repeated by Jacob in Jacob 1:19 and pronounced by King Benjamin (who assembled his people in order to rid his garments of their blood [Mosiah 2:28]), by Alma (who asks his brethren how they will feel at the bar of God with their "garments stained with blood and all manner of filthiness" [Alma 5:22]), and by Mormon and Moroni—whose testimonies help them "rid [their] garments of the blood of [their] brethren" (Mormon 9:35; Ether 12:38).

27. For a chiastical and rhetorical approach to part of Alma 13, see James T. Duke, "The Literary and Doctrinal Significance of Alma 13:1–9," *Journal of Book of Mormon Studies* 5 (1996): 103–18.

28. This is a point Jacob Neusner, noted Jewish scholar, makes about Genesis in his book *Christian Faith and the Bible of Judaism: The Judaic Encounter with Scripture* (Grand Rapids, Mich.: Eerdmans, 1987), 20. It applies well to a number of situations in the Book of Mormon in which nature and history correlate with each other.

29. Steven L. Olsen, "Patterns of Prayer: Humility or Pride," *Ensign* 22 (August 1992): 10, says, "Mormon's entire account of the mission to the Zoramites teaches a powerful lesson on true worship, carefully drawn from the historical details of the records and woven around the poignant contrast between Alma's prayer and the prayers of the Zoramites."

30. Amos N. Wilder, in *Early Christian Rhetoric: The Language of the Gospel* (Cambridge: Harvard University Press, 1971), 43, finds three particular speech patterns in the oldest period of the Gospels: the dialogue, the story, and the poem. The dialogue-form, he says, "takes us to the heart of biblical religion, namely prayer itself" (45).

31. Wilder, *Early Christian Rhetoric*, 25, says, "In all genuine artifacts, including language-forms, shape and substance are inseparable and mutually determinative." In my analyses of Book of Mormon sermons, I have been aided by a number of examinations of the New Testament as literature. Leland Ryken in *How to Read the Bible as Literature* (Grand Rapids, Mich.: Academie Books, 1984), for example, discusses examples of rhetorical patterns found in the New Testament. These include parallelism, rhetorical questions, question-and-answer constructions, imaginary dialogues, the aphoristic conciseness of a proverb, and any highly patterned arrangement of clauses or phrases. Forceful and imaginative language in the New Testament, Ryken finds, uses rhetorical devices to break through the clichés of ordinary language and to reveal truth with power.

CHAPTER 6
"Their Fathers"
LETTERS AND AUTOBIOGRAPHY

1. For a discussion of the various styles of writing in the Book of Mormon, see Robert K. Thomas, "A Literary Critic Looks at the Book of Mormon," in *To the Glory of God*, ed. Charles D. Tate Jr. and Truman G. Madsen (Salt Lake City:

Deseret Book, 1972), 149–61. For extensive treatments of individual personalities and family relationships, see *The Book of Mormon: It Begins with a Family,* a compilation of essays first printed in the *Ensign* on Book of Mormon persons (Salt Lake City: Deseret Book, 1983); E. Douglas Clark and Robert S. Clark, *Fathers and Sons in the Book of Mormon* (Salt Lake City: Deseret Book, 1991); and John S. Tanner, "Jacob and His Descendants as Authors," in *Rediscovering the Book of Mormon,* ed. John L. Sorenson and Melvin J. Thorne (Salt Lake City: Deseret Book and FARMS, 1991), 52–66.

2. Jonathan Edwards, Personal Narrative, in *The Works of President Edwards* (1847; reprint, New York: Burt Franklin, 1968), 1:29, 33.

3. Erich Auerbach, *Mimesis: The Representation of Reality in Western Literature,* trans. Willard R. Trask (Princeton: Princeton University Press, 1953), 8.

4. Ibid., 11.

5. Ibid.

6. John W. Welch, "Chiasmus in the Book of Mormon," in *Chiasmus in Antiquity: Structures, Analyses, Exegesis,* ed. John W. Welch (Hildesheim, West Germany: Gerstenberg, 1981), 207. Welch also says, "It is difficult to imagine a more paradigmatic or a more effective use of chiasmus than this. Alma 36 is worthy in form to the best of any ancient chiastic writer."

7. Moroni's witness account is put in a larger context by Lisa Bolin Hawkins and Gordon C. Thomasson in "I Only Am Escaped Alone to Tell Thee: Survivor-Witnesses in the Book of Mormon" (Provo, Utah: FARMS, 1984).

8. Horace Walpole, quoted by Henry B. Wheatley in "Letter Writers," in *The Cambridge History of English Literature,* ed. A. W. Ward and A. R. Waller (New York: Macmillan, 1933), 10:284.

9. Harold C. Binkley, "Essays and Letter Writing," *PMLA* 41 (June 1926): 346 [342–61].

10. Ronald J. Corthell, "'Friendships Sacraments': John Donne's Familiar Letters," *Studies in Philology* 78 (Fall 1981): 410 [409–25].

11. Norman Perrin in *The New Testament: An Introduction* (New York: Harcourt Brace Jovanovich, 1974), 96, says the Greek word *epistole* may be translated either as "epistle" or "letter" but then notes that "in the ancient world a 'letter' was a personal communication between individuals or groups" and was intended to be direct and personal, while an "epistle" was a "deliberate literary creation intended for wide dissemination." Given this distinction, most of these Book of Mormon pieces would more appropriately be called *letters.*

12. Sidney B. Sperry in *Our Book of Mormon* (Salt Lake City: Bookcraft, 1947), 102–9, finds a ninth epistle in Ether 5—"Moroni's instructions to the future translator of the Book of Mormon" (106). He calls the first six of the eight we are considering "war epistles" and the letters from Mormon "pastoral epistles."

13. Hugh Nibley, in his analysis of the exchange between Moroni and Ammoron in *Teachings of the Book of Mormon; Semester 3 Transcripts (1988–90)* (Provo, Utah: FARMS, n.d.), 164, says what Moroni does here is

"accepted procedure for generals. . . . In epic literature, whether it's Homer or whether it's the *Aeneid,* the heroes or leaders of the hosts always before the battle have to stand up and at least spiel off a whole book, sometimes two books, of imprecations against the enemy—tell him how often he has done wrong, how evil he is, and the terrible things you are going to do with him. Then he comes and replies."

14. The phrase comes from an introduction to the letters of Keats by Harold Bloom and Lionel Trilling in *The Oxford Anthology of English Literature,* ed. Harold Bloom et al. (New York: Oxford University Press, 1973), 2:764. They note that good letters "are those which are free from self-consciousness, which claim their right to be spontaneous and immediate, and even, if the mood dictates and the occasion allows, casual or willful. Yet some of the conventional standards of literary excellence do apply, of which substantiality of subject matter, cogency of observation and reasoning, and sincerity and force of utterance are salient."

15. George A. Kennedy, *Classical Rhetoric and Its Christian and Secular Tradition from Ancient to Modern Times* (Chapel Hill: University of North Carolina Press, 1980), 4. Of course, rhetorical devices are found in various cultures down through time. As Kennedy says in *Classical Rhetoric,* "Traditional or natural rhetoric occurs in all societies," and when conceptualized, many of the qualities are "not dissimilar to categories of Greek rhetoric" (6, 7).

16. Edward P. J. Corbett, *Classical Rhetoric for the Modern Student* (New York: Oxford University Press, 1990); Northrop Frye, Sheridan Baker, and George Perkins, *The Harper Handbook to Literature* (New York: Harper & Row, 1985), 395.

17. Corbett, *Classical Rhetoric for the Modern Student,* 438.

18. I treat this more fully in an essay called "Purpose of the War Chapters in the Book of Mormon," in *Warfare in the Book of Mormon,* ed. Stephen D. Ricks and William J. Hamblin (Salt Lake City: Deseret Book and FARMS, 1990), 29–32.

19. Nibley, *Since Cumorah* (Salt Lake City: Deseret Book, 1967), 360.

20. Ibid., 362.

21. Michael Goulder, "The Pauline Epistles," in *The Literary Guide to the Bible,* ed. Robert Alter and Frank Kermode (Cambridge: Harvard University Press, 1987), 482.

22. Mark Thomas, "Listening to the Voice from the Dust: Moroni 8 as Rhetoric," *Sunstone* 24, no. 10 (1979): 22–24.

CHAPTER 7

"Not Cast Off Forever"
IMAGERY

1. C. Day Lewis, quoted by N. Friedman, "Imagery," *Princeton Encyclopedia of Poetry and Poetics,* ed. Alex Preminger (Princeton: Princeton University Press, 1974), 363.

2. Friedman, "Imagery," *Princeton Encyclopedia,* 363.

3. Tremper Longman III, *Literary Approaches to Biblical Interpretation* (Grand Rapids, Mich.: Academie Books, 1987), 129–30.

4. Longman, *Literary Approaches,* 131–32.

5. Another interesting example of a simile curse is found in the declaration of the soldier who has taken off the scalp of the Lamanite leader Zerahemnah: "Even as this scalp has fallen to the earth, which is the scalp of your chief, so shall ye fall to the earth except ye will deliver up your weapons of war and depart with a covenant of peace" (Alma 44:14). This is one of several curses discussed by Mark J. Morrise in "Simile Curses in the Ancient Near East, Old Testament, and Book of Mormon" (*Journal of Book of Mormon Studies* 2, no. 1 (1993): 124–38). Morrise concludes: "The simile curse appears in the same contexts in the Book of Mormon as it does in ancient Near Eastern and Old Testament texts, namely: treaties, religious covenants, and prophecies" (132).

6. T. R. Henn, *The Bible as Literature* (New York: Oxford University Press, 1970), 63–64.

7. Mircea Eliade makes this point in *The Myth of the Eternal Return,* trans. Willard R. Trask (1949, reprint ed.; New York: Pantheon Books for Bollingen Foundation, 1954) and in *Cosmos and History* (Princeton: Princeton University Press, 1971), 34.

8. Northrop Frye, *Anatomy of Criticism* (Princeton: Princeton University Press, 1957), 146.

9. Joseph Smith puts this concept in another context: "'By proving contraries,' truth is made manifest" (*History of The Church of Jesus Christ of Latter-day Saints,* ed. B. H. Roberts, 2d ed. rev. [Salt Lake City: The Church of Jesus Christ of Latter-day Saints, 1932–51] 6:428). Supporting the same point, Carl Jung says in *The Archetypes and the Collective Unconscious* (Bollingen Series 20, vol. 9, pt. 1. [Princeton: Princeton University Press, 1959], 36), "The balanced co-operation of moral opposites is a natural truth."

10. Henn, *Bible as Literature* (64–65) says: "Fire-imagery, in all literatures, may connote destruction, inspiration, purification (as in the lips touched with fire), inspiration (Ezekiel, and the Cloven Tongues of Pentecost); the intensities of love or lust." Northrop Frye in *The Great Code: The Bible and Literature* (New York: Harcourt Brace Jovanovich, 1982), 161, comments on the ironies and oppositions regarding fire: "Man in his present state cannot live in fire, but, as with water, there is a fire of life and a fire of death. The fire of life burns without burning *up;* there is light and heat but no pain or destruction."

11. This is a good example of the linkage between violence and the sacred that René Girard finds in *Violence and the Sacred* (Baltimore: Johns Hopkins University Press, 1977).

12. The Puritan poet Edward Taylor considered the Living Water and the Tree of Life to be synonymous: "A Well of Living Water: Tree of Life / From whom Life comes to every thing alive" (Donald E. Stanford, ed., *The Poems of Edward Taylor* [New Haven: Yale University Press, 1960], 1:167). In Charles

W. Mignon, ed., *Upon the Types of the Old Testament* (Lincoln: University of Nebraska Press, 1989), 2:744, Taylor says Christ is "the Tree of Life in the midst of the Paradise of God." Robert Murray, in *Symbols of Church and Kingdom: A Study in Early Syriac Tradition* (London: Cambridge University Press, 1975), 127, expands this idea: "Just as Christ is now grape, now wine, so he is now fruit of the Tree of Life, now the tree itself, antitype of the tree in Eden." Bruce W. Jorgensen, in "The Dark Way to the Tree: Typological Unity in The Book of Mormon," in *Literature of Belief: Sacred Scripture and Religious Experience* (ed. Neal E. Lambert [Provo, Utah: Brigham Young University Religious Studies Center, 1981], 217–31), sees Jacob's story of the olive vineyard as a comple-ment of Lehi's dream. Noting that "in some Jewish legends the tree of life is an olive" (224), Jorgensen finds that "like Lehi desiring the fruit of the tree of life, the vineyard's Lord also looks toward 'most precious' fruit in which he will rejoice, a fruit that Jacob suggests represents the perfected love of man toward God . . . (Jacob 6:5–7)" (225). Ad de Vries in *Dictionary of Symbols and Imagery* (London: North-Holland, 1974), 474, says that in Hebrew tradi-tion the tree of life took forms of a vine branch, an olive tree, or a wheat ear. An extensive treatment of the olive tree is found in Stephen D. Ricks and John W. Welch, eds., *The Allegory of the Olive Tree* (Salt Lake City: Deseret Book and FARMS, 1994). The editors affirm that Zenos's allegory of the olive tree is "one of the most magnificent allegories in all the sacred literature of the Judeo-Christian tradition" (ix).

13. For an extended treatment of images such as these that serve as sym-bols inspiring readers to flee degradation and partake of eternal life, see Richard Dilworth Rust, "Taste and Feast: Images of Eating and Drinking in the Book of Mormon," *Brigham Young University Studies* 33, no. 4 (1993): 743–52.

14. Irene M. Briggs, "The Tree of Life Symbol: Its Significance in Ancient American Religion" (master's thesis, Brigham Young University, 1950), 164–65.

15. Constance Irwin, *Fair Gods and Stone Faces* (New York: St. Martin's Press, 1963), 166.

16. Joseph Campbell, *The Hero with a Thousand Faces* (Princeton: Princeton University Press, 1968), 41.

17. E. A. S. Butterworth, *The Tree at the Navel of the Earth* (Berlin: Walter de Gruyter, 1970), 7.

18. Thomas Barns, "Trees and Plants," in *Encyclopaedia of Religion and Ethics*, ed. James Hastings (New York: Charles Scribners Sons, 1922), 12:454.

19. Arnold Whittick, *Symbols, Signs, and Their Meaning* (London: Leonard Hill, 1960), 278.

20. E. O. James, *The Tree of Life: An Archaeological Study* (Leiden: E. J. Brill, 1966), 78.

21. C. Wilfred Griggs, "The Tree of Life in Ancient Cultures," *Ensign* 18 (June 1988): 26–31.

22. Henn, *Bible as Literature* (74) says "the dust is the serpent's meat. It is

an emblem of misery, degradation, and earth's ultimate reduction of man. It has overtones of the desert and the waste places."

23. Ralph Waldo Emerson, *Nature, Addresses, and Lectures,* vol. 1 of *The Collected Works of Ralph Waldo Emerson,* ed. Robert E. Spiller and Alfred R. Ferguson (Cambridge: Belknap Press of Harvard University Press, 1971), 21.

24. Hugh Nibley in *The Message of the Joseph Smith Papyri* (Salt Lake City: Deseret Book, 1976), 147, says, "Sleep, like water, is one of those things in which reality and symbol meet and fuse. It is both the rest of the body and the freeing of the spirit." Nibley quotes A. Altmann on "the Gnostic idea that sleep represents spiritual death, the 'Forgetfulness of man's divine origin.'"

25. Another angle that has some relevance to what I am saying here is found in Daniel J. Schneider's *Symbolism: The Manichean Vision* (Lincoln: University of Nebraska Press, 1975), 17. Schneider says, "To ascend a staircase is often (as in Yeats and Eliot) to cast off the flesh and to advance toward a condition of pure spirituality. To move downward, into a pit, marsh, mire, or jungle, is to fall into the corporeal world, usually sinful, often terrifying." However, the Book of Mormon affirms, unlike the Manicheans, that this contrast is necessary to salvation.

26. John L. Sorenson, in *An Ancient American Setting for the Book of Mormon* (Salt Lake City: Deseret Book and FARMS, 1985), considers that Book of Mormon towers were pyramids or "cosmic mountains" (172). "Height, not shape, must be the main criterion" (174).

27. Anciently in a temple-building society, as Hugh Nibley points out in "Tenting, Toll, and Taxing," *Western Political Quarterly* 19, no. 4 (1966): 604–5, the first temples were tents. (This article is reprinted in Nibley, *The Ancient State: The Rulers and the Ruled* [Salt Lake City: Deseret Book and FARMS, 1991].)

28. For an elaboration of the importance of the temple as an *axis mundi* (center of the earth and a connecting point between heaven and earth), see Steven L. Olsen, "Cosmic Urban Symbolism in the Book of Mormon," *Brigham Young University Studies* 23, no. 1 (1983): 79–92.

29. Nibley in *An Approach to the Book of Mormon* (Salt Lake City: Deseret Book and FARMS, 1988), 218–20, cites tenth-century Jewish lore about two remnants of Joseph's garment, one of which remained undecayed.

30. Regarding the importance of metaphors, Northrop Frye in *Words with Power: Being a Second Study of the Bible and Literature* (New York: Harcourt Brace Jovanovich, 1990), 28, asserts that "all intensified language sooner or later turns metaphorical" and that "literature is not only the obvious but the inescapable guide to higher journeys of consciousness."

31. The power of the oasis imagery in the Bible has relevance here as well. In *The Great Code,* Frye says, "For a people who were originally desert dwellers, the oasis is the inevitable image of providential order, a garden directly created and sustained by God, a habitation that makes sense in human

terms without human transformation, the visible form of the invisible divine creation" (142).

CHAPTER 8
"That Jesus Is the Christ"
TYPOLOGY

1. Notable treatments of Book of Mormon typology are by Hugh Nibley, *Since Cumorah* (Salt Lake City: Deseret Book and FARMS, 1988); Bruce R. McConkie in *The Promised Messiah: The First Coming of Christ* (Salt Lake City: Deseret Book, 1978), chapters 21–24; and Bruce W. Jorgensen, "The Dark Way to the Tree: Typological Unity in the Book of Mormon" (217–31), Richard Dilworth Rust, "'All Things Which Have Been Given of God . . . Are the Typifying of Him': Typology in the Book of Mormon" (234–43), and George S. Tate, "The Typology of the Exodus Pattern in the Book of Mormon" (245–62) in *Literature of Belief: Sacred Scripture and Religious Experience*, ed. Neal E. Lambert (Provo, Utah: BYU Religious Studies Center, 1981). Instruction of the Lord to Adam expresses more fully the idea presented by Nephi: "And behold, all things have their likeness, and all things are created and made to bear record of me, both things which are temporal, and things which are spiritual; things which are in the heavens above, and things which are on the earth, and things which are in the earth, and things which are under the earth, both above and beneath: all things bear record of me" (Moses 6:63).

2. Some additional Old Testament types of Christ clearly set forth as such are manna (John 6:51), water coming out of the rock (1 Corinthians 10:4), Jonah in the belly of the fish for three days and three nights (Matthew 12:40), and the Passover (1 Corinthians 5:7). A thorough, even encyclopedic, treatment of Old Testament typology is by the Puritan minister Samuel Mather, *The Figures or Types of the Old Testament* (London, 1705; reprint ed., New York: Johnson Reprint Company, 1969, intro. and notes by Mason I. Lowance Jr.). Mather defines a type as "some outward or sensible thing ordained of God under the Old Testament, to represent and hold forth something of Christ in the New" (52). Besides being contained within the perpetual system of Mosaic ceremonies, sacrifices, and festivals, types, as Mather shows, can be found as well in occasional persons, things, and events. As a work that can profitably be consulted along with Mather's, *Upon the Types of the Old Testament* (Lincoln: University of Nebraska Press, 1989) is a recently discovered series of sermons on typology by the great Puritan poet Edward Taylor.

3. Northrop Frye, *The Great Code: The Bible and Literature* (New York: Harcourt Brace Jovanovich, 1982), 79.

4. Ibid., 80–81.

5. Erich Auerbach, "Figura," trans. Ralph Manheim, in *Scenes from the Drama of European Literature* (New York: Meridian, 1959), 53.

6. Perry Miller, introduction to *Images or Shadows of Divine Things,* by Jonathan Edwards (New Haven: Yale University Press, 1948), 6. Ursula Brumm, *American Thought and Religious Typology* (New Brunswick, N.J.: Rutgers University Press, 1970), 24. Van Mildert, *An Inquiry into the General Principles of Scripture-Interpretation* (Oxford, 1815), quoted in the *Encyclopaedia of Religion and Ethics,* ed. James Hastings (New York: Charles Scribner's Sons, 1958), 12:500. Mason I. Lowance Jr., "Images or Shadows of Divine Things: The Typology of Jonathan Edwards," *Early American Literature* 5 (Spring 1970): 141. Mason I. Lowance Jr., *The Language of Canaan: Metaphor and Symbol in New England from the Puritans to the Transcendentalists* (Cambridge, Mass.: Harvard University Press, 1980), 39.

7. Auerbach, *Mimesis: The Representation of Reality in Western Literature,* trans. Willard R. Trask (Princeton: Princeton University Press, 1953), 73–74.

8. Jonathan Edwards, "Types of the Messiah," in *The Works of President Edwards* (1847; reprint ed., New York: Burt Franklin, 1968), 9:493.

9. Hugh Nibley, *Temple and Cosmos* (Salt Lake City: Deseret Book and FARMS, 1992), 203.

10. McConkie, *Promised Messiah,* 377.

11. Nibley in *Since Cumorah* (202–5) shows how the ancient apocrypha, like the Book of Mormon, "give a peculiar importance to the figure of Joseph, who is both a real person and a symbol."

12. Nibley, *Since Cumorah,* 204.

13. Nibley in *An Approach to the Book of Mormon* (Salt Lake City: Deseret Book and FARMS, 1988), 211–13, 218–21, develops the typical apocryphal variations of this theme of the rent garment of Joseph. With respect to the typological way of thinking, Nibley says (212): "To the modern and the western mind all this over-obvious dwelling on types and shadows seems a bit overdone, but not to the ancient or Oriental mind. The whole Arabic language is one long commentary on the deep-seated feeling, so foreign to us but so characteristic of people who speak synthetic languages, that if things are *alike* they are the *same.*"

14. An extensive discussion of Ammon as a type of Christ is found in Camille Fronk's essay, "'Show Forth Good Examples in Me': Alma 17–23," in *1 Nephi to Alma 29,* ed. Kent P. Jackson, Studies in Scripture Series, vol. 7 (Salt Lake City: Deseret Book, 1987), 323–29.

15. Tate, "Typology," 252.

16. Ibid., 257.

17. Bible Dictionary, LDS edition of the Bible (1983), s.v. "Babylon or Babel."

18. Ezra Taft Benson, "I Testify," *Ensign* 18 (November 1988): 87.

19. "We Are All Enlisted," *Hymns of The Church of Jesus Christ of Latter-day Saints* (Salt Lake City: The Church of Jesus Christ of Latter-day Saints, 1985), no. 250.

20. See Mosiah 7:20; Alma 9:10; 19:27; 29:11; 36:28–29; 60:20; 62:50; 3 Nephi 3:25; 4:8, 29–33.

21. Benson, "I Testify," 87.

22. Hugh Nibley amplifies this point in his article "Treasures in the Heavens: Some Early Christian Insights into the Organizing of Worlds," *Dialogue* 8, nos. 3–4 (1973): 76–98.

CHAPTER 9

"At the Judgment-Seat of Christ"
SUMMARY

1. From *Following the Equator,* in *The Portable Mark Twain,* ed. Bernard DeVoto (New York: Viking Press, 1946), 564.

2. John W. Welch, "Study, Faith, and the Book of Mormon," *BYU 1987–88 Devotional and Fireside Speeches* (Provo, Utah: Brigham Young University Press, 1988), 148; see also Hugh Nibley, *The World of the Jaredites* (Salt Lake City: Deseret Book and FARMS, 1988), 153.

3. See 2 Nephi 9:22–46; 33:11–15; Jacob 6:9, 13; Mosiah 3:24; 16:10; Alma 5:22; 9:15; 11:44; 12:27; 33:22; Helaman 8:25; 3 Nephi 26:3–5; Mormon 7:7–10; 9:13–14; Moroni 10:27, 34.

4. In *The Rites of Passage* (Chicago: University of Chicago Press, 1960), 11, Arnold van Gennep defines a rite of transition as being a liminal rite between a rite of separation and one of incorporation. Some examples of liminal rites are initiations, "rites of attachment to the deity," and those "enacting death in one condition and resurrection in another" (12–13).

5. Victor Turner, *The Ritual Process: Structure and Anti-Structure* (Chicago: Aldine Press, 1969), 95.

6. van Gennep, *Rites of Passage,* 20.

7. Ibid., 20, 62.

8. Victor Turner, *Dramas, Fields, and Metaphors: Symbolic Action in Human Society* (Ithaca, N. Y.: Cornell University Press, 1974), 49, 202.

9. John A. Tvedtnes, "King Benjamin and the Feast of Tabernacles," in *By Study and Also by Faith: Essays in Honor of Hugh W. Nibley,* ed. John M. Lundquist and Stephen D. Ricks (Salt Lake City: Deseret Book and FARMS, 1990), 2:197–237.

10. Hugh Nibley, *An Approach to the Book of Mormon* (Salt Lake City: Deseret Book and FARMS, 1988), 296–97. Interior quotation is from Nibley, "The Hierocentric State," *Western Political Quarterly* 4 (1951): 226–27.

11. According to Gabriel Josipovici in *The Book of God: A Response to the Bible* (New Haven: Yale University Press, 1988), 242, there is an appropriate connection between repentance and ancient New Year rites. Josipovici says, "In the Hebrew Bible, and in Judaism till the present day, the term for repentance is *testuvah,* a turning. You have gone astray in this way or that and now you recognize and admit this and turn back to the right way. The great series

of feasts connected with the new year culminates in the Day of Atonement, when, having repented fully, you are forgiven and so can start afresh with the slate wiped clean."

12. Victor Turner, *The Forest of Symbols: Aspects of Ndembu Ritual* (Ithaca, N. Y.: Cornell University Press, 1969), 96.

13. Although it is a somewhat trivial analogy, this centering and surrounding is like Wallace Stevens's jar in "Anecdote of the Jar":

> I placed a jar in Tennessee,
> And round it was, upon a hill.
> It made the slovenly wilderness
> Surround that hill.
>
> . . . .
>
> It took dominion everywhere.

14. Mircea Eliade, *Cosmos and History,* trans. Willard R. Trask (Princeton: Princeton University Press, 1971), 12.

15. For a thorough and convincing treatise on the implications of this with respect to temple ordinances and covenants, see John W. Welch, *The Sermon at the Temple and the Sermon on the Mount: A Latter-day Saint Approach* (Salt Lake City: Deseret Book, 1990).

16. M. Catherine Thomas, "Types and Shadows of Deliverance in the Book of Mormon," in *Doctrines of the Book of Mormon: The 1991 Sperry Symposium,* ed. Bruce A. Van Orden and Brent L. Top (Salt Lake City: Deseret Book, 1992), 186–87.

17. This specifies what is to be found in the sealed part of the Book of Mormon—which will come forth and be translated in "the own due time of the Lord . . . ; for behold, they reveal all things from the foundation of the world unto the end thereof" (2 Nephi 27:10; see also 2 Nephi 30:3; Ether 5:1). What is said about the vision of the brother of Jared applies as well to the sealed part of the Book of Mormon: "Ye shall write them and shall seal them up, that no one can interpret them, . . . and I will show them in mine own due time unto the children of men" (Ether 3:22, 27). Moroni then spells out his instructions: "I have written upon these plates the very things which the brother of Jared saw [see v. 25]; and there never were greater things made manifest than those which were made manifest unto the brother of Jared. . . . And [the Lord] commanded me that I should seal them up. . . . For the Lord said unto me: They shall not go forth unto the Gentiles until the day that they shall repent of their iniquity, and become clean before the Lord. And in that day that they shall exercise faith in me, saith the Lord, . . . then will I manifest unto them the things which the brother of Jared saw, even to the unfolding unto them all my revelations. . . . Come unto me, O ye Gentiles, and I will show unto you the greater things, the knowledge of which is hid up because of unbelief" (Ether 4:4–7, 13).

18. Northrop Frye, *The Great Code: The Bible and Literature* (New York: Harcourt Brace Jovanovich, 1982), 106.

19. Ibid., 108.

20. Eliade, *Cosmos and History,* 9–10.

21. Frye, *Great Code,* 136, 137.

22. The term *Lamanites* has several different meanings in the Book of Mormon. At one point, after the Savior's visit and the conversion of the people, there cease to be Lamanites altogether, but then the name is revived to apply to unbelievers (4 Nephi 1:17, 38). After the eventual destruction of the Nephites as a people, all those who remain are considered Lamanites (Alma 45:14). The term as I use it here in reference to latter-day Lamanites applies generally to all the living descendants of Lehi. That is the way Nephi uses it when he says that "the remnant of our seed" will receive the Book of Mormon (2 Nephi 30:3).

23. Joseph Smith is so called in early versions of the Doctrine and Covenants (78:9; 82:11; 104:26, 43). A possible meaning of the name *Gazelem* is given by George Reynolds and Janne M. Sjodahl in *Commentary on the Book of Mormon* (Salt Lake City: Deseret Book, 1973), 4:162. They say it is "a name given to a servant of God. The word appears to have its roots in Gaz—a stone, and Aleim, a name of God as a revelator, or the interposer in the affairs of men. If this suggestion is correct, its roots admirably agree with its apparent meaning—a seer."

24. In an appendix to my essay, "Taste and Feast: Images of Eating and Drinking in the Book of Mormon," *Brigham Young University Studies* 33 (1993): 751–52, I provide a guide to the direct words of Christ in the book.

25. Regarding the relationship of metaphor to poetry, in *The Biblical Web* (Ann Arbor: University of Michigan Press, 1994), 109, Ruth apRoberts analyzes the contribution of Robert Lowth to biblical literary criticism and says he cites the two Hebrew words for poem, *mizmor* and *mashal,* with *mizmor* expressing the principle of parallelism and *mashal* meaning *"he likened, he spoke in parables,* and this expresses the characteristic of figurative language."

26. Spoken in October 1996 general conference; quoted in *Church News,* 12 October 1996, 24.

27. Wesley A. Kort makes the same point about the Bible in *Story, Text, and Scripture: Literary Interests in Biblical Narrative* (University Park, Pennsylvania: Pennsylvania State University Press, 1988), xi. He says, "The religious meaning and significance of biblical material and its literary and textual form are inseparable." It should be added that just as Harold Fisch says regarding the Bible in *Poetry with a Purpose: Biblical Poetics and Interpretation* (Bloomington: Indiana University Press, 1988), so with the Book of Mormon: The book is not merely an aesthetic work; the creation does not stop with beauty: it continues.

WORKS CITED

Abrams, M. H. *A Glossary of Literary Terms*. 6th ed. Fort Worth: Harcourt Brace Jovanovich, 1993.

Ackerman, James S. "Joseph, Judah, and Jacob." In *Literary Interpretations of Biblical Narratives,* edited by Kenneth R. R. Gros Louis. Vol. 2. Nashville: Abingdon, 1982. 85.

Alter, Robert. "Psalms." In *The Literary Guide to the Bible,* edited by Robert Alter and Frank Kermode. Cambridge, Mass.: Harvard University Press, 1987.

———. *The Art of Biblical Narrative*. New York: Basic Books, 1981.

———. *The Art of Biblical Poetry*. New York: Basic Books, 1985.

apRoberts, Ruth. "Old Testament Poetry: The Translatable Structure." *PMLA* 92 (1977): 987–1003.

———. *The Biblical Web*. Ann Arbor: University of Michigan Press, 1994.

Arnold, Marilyn. *Sweet Is the Word: Reflections on the Book of Mormon, Its Narrative, Teachings, and People*. American Fork, Utah: Covenant, 1996.

Auerbach, Erich. "Figura." Translated by Ralph Manheim. In *Scenes from the Drama of European Literature*. New York: Meridian, 1959.

———. *Mimesis: The Representation of Reality in Western Literature*. Translated by Willard R. Trask. Princeton: Princeton University Press, 1953.

Barns, Thomas. "Trees and Plants." *Encyclopaedia of Religion and Ethics*. Ed. James Hastings. Vol. 12. New York: Charles Scribners Sons, 1922.

Bassett, Arthur R. "Jesus' Sermon to the Nephites." In *The Book of Mormon: It Begins with a Family*. Salt Lake City: Deseret Book, 1983.

Benson, Ezra Taft. "I Testify." *Ensign* 18 (November 1988): 86–87.

———. "The Book of Mormon: Keystone of Our Religion." *Ensign* 16 (November 1986): 4–6.

———. "The Book of Mormon Is the Word of God," *Ensign* 5 (May 1975): 63–65.

Bible Dictionary, LDS edition of the King James Version of the Bible. Salt Lake City: The Church of Jesus Christ of Latter-day Saints, 1983.

Binkley, Harold C. "Essays and Letter Writing." *PMLA* 41 (June 1926): 342–61.

Black, Susan Easton. *Finding Christ through the Book of Mormon*. Salt Lake City: Deseret Book, 1987.

Bloom, Harold, and Lionel Trilling. *The Oxford Anthology of English Literature*. Ed. Harold Bloom, et al. Vol. 2. New York: Oxford University Press, 1973.

Book of Mormon Critical Text: A Tool for Scholarly Reference. 3 vols. Provo, Utah: FARMS, 1984–87.

Book of Mormon, The. Salt Lake City: The Church of Jesus Christ of Latter-day Saints, 1981. Subsequently published as The Book of Mormon: Another Testament of Jesus Christ.

Book of Mormon, The: It Begins with a Family. Salt Lake City: Deseret Book, 1983.

Briggs, Irene M. "The Tree of Life Symbol: Its Significance in Ancient American Religion." Master's thesis, Brigham Young University, 1950.

Brooks, Cleanth, R. W. B. Lewis, and Robert Penn Warren. *American Literature: The Makers and the Making*. Vol. 2. New York: St. Martin's Press, 1973.

Brown, S. Kent. "The Exodus Pattern in the Book of Mormon." *Brigham Young University Studies* 30, no. 3 (1990): 111–42.

———. "The Prophetic Laments of Samuel the Lamanite." *Journal of Book of Mormon Studies* 1 (Fall 1992): 163–80.

Brown, Wade. *The God-Inspired Language of the Book of Mormon: Structure and Commentary*. Clackamas, Oreg.: Rainbow Press, 1988.

Brumm, Ursula. *American Thought and Religious Typology*. New Brunswick, N. J.: Rutgers University Press, 1970.

Burgon, Glade L. "An Analysis of Style Variations in the Book of Mormon." Master's thesis, Brigham Young University, 1958.

Butterworth, E. A. S. *The Tree at the Navel of the Earth*. Berlin: Walter de Gruyter, 1970.

Campbell, Joseph. *The Hero with a Thousand Faces*. Princeton: Princeton University Press, 1968.

Chase, Mary Ellen. *The Bible and the Common Reader*. New York: Macmillan, 1956.

Clark, E. Douglas, and Robert S. Clark. *Fathers and Sons in the Book of Mormon*. Salt Lake City: Deseret Book, 1991.

Clemens, Samuel Langhorne. *Following the Equator*. In *The Portable Mark Twain*. New York: Viking Press, 1946.

Coleridge, Samuel Taylor. *Biographia Literaria* [selections]. In *English Romantic Poetry and Prose,* edited by Russell Noyes. New York: Oxford University Press, 1956.

Corbett, Edward P. J. *Classical Rhetoric for the Modern Student*. 3d ed. New York: Oxford University Press, 1990.

Corthell, Ronald J. "'Friendships Sacraments': John Donne's Familiar Letters." *Studies in Philology* 78 (Fall 1981): 409–25.

Cracroft, Paul. "A Clear Poetic Voice." *Ensign* 14 (January 1984): 28–31.

Crowell, Angela M. "The Hebrew Literary Structure of the Book of Mormon." In *Restoration Studies V,* edited by Darlene Caswell. Independence, Mo.: Herald Publishing House, 1993.

——. "Hebrew Poetry in the Book of Mormon." *Zarahemla Record,* 32 and 33 (1986): 2–9; 34 (1986): 7–12.

Dartmouth Bible, The: An Abridgment of the King James Version, with Aids to Its Understanding as History and Literature, and as a Source of Religious Experience. Boston: Houghton Mifflin, 1950.

de Vries, Ad. *Dictionary of Symbols and Imagery.* London: North-Holland, 1974.

Duke, James T. "The Literary Structure and Doctrinal Significance of Alma 13:1–9." *Journal of Book of Mormon Studies* 5 (Spring 1996): 103–18.

Dyer, Alvin R. Quoted in "A Thought from the Scriptures." *Church News,* 12 October 1996, 24.

Edwards, Jonathan. *The Works of President Edwards.* 10 vols. 1847. Reprint. New York: Burt Franklin, 1968.

Eliade, Mircea. *Cosmos and History.* Princeton, N. J.: Princeton University Press, 1971.

——. *The Myth of the Eternal Return.* Translated by Willard R. Trask. 1949. Reprint. New York: Pantheon Books for Bollingen Foundation, 1954.

Emerson, Ralph Waldo. "The Poet." *Essays: First and Second Series.* New York: Vintage Books and Library of America, 1990.

——. "Address at the Opening of the Concord Free Public Library." In *Miscellanies.* Vol. 11 of *The Complete Works of Ralph Waldo Emerson.* Boston: Houghton Mifflin Company, 1911.

Everson, William. Note to *American Bard,* by Walt Whitman. New York: Viking Press, 1982.

Fisch, Harold. *Poetry with a Purpose: Biblical Poetics and Interpretation.* Bloomington: Indiana University Press, 1988.

Freedman, David Noel. "Pottery, Poetry, and Prophecy: An Essay on Biblical Poetry." In *The Bible in Its Literary Milieu,* edited by John Maier and Vincent Toller. Grand Rapids, Mich.: Eerdmans, 1979.

——. Preface to *Chiasmus in Antiquity: Structures, Analyses, Exegisis,* edited by John W. Welch. Hildesheim, West Germany: Gerstenberg, 1981.

Friedman, N. "Imagery." In *Princeton Encyclopedia of Poetry and Poetics,* edited by Alex Preminger. Princeton: Princeton University Press, 1974.

Fronk, Camille. "'Show Forth Good Examples in Me': (Alma 17–23)." In *1 Nephi to Alma 29,* edited by Kent P. Jackson. Studies in Scripture Series, vol. 7. Salt Lake City: Deseret Book, 1987.

Frost, Robert. "Education by Poetry: A Meditative Monologue" and "The Constant Symbol." In *Robert Frost: An Introduction,* edited by Robert A. Greenberg and James G. Hepburn. New York: Holt, Rinehart and Winston, 1961.

Frye, Northrop. *Anatomy of Criticism: Four Essays*. Princeton: Princeton University Press, 1957.

———. *The Great Code: The Bible and Literature*. New York and London: Harcourt Brace Jovanovich, 1982.

———. *Words with Power: Being a Second Study of the Bible and Literature*. San Diego, New York, London: Harcourt Brace Jovanovich, 1990.

Frye, Northrop, Sheridan Baker, and George Perkins. *The Harper Handbook to Literature*. New York: Harper & Row, 1985.

Geary, Edward. "A Conversation with Clinton F. Larson." *Dialogue* 4 (Autumn 1969): 74–79.

Girard, René. *Violence and the Sacred*. Baltimore: Johns Hopkins University Press, 1977.

Goulder, Michael. "The Pauline Epistles." In *The Literary Guide to the Bible,* edited by Robert Alter and Frank Kermode. Cambridge, Mass.: Harvard University Press, 1987.

Greenberg, Moshe. "Job." In *The Literary Guide to the Bible,* edited by Robert Alter and Frank Kermode. Cambridge, Mass.: Harvard University Press, 1987.

Griggs, C. Wilfred. "The Tree of Life in Ancient Cultures." *Ensign* 18 (June 1988): 26–31.

Hardy, Grant R. "Mormon as Editor." In *Rediscovering the Book of Mormon,* edited by John L. Sorenson and Melvin J. Thorne. Salt Lake City: Deseret Book, 1991.

Harris, Franklin S., Jr. "The Book of Mormon as Literature." *The Book of Mormon Message and Evidences*. Salt Lake City: Corporation of the President of the Church of Jesus Christ of Latter-day Saints, 1953.

Hawkins, Lisa Bolin, and Gordon C. Thomasson. "I Only Am Escaped Alone to Tell Thee: Survivor-Witnesses in the Book of Mormon." Provo, Utah: FARMS, 1984.

Hawthorne, Nathaniel. *The Scarlet Letter.* Vol. 1 of *The Centenary Edition of the Works of Nathaniel Hawthorne,* edited by William Charvat, et al. Columbus: Ohio State University Press, 1962.

Henn, T. R. *The Bible as Literature*. New York: Oxford University Press, 1970.

———. "The Bible as Literature." In *Peake's Commentary on the Bible,* edited by Matthew Black and H. H. Rowley. Surrey: Thomas Nelson & Sons, 1962.

Hinckley, Gordon B. "An Angel from on High, the Long, Long Silence Broke." *Ensign* 9 (November 1979): 7–9.

Irwin, Constance. *Fair Gods and Stone Faces*. New York: St. Martin's Press, 1963.

Jackson, Kent P. "Nephi and Isaiah." In *1 Nephi to Alma 29,* edited by Kent P. Jackson. Studies in Scripture Series, vol. 7. Salt Lake City: Deseret Book, 1987.

James, E. D. *The Tree of Life: An Archaeological Study*. Leiden: E. J. Brill, 1966.

Jones, Phyllis M., and Nicholas R. Jones, eds. *Salvation in New England: Selections from the Sermons of the First Preachers.* Austin: University of Texas Press, 1977.

Jorgensen, Bruce W. "The Dark Way to the Tree: Typological Unity in the Book of Mormon." In *Literature of Belief: Sacred Scripture and Religious Experience,* edited by Neal E. Lambert. Provo, Utah: Brigham Young University Religious Studies Center, 1981. First published in *Encyclia* 54 (1977): 16–24.

Josipovici, Gabriel. *The Book of God: A Response to the Bible.* New Haven: Yale University Press, 1988.

Jung, C. G. *The Archetypes and the Collective Unconscious.* Bollingen Series 20, vol. 9, pt. 1. New York: Pantheon Books, 1959.

Kennedy, George A. *Classical Rhetoric and Its Christian and Secular Tradition from Ancient to Modern Times.* Chapel Hill: University of North Carolina Press, 1980.

———. *New Testament Interpretation through Rhetorical Criticism.* Chapel Hill: University of North Carolina Press, 1984.

Kermode, Frank. "Matthew." In *The Literary Guide to the Bible,* edited by Robert Alter and Frank Kermode. Cambridge, Mass.: Harvard University Press, 1987.

King, Arthur Henry. "Language Themes in Jacob 5: 'The vineyard of the Lord of hosts is the house of Israel (Isaiah 5:7).'" In *The Allegory of the Olive Tree: The Olive, the Bible, and Jacob 5,* edited by Stephen D. Ricks and John W. Welch. Salt Lake City: Deseret Book and FARMS, 1994.

Kort, Wesley A. *Story, Text, and Scripture: Literary Interests in Biblical Narrative.* University Park: Pennsylvania State University Press, 1988.

Kugel, James L. *The Idea of Biblical Poetry: Parallelism and Its History.* New Haven and London: Yale University Press, 1981.

Longman, Tremper, III. *Literary Approaches to Biblical Interpretation.* Grand Rapids, Mich.: Academie Books, 1987.

Lowance, Mason I., Jr. *The Language of Canaan: Metaphor and Symbol in New England from the Puritans to the Transcendentalists.* Cambridge, Mass., and London: Harvard University Press, 1980.

Ludlow, Daniel H. "The Book of Mormon Was Written for Our Day." *Instructor,* July 1966, 265–67.

Ludlow, Victor L. *Isaiah: Prophet, Seer, and Poet.* Salt Lake City: Deseret Book, 1982.

Lundquist, John M., and John W. Welch. "Kingship and Temple in 2 Nephi 5–10." In *Reexploring the Book of Mormon,* edited by John W. Welch. Salt Lake City: Deseret Book and FARMS, 1992.

Mather, Samuel. *The Figures or Types of the Old Testament,* 2d ed. 1705. Reprint. New York: Johnson Reprint Co., 1969. Introduction and notes by Mason I. Lowance Jr.

McConkie, Bruce R. *The Promised Messiah: The First Coming of Christ*. Salt Lake City: Deseret Book, 1978.

McWilliams, John P. Jr. *The American Epic: Transforming a Genre, 1770–1860*. New York: Cambridge University Press, 1989.

Metcalfe, Brent Lee. Preface to *New Approaches to the Book of Mormon*. Edited by Brent Lee Metcalfe. Salt Lake City: Signature Books, 1993.

Mildert, Van. *An Inquiry into the General Principles of Scripture-Interpretation*. Oxford, 1815. Quoted in the *Encyclopaedia of Religion and Ethics*, edited by James Hastings. 12 vols. New York: Charles Scribner's Sons, 1958, 12:500.

Miller, Perry. Introduction to *Images or Shadows of Divine Things*, by Jonathan Edwards. New Haven: Yale University Press, 1948.

———. *The New England Mind: The Seventeenth Century*. Cambridge, Mass.: Harvard University Press, 1954.

Morrise, Mark J. "Simile Curses in the Ancient Near East, Old Testament, and Book of Mormon." *Journal of Book of Mormon Studies* 2, no. 1 (1993): 124–38.

Murdock, Kenneth R. "The Colonial and Revolutionary Period." In *The Literature of the American People*, edited by Arthur Hobson Quinn. New York: Appleton-Century-Crofts, 1951.

Murray, Robert. *Symbols of Church and Kingdom: A Study in Early Syriac Tradition*. London: Cambrdige University Press, 1975.

Neusner, Jacob. *Christian Faith and the Bible of Judaism: the Judaic Encounter with Scripture*. Grand Rapids, Mich.: Eerdmans, 1987.

Nibley, Hugh. *An Approach to the Book of Mormon*. Salt Lake City: Deseret Book and FARMS, 1988.

———. *Message of the Joseph Smith Papyri, The*. Salt Lake City: Deseret Book, 1976.

———. *Prophetic Book of Mormon, The*. Salt Lake City: Deseret Book and FARMS, 1989.

———. *Since Cumorah*. Salt Lake City: Deseret Book and FARMS, 1988.

———. *Teachings of the Book of Mormon: Semester 3 Transcripts (1988–90)*. Provo, Utah: FARMS, n.d.

———. *Temple and Cosmos*. Salt Lake City: Deseret Book, 1954; and Deseret Book and FARMS, 1988.

———. *World and the Prophets, The*. Salt Lake City: Deseret Book, 1954; and Deseret Book and FARMS, 1987.

———. *World of the Jaredites, The*. Salt Lake City: Deseret Book and FARMS, 1988.

———. "Tenting, Toll, and Taxing." *Western Political Quarterly* 19, no. 4 (1966): 599–630. Reprinted in *The Ancient State: The Rulers and the Ruled*. Salt Lake City: Deseret Book and FARMS, 1991.

———. "The Hierocentric State." *Western Political Quarterly* 4 (1951): 226–53.

———. "Treasures in the Heavens: Some Early Christian Insights into the Organizing of Worlds," *Dialogue* 8 (Autumn/Winter 1973): 76–98.

Olsen, Steven L. "Cosmic Urban Symbolism in the Book of Mormon." *Brigham Young University Studies* 23, no. 1 (1983): 79–92.

———. "Patterns of Prayer: Humility or Pride." *Ensign* 22 (August 1992): 8–10.

Packer, Boyd K. *Teach Ye Diligently*. Salt Lake City: Deseret Book, 1975.

Parry, Donald W. *The Book of Mormon Text Reformatted According to Parallelistic Patterns*. Provo, Utah: FARMS, 1992.

———. "Climactic Forms in the Book of Mormon." In *Reexploring the Book of Mormon,* edited by John W. Welch. Salt Lake City: Deseret Book and FARMS, 1992.

———. "Poetic Parallelisms of the Book of Mormon." Provo, Utah: FARMS, 1988.

Perrin, Norman. *The New Testament: An Introduction*. New York: Harcourt Brace Jovanovich, 1974.

Poe, Edgar Allan. "*Twice-Told Tales,* by Nathaniel Hawthorne: A Review." *Graham's Magazine* 20 (May 1842): 298–300.

Reynolds, George, and Janne M. Sjodahl. *Commentary on the Book of Mormon*. Vol. 4. Reprint. Salt Lake City: Deseret Book, 1973.

Ricks, Stephen D. "King, Coronation, and Covenant in Mosiah 1–6." In *Rediscovering the Book of Mormon,* edited by John L. Sorenson and Melvin J. Thorne. Salt Lake City: Deseret Book, 1991.

———. "The Ideology of Kingship in Mosiah 1–6." In *Reexploring the Book of Mormon,* edited by John W. Welch. Salt Lake City: Deseret Book and FARMS, 1992.

———. "The Treaty/Covenant Pattern in King Benjamin's Address (Mosiah 1–6)." *Brigham Young University Studies* 24 (Spring 1984): 151–62.

Ricks, Stephen D., and John W. Welch, eds. *The Allegory of the Olive Tree: The Olive, the Bible, and Jacob 5*. Salt Lake City: Deseret Book and FARMS, 1994.

Riddle, Chauncey C. "Korihor." *The Book of Mormon: It Begins with a Family*. Salt Lake City: Deseret Book, 1983.

Rust, Richard Dilworth. "'All Things Which Have Been Given of God . . . Are the Typifying of Him': Typology in the Book of Mormon." In *Literature of Belief: Sacred Scripture and Religious Experience,* edited by Neal E. Lambert. Provo, Utah: Brigham Young University Religious Studies Center, 1981.

———. "Book of Mormon Poetry." *New Era* 13 (March 1983): 46–50.

———. "Purpose of the War Chapters in the Book of Mormon." In *Warfare in the Book of Mormon,* edited by Stephen D. Ricks and William J. Hamblin. Salt Lake City: Deseret Book, 1990.

———. "Taste and Feast: Images of Eating and Drinking in the Book of Mormon." *Brigham Young University Studies* 33, no. 4 (1993): 743–52.

Ryken, Leland. *How to Read The Bible as Literature*. Grand Rapids, Mich.: Academie Books, 1984.

———. *Words of Delight: A Literary Introduction to the Bible*. Grand Rapids, Mich.: Baker, 1987.

Schneider, Daniel J. *Symbolism, The Manichean Vision: A Study of Symbolism in the Art of James, Conrad, Woolf, and Stevens*. Lincoln: University of Nebraska Press, 1975.

Shute, Evan. "The Book of Mormon as Literature." *The Saints' Herald*, 27 · February 1943, 7–9, 22.

Smith, Joseph. *History of The Church of Jesus Christ of Latter-day Saints*. Edited by B. H. Roberts, 2d ed. rev. Vol. 1. Salt Lake City: The Church of Jesus Christ of Latter-day Saints, 1932–51.

Snow, Edgar C., Jr. "Narrative Criticism and the Book of Mormon." *Journal of Book of Mormon Studies* 4, no. 2 (1995): 93–106.

Sondrup, Stephen P. "The Psalm of Nephi: A Lyric Reading." *Brigham Young University Studies* 21 (1981): 357–72.

Sorenson, John L. *An Ancient American Setting for the Book of Mormon*. Salt Lake City: Deseret Book and FARMS, 1985.

Sperry, Sidney B. *Book of Mormon Compendium*. Salt Lake City: Bookcraft, 1968. Expanded in *Our Book of Mormon*. Salt Lake City: Bookcraft, 1947. Reprinted (much of it) in *Journal of Book of Mormon Studies* 4, no. 1 (1995).

Stendahl, Krister. "The Sermon on the Mount and Third Nephi." In *Reflections on Mormonism: Judaeo-Christian Parallels*, edited by Truman G. Madsen. Provo, Utah: Brigham Young University Religious Studies Center, 1978.

Stevens, Wallace. *Poems by Wallace Stevens*. New York: Vintage, 1957.

Tabor, Susan. "Mormon's Literary Technique." *Mormon Letters Annual*, 1983, 113–25.

Talmage, James E. *The Articles of Faith*. Salt Lake City: The Church of Jesus Christ of Latter-day Saints, 1924.

Tanner, John S. "Jacob and His Descendants as Authors." In *Rediscovering the Book of Mormon*, edited by John L. Sorenson and Melvin J. Thorne. Salt Lake City: Deseret Book, 1991.

Tate, George S. "The Typology of the Exodus Pattern in the Book of Mormon." In *Literature of Belief: Sacred Scripture and Religious Experience*, ed. Neal E. Lambert. Provo, Utah: Brigham Young University Religious Studies Center, 1981.

Taylor, Edward. *The Poems of Edward Taylor*. Ed. Donald E. Stanford. New Haven: Yale University Press, 1960.

———. *Upon the Types of the Old Testament*. Ed. Charles W. Mignon. 2 vols. Lincoln: University of Nebraska Press, 1989.

Thomas, M. Catherine. "Types and Shadows of Deliverance in the Book of Mormon." In *Doctrines of the Book of Mormon: The 1991 Sperry*

Symposium, edited by Bruce A. Van Orden and Brent L. Top. Salt Lake City: Deseret Book, 1992.

Thomas, Mark. "Listening to the Voice from the Dust: Moroni 8 as Rhetoric." *Sunstone* (January-February 1979): 22–24.

Thomas, Robert K. "A Literary Analysis of the Book of Mormon." Bachelor of arts thesis, Reed College, 1947.

———. "A Literary Critic Looks at the Book of Mormon." In *To the Glory of God,* edited by Charles D. Tate Jr. and Truman G. Madsen. Salt Lake City: Deseret Book, 1972.

Thomasson, Gordon C. "Expanding Approaches to the Book of Mormon: Pre-exilic Israelite Religious Patterns." Photocopy of unpublished manuscript.

———. "Mosiah: The Complex Symbolism and the Symbolic Complex of Kingship in the Book of Mormon." *Journal of Book of Mormon Studies* 2, no. 1 (1993).

Tillyard, E. M. W. *The English Epic and Its Background.* New York: Barnes and Noble, 1966.

Turner, Victor. *Dramas, Fields, and Mataphors: Symbolic Action in Human Society.* Ithaca, N. Y.: Cornell University Press, 1974.

———. *The Forest of Symbols: Aspects of Ndembu Ritual.* Ithaca, N. Y.: Cornell University Press, 1969.

———. *The Ritual Process: Structure and Anti-Structure.* Chicago: Aldine Press, 1969.

Tvedtnes, John A. "King Benjamin and the Feast of Tabernacles." In *By Study and Also by Faith: Essays in Honor of Hugh W. Nibley,* vol. 2, edited by John M. Lundquist and Stephen D. Ricks. Salt Lake City: Deseret Book and FARMS, 1990.

———. "*Rod* and *Sword* as the Word of God." *Journal of Book of Mormon Studies* 5, no. 2 (1996): 148–55.

van Gennep, Arnold. *The Rites of Passage.* Translated by Monika B. Vizedom and Gabrielle L. Caffee. Chicago: University of Chicago Press, 1960.

Walker, Gary Lee. "The Downfall of the Nephite Nation: Lessons for Our Time (3 Nephi 6–10)." In *Alma 30 to Moroni,* edited by Kent P. Jackson. Studies in Scripture Series, vol. 8. Salt Lake City: Deseret Book, 1988.

Walpole, Horace. Quoted by Henry B. Wheatley in "Letter Writers." In *The Cambridge History of English Literature,* vol. 10, edited by A. W. Ward and A. R. Waller. New York: Macmillan, 1933.

Warner, C. Terry. "Jacob." *The Book of Mormon: It Begins with a Family.* Salt Lake City: Deseret Book, 1983.

Washburn, J. N. *The Miracle of the Book of Mormon.* Orem, Utah: Book Production Services, 1984.

Watson, Wilford G. E. *Classical Hebrew Poetry: A Guide to Its Techniques.* Sheffield, England: JSOT Press, 1984.

———. *Hebrew Poetry: Traditional Techniques in Classical Hebrew Verse.* Sheffield, England: Sheffield Academic Press, 1994.

Welch, John W. *The Sermon at the Temple and the Sermon on the Mount: A Latter-Day Saint Approach*. Salt Lake City: Deseret Book, 1990.

———. "Benjamin's Speech: A Classic Ancient Farewell Address." In *Reexploring the Book of Mormon*, edited by John W. Welch. Salt Lake City: Deseret Book and FARMS, 1992.

———. "Chiasmus in the Book of Mormon." *Brigham Young University Studies* 10 (Autumn 1969): 69–84.

———. "Chiasmus in the Book of Mormon." In *Chiasmus in Antiquity: Structures, Analyses, Exegisis,* edited by John W. Welch. Hildesheim, West Germany: Gerstenberg, 1981.

———. "Jacob's Ten Commandments." In *Reexploring the Book of Mormon,* edited by John W. Welch. Salt Lake City: Deseret Book and FARMS, 1992.

———. "Study, Faith, and the Book of Mormon." In *Brigham Young University 1987–88 Devotional and Fireside Speeches*. Provo, Utah: Brigham Young University, 1988.

———. "The Temple in the Book of Mormon." In *Temples of the Ancient World,* edited by Donald W. Parry. Salt Lake City: Deseret Book and FARMS, 1994.

West, Roy A. *An Introduction to the Book of Mormon*. Salt Lake City: LDS Department of Education, 1940.

Whitney, Orson F. "Joseph Smith in Literature." *Improvement Era* 9 (December 1905): 135–53.

———. "Oratory, Poesy and Prophecy." *Improvement Era* 29 (March-July 1926): 401–04, 530–33, 628–31, 714–16, 857–60.

Whittick, Arnold. *Symbols, Signs, and Their Meaning*. London: Leonard Hill, 1960.

Wilder, Amos N. *Early Christian Rhetoric: The Language of the Gospel*. Cambridge, Mass.: Harvard University Press, 1971.

Wordsworth, William. "Preface to the *Lyrical Ballads*." In *English Romantic Poetry and Prose,* edited by Russell Noyes. New York: Oxford University Press, 1956.

INDEX

65; poetry testifies of, 75, 100; testimonies of, 79, 236; second coming of, 81; and Zenos's prayer, 86; poetic instruction of, 95–96; taking name of, 101; sermon of, on Israel, 101, 103; sanctification in, 103; King Benjamin clarifies judgment of, 107; name of Redeemer given as, 119; sermon of, on Israel, 137–40; incorporates teachings of Isaiah, 138–39, 140; the Child, 164; crucifixion of, 174; and fire, 174; word of, as guide, 179; imagery and atoning power of, 182; condescension of, 185; as rock, 188; typology of, 196, 208; audience of, 211; disciples of, 223; resurrected, 232; direct quotations of, 244–45; Book of Mormon as literary testimony of, 246

Jews: Book of Mormon directed to, 9, 19, 211, 234; promises to, 119; Lord preaches to, 138–39; Book of Mormon testifies to, of Messiah, 247

Jonah, 210–11; saving power of, 228

Josipovici, Gabriel, 52

Journey, spiritual, 44–45

Joy, 108

Judges, 128–29

Judgment, 91, 131, 231, 249; King Benjamin clarifies, of Christ, 107; day, 220–21

Justice, 117; sword of, 217

Kennedy, George, 105, 109, 114, 119; on rhetorical devices, 152

Keystone, Book of Mormon as, 10

King-men, 159

Kishkumen, 24

Knowing and knowledge, conflict of, 35

Korihor, 36–40, 133

Laban, 24, 28; sword of, 190

Lachoneus, letter from Giddianhi to, 149, 161–62

Laman and Lemuel: patriarchal blessings of, 47–48; false traditions of, 144–45

Lamanite-Nephite conflict, 150–51, 155

Lamanites, 193, 203; Book of Mormon directed to, 9, 15, 19, 211; false tradition of, 48; Lord preaches to, 138; gospel to be preached to, 140; Mormon speaking to, 144; brutality of, 165; degradation of, 192; conversion of, 209, 234; and deliverance, 247

Lamentation, Mormon's, 91–93

Lamoni, King, 30–32, 175

Language of Book of Mormon, 13; figurative, 135–36

Larson, Clinton F., 84

Lawyers, 127–29

Lehi: patriarchal blessings of, 47–48; in Heroic Age, 52; tree of life dream of, 54, 60, 173, 175, 224; poetry of, 66; and sea, 181; and tents, 185–86

Lehites, 54

Letters in the Book of Mormon, 149–66; Mormon's pastoral, 162–63

Liahona, 59, 171, 179, 198; Book of Mormon as, 44; and word of Christ, 191

Life and death, 182

Light and darkness, 174–76

Limhi, people of, 242

Liminality, 221

Literary: forms, Book of Mormon shaped through ancient, 10; Jesus uses, techniques, 138

Literature, Book of Mormon as sacred, 1, 149

Logos, 106–7, 109

Longman, Tremper, 167–68

Love, 164

WHAT IS FARMS?

The Foundation for Ancient Research and Mormon Studies (FARMS) encourages and supports research about the Book of Mormon: Another Testament of Jesus Christ and other ancient scriptures.

FARMS is a nonprofit educational foundation, independent of all other organizations. Its main research interests include ancient history, language, literature, culture, geography, politics, and law relevant to the scriptures. Although such subjects are of secondary importance when compared with the spiritual and eternal messages of the scriptures, solid research and academic perspectives alone can supply certain kinds of useful information, even if only tentatively, concerning many significant and interesting questions about the ancient backgrounds, origins, composition, and meanings of scripture.

The Foundation works to make interim and final reports about this research available widely, promptly, and economically. As a service to teachers and students of the scriptures, research results are distributed in both scholarly and popular formats.

It is hoped that this information will help all interested people to "come unto Christ" (Jacob 1:7) and to understand and take more seriously these ancient witnesses of the atonement of Jesus Christ, the Son of God.

For more information about FARMS, call toll free 1-800-327-6715, or write to FARMS, P.O. Box 7113, University Station, Provo, Utah 84602.